Naples

Nick Bruno

D0898348

Credits

Footprint credits

Editor: Nicola Gibbs
Production and layout: Emma Bryers
Maps: Kevin Feeney
Cover: Pepi Bluck

Publisher: Patrick Dawson
Managing Editor: Felicity Laughton
Advertising: Elizabeth Taylor
Sales and marketing: Kirsty Holmes

Photography credits
Front cover: edella/Shutterstock.com
Back cover: Natalia Barsukova/
Shutterstock.com

Printed and bound in the United
States of America

Every effort has been made to ensure that
the facts in this guidebook are accurate.
However, travellers should still obtain advice
from consulates, airlines, etc, about travel
and visa requirements before travelling.
The authors and publishers cannot accept
responsibility for any loss, injury or
inconvenience however caused.

Publishing information
Footprint *Focus Naples*
1st edition
© Footprint Handbooks Ltd
September 2013

ISBN: 978 1 908206 94 7
CIP DATA: A catalogue record for this book
is available from the British Library

® Footprint Handbooks and the Footprint
mark are a registered trademark of
Footprint Handbooks Ltd

Published by Footprint
6 Riverside Court
Lower Bristol Road
Bath BA2 3DZ, UK
T +44 (0)1225 469141
F +44 (0)1225 469461
footprinttravelguides.com

Distributed in the USA by Globe Pequot
Press, Guilford, Connecticut

The content of Footprint *Focus Naples*
has been taken directly from Footprint's
Naples & Amalfi Coast, which was
researched and written by Nick Bruno.

Contents

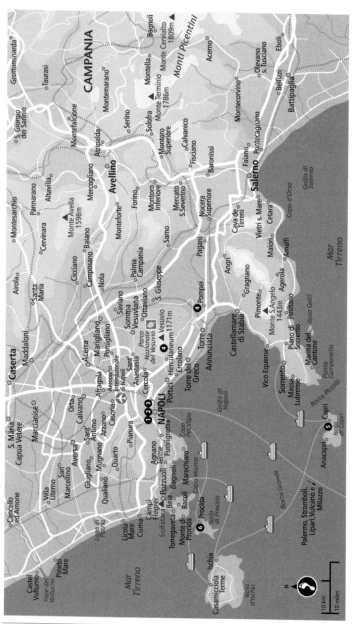

Set in the most spectacular and fertile bay imaginable, Naples oozes deadly gorgeous dollops of history, culture, food and vulcanism. Some 2500 years of life have created an intoxicating tragicomedy that is *Napoli, La Città* – Naples, the City. It's dirty, loud, chaotic and infuriating at one turn; compelling, exhilarating and gorgeous at the next. Labyrinthine layers of history have created architecture, customs and language that barely feel Italian let alone European.

However, Naples is not just one mad city with an addictive rhythm. Campi Flegrei – the Phlegrean Fields – fizz with fumaroles, springs and Graeco-Roman spas where emperors indulged, plotted and then often lost the plot. Feel the forces of nature around Vesuvius and the archaeological sites, walking on the crater rim of mainland Europe's only active volcano and exploring AD 79 time capsules at Pompeii, Herculaneum, Oplontis and Stabiae. Towering limestone cliffs shelter cute fishing villages, limpid emerald-blue inlets, fairytale castle gardens and majolica-domed churches on the Sorrentine Peninsula. Serenity, glamour and shimmering beauty abound on the Islands of Capri, Ischia and Procida. Capri is all about drama, escapism and the *molto chic*; Ischia heals with its thermal springs, lush valleys and sandy beaches; while Procida has down-to-earth charm and pastel-painted villages straight out of a Neapolitan *presepe* (nativity scene).

Planning your trip

Best time to visit Naples

The southern Italian climate makes Naples an attractive holiday destination all year round. For those who enjoy the blistering heat of a *Mezzogiorno* summer and a beach holiday with fabulous food then mid-June to September is the period to visit. Be warned though: temperatures often exceed 30°C and air quality in the city can suffer, which makes getting around a stifling experience. For days of warm sunshine but less oppressive temperatures visit mid-April to early June, or in October, when average temperatures are around 22°C. Even in these months, the days can reach a sweltering 30°C, often interrupted by rain showers. In early November, the climate can change overnight as weather fronts from the far north displace the southerly hot, dry scirocco winds from Africa. November is the wettest month and there can be cold and rainy days through until March. However, warm spring-like days are also possible, and even at Christmas there's the chance to enjoy Mediterranean fruits, vegetables and seafood.

What to see in Naples

Naples is one crazy *mamma* of a city that yields fascinating ancient baggage and stupefying surroundings: a natural bounty that an endless stream of foreign suitors has coveted. The sparkling gulf of Napoli has a spectacular coastline, islands and volcanoes that have spawned Graeco-Roman myths, hedonistic shenanigans and seismic episodes. Despite its natural dangers and perennial troubles, the Campania region offers unparalleled drama, beauty and flavour, including a life-affirming walk on the lip of snoozing Vesuvius.

Naples

Naples seeps into you: its relentless rhythm defies the rational as it makes its own rules. Ignore the overstated negative reputation and experience it for yourself. With a long history of foreign influence – including Greek, Roman, Norman, Arab, Swabian, Spanish and French – Naples is a city whose architecture, customs and language barely feel Italian, let alone European. In his 1947 novel *La Pelle* (*The Skin*), Curzio Malaparte wrote: "Naples is the most mysterious city in Europe. It is the only city of the Ancient world that has not perished…It is not a city: it's a world – the ancient pre-Christian world, which has survived intact on the surface of the modern world." Naples is a tangle of intense flavours and vibrant culture. It's the home of pizza, coffee, ice cream, pasta and the fruits of the Campania Felix. Down in the old Graeco-Roman *decumani* streets, amid the layers of architecture and *arte d'arrangiarsi* ('arrange yourself': make ends meet), the languidly sensual *teatro napoletano* is played out with stop-start bursts of energy. Compelling atmospheres fill the city's *rioni* (quarters), from elegant Chiaia to palatial Capodimonte. The muggy air and glimpses of Vesuvius add to the dreamlike spectacle. Neapolitans infuse their Baroque everyday dealings with hedonism and macabre superstition laced with humour. Once Naples gets under your skin, that nonchalant Neapolitan shrug towards the city's perennial woes begins to make some sense. With Campania's beauty and fertility comes the Camorra's grip and volcanic menace. Neapolitans "dwell on the confines of heaven and hell-fire", as the Enlightenment scholar Edwin Gibbon said, so they are bound to behave a little differently.

A T-shirt mimicking the warning on a cigarette packet sums up the city's deadly allure: *Napoli non è una città, ma uno stato d'animo* – Naples is not a city, it's a mood, an atmosphere.

Campi Flegrei

Dubbed the "Fiery Fields" by the ancients, this 13-km-wide volcanic caldera west of Naples is picturesquely pocked with craters, steaming sights and Graeco-Roman ruins. Mythmakers Virgil and Homer saw this as a land of fatal contrasts: a heavenly Arcadian landscape scarred by a fiery Hades, the entrance to the underworld. Eerily beautiful Lake Averno and the sulphuric moonscape of Solfatara certainly have the whiff of myth about them. At Pozzuoli, Baia and Bacoli, remains of the most lavish spa resort and grandiose Roman buildings, including the Anfiteatro Flavio, mingle with a new wave of swanky beach clubs, restaurants and hotels. Amid the scenic architectural fragments at Cuma, where the Greeks founded Magna Graecia, is a trapezoidal tunnel with fantastical stories attached to a prophetess, the Cumean Sybil. Piscina Mirabilis, a cathedral-like underground cistern, held the water of one of Rome's finest feats of engineering, the Serino Aqueduct. At Bagnoli, an industrial wasteland is slowly being reclaimed as a destination of innovation and pleasure; while at Fuorigrotta, a piece of monumental Fascist architecture, the Mostra d'Oltremare, sits among theme parks, SSC Napoli's Stadio San Paolo and the zoo.

Vesuvius, Herculaneum and Pompeii

Below Vesuvius, compelling time capsules of Roman life continue to astonish archaeologists and visitors. This is *La Zona Rossa*, the Red Zone, the area that will feel the true force of mainland Europe's only active volcano one day. For a heart-pounding dose of humble pie, take a walk around the crater rim of Vesuvius and peer into its depths. There are incredible walks in the Parco Nazionale di Vesuvio and time-travel explorations at Pompeii, Ercolano, Oplontis, Boscoreale and Stabiae. Combine a walk around the ancient well-heeled beachside resort of Herculaneum, where skeletons, jewels and the Villa dei Papiri's priceless library of scrolls are still coming to light, with a journey around mind-blowing Pompeii. Along the *Miglio d'Oro* (the Golden Mile) there are dozens of 18th-century, Bourbon-era *Ville Vesuviane*. Vesuvian soil yields the tastiest produce, particularly San Marzano tomatoes, apricots, artichokes, persimmons, and grapes that produce the white Vesuvio DOC and Lacryma Christi wines.

Capri, Ischia and Procida

These three islands offer their own unique dreams and adventures. Glamour, glitz and the jet-set are synonymous with Capri, the largest and bluest chip off the old Sorrentine

Peninsula's limestone rock. So hilly and craggy is Capri that you can easily escape the daily invasion of mass tourism and bask in the island's wild wonders by ducking down a scented lane or by chartering a boat. Emperors Augustus and Tiberius, and writers such as Graham Greene and Axel Munthe, have all added to its allure as an idyllic retreat of rustic epicurean pleasures and hedonistic japes.

Both Ischia and Procida were plopped into the bay by the Campi Flegrei volcanic caldera. Vestiges of its heated volcanic past can be seen in Ischia's thermal springs, while Procida is made up of four curvy craters that form stunning bays backed by honey-hued tufa rock. Ischia's 46 sq km contain a dead volcano – Monte Epomeo – subtropical gardens and beaches of volcanic sand fizzing with fumaroles. Tiny Procida is all about intimacy, earthiness and relaxation – its leafy lanes lead to pastel-coloured fishing villages and beaches.

Getting to Naples

Air

From UK and Ireland Flying to Naples International Airport (Aeroporto Internazionale di Napoli, also known as Aeroporto Capodichino) is the most convenient option as it's within easy reach of the city and other attractions. Year-round direct flights leave from Dublin, London Heathrow, London Gatwick and London Stansted airports. The main airlines providing year-round direct flights are **Alitalia**, **Aerlingus**, **British Airways** and **easyJet**. Some carriers, such as **Thomson**, run charter flights in the spring and summer months from London and other UK airports including Belfast, Birmingham, Bristol, East Midlands, Glasgow, Manchester and Newcastle. Edinburgh and Liverpool are served by **easyJet** from April to October.

From North America There are no year-round direct flights to Naples from North America. Rome Fiumincino is the nearest airport you can fly direct to, with **Alitalia** and **Delta** flights from New York and Toronto. **Alitalia**, **Air Canada**, **Air France**, **British Airways**, **Delta** and **KLM** also fly to the large Italian airports of Milan Malpensa and Venice Marco Polo. London, Munich and Paris are other possible hubs with lots of connecting flights to Naples.

From rest of Europe There are direct flights to Naples from many European cities including Amsterdam, Athens, Barcelona, Basel, Berlin, Brussels, Bucharest, Frankfurt, Geneva, Hanover, Kiev, Madrid, Monaco, Munich, Paris, Prague, Stockholm, Stuttgart, Vienna and Zurich. Carriers include **Aerosvit**, **Air One**, **Air France**, **Alitalia**, **Brussels Airlines**, **easyJet**, **Clickair**, **Iberia**, **Lufthansa**, **Meridiana**, **Tuifly**, **Vueling** and **Sky Europe**.

Airport information **Naples International Airport (NAP)** ① *T081-751 5471/081-789 6259, www.gesac.it*, also known as Capodichino Airport, is situated about 7 km northeast of the centre of Naples. Recent additions to the airport complex have not drastically changed its feel as a small airport of a manageable size. Buses to central Naples are fairly reliable – they all stop at the main train station, Napoli Centrale, and many drop passengers near the port, so connections with other transport services are usually straightforward. In the Arrivals hall there's an EPT (local tourist board) desk where you can find out tourist information and buy the **Artecard** (see box, page 22), and car hire desks including **Avis** ① *T081-780 5790, www.avis.co.uk*, **Europcar** ① *T081-780 5643, www.europcar.co.uk*, and **Hertz** ① *T081-780 2971, www.hertz.co.uk*.

Airport transfer options The **Alibus** runs every 30 minutes from 0630 to 2330 between the airport, piazza Garibaldi (20 minutes) and the port terminal at piazza Municipio (35 minutes). Tickets cost €4 and can be bought on board. If you opt for a taxi, you are plunged into Neapolitan chaos at the taxi rank outside Arrivals. Make sure you get an authorized cab (most are white and should have a laminated card with tariff list on the back seat) and either agree to a *prezzo fisso* (fixed price: a journey to central Naples should cost €19-25) or that the *tassista* (taxi driver) puts on his *tassimetro* (metre). You could travel in style with a reputable private chauffeur such as **Benvenuto Limos** ① *T346-684 0226, www.benvenutolimos.com*.

To reach destinations outside of the city, **Curreri Viaggi** ① *T081-801 5420, www.curreriviaggi.it, services 0900-1930, €10 one way*, runs infrequent buses to and from Pompeii and along the Sorrentine Peninsula. Otherwise, less direct routes involve taking the **ANM Alibus**, or a taxi, to Naples – the region's transport hub for Circumvesuviana rail, mainline rail and seaborne services along the coast or to the islands (see Sea, below).

Rail
There are no direct rail links to Naples from the UK. However there are train services to Milan, Turin, Venice, Padua and Verona from European cities, including Paris, Munich, Vienna and Geneva; you can then use **Trenitalia** ① *www.trenitalia.com*, trains to reach Naples. Travel by rail from the UK involves taking the **Eurostar** ① *www.eurostar.com*, service from London St Pancras to Paris Gare du Nord (two hours 25 minutes) and then crossing Paris to the Gare de Bercy to catch a direct overnight sleeper to Milan or Venice Santa Lucia in northern Italy, from where you can catch a train to Naples, which takes another six hours. Daytime travel is also possible but you'll have to spend a night in either Paris, Milan or Geneva. Another alternative is an overnight train from Paris Bercy to Roma Termini, which takes 18 hours. Buy tickets through **Rail Europe** ① *T0844 848 4064, www.raileurope.co.uk, www.raileurope.com*, or **SNCF** ① *www.voyages-sncf.com*. For comprehensive information on rail travel throughout Europe, consult www.seat61.com.

Road
Car If you're up for the 2000-km journey and can afford the petrol, you could drive from the UK to Naples in a leisurely 30 hours (if you're lucky) – a couple of overnight stops on the way would make for a more pleasant adventure. The classic route from the UK is through France, entering Italy through the Mont Blanc tunnel where you will arrive in the gorgeous Italian Alps, just north of Turin. Italian *autostrade* take you down to Naples; perhaps choose a route to take in some towns and sights on the way. Having a car is a bonus if you want to explore Campania but it's more of a hindrance for those based in Naples itself as Neapolitan traffic can be a frightening prospect, especially for the uninitiated. Car theft and parking is also a big problem in the city so think thrice before opting to drive in Naples.

Bus/coach Eurolines ① *T0871-781 8178, www.eurolines.com*, run long-distance coaches across Europe. The tortuous journey from London to Naples takes about 36 hours, stopping at Paris and Milan on the way.

Sea
Naples is very much on the Mediterranean cruise liner route. Colossal ships dock around the impressive Fascist-era **Stazione Marittima** ① *T081-551 4448, www.terminalnapoli.it*, terminal building on the Molo Angioino. A good place to research into the pros and cons of cruise holidays and operators is www.cruises.co.uk, which contains a wealth of reviews.

Transport in Naples

Getting around

By foot The easiest way to get around the Centro Antico is on foot. Traffic in Naples is notoriously anarchic and takes some getting used to. Drivers obey a very Neapolitan game plan which is much like playing bumper-cars at the fair: whizzing scooters and vehicles largely ignore traffic lights, and *clacsons* are used constantly to communicate a laconic "oi watch it!" All this makes crossing the road in Naples an art form in itself.

By public transport Naples has a comprehensive transport system of buses, trams, funiculars and metro trains. For up-to-date timetables consult the latest *Qui Napoli* booklet, now available only online (www.inaples.it) as a PDF. Tickets are available from *tabacchi* (tobacconists – look out for the big 'T') as well as from ticket offices, some bars and news-stands. The **UnicoNapoli** travel cards provide unlimited travel in the city and beyond: 60 minutes for €1.30; 24 hours on weekdays for €3.70; 24 hours at the weekend for €3.10; 72 hours throughout Campania including the islands for €20; and 72 hours in conjunction with the **Artecard** for €27.

Napoli's metro system, **Metronapoli** ① *www.metro.na.it*, is currently undergoing redevelopment and, when finished (2015 and counting… it's years behind schedule), will consist of 10 lines. Two existing lines are particularly useful: Linea 1 or *Metro d'Arte*, with contemporary art installations, runs from piazza Dante and Museo to Vomero; while Linea 2 crosses the city from east to west, linking Pozzuoli to Gianturco. When – and if – completed Linea 1 will run in a circle between Napoli Centrale train station and Capodichino Airport.

Buses and trams run from 0500-2400. There are three colour-coded types: red buses (marked 'R') are supposedly fast and frequent; orange buses are the most common; blue buses serve the outlying areas. Night buses (*linee notturne*) are best avoided. Useful buses include R2 linking piazza Garibaldi and piazza Trieste e Trento; R3 running from piazza Carità to Mergellina via the Galleria Umberto I and Chiaia; and R4 linking the port area with the Museo Archeologico.

Regional and local buses arrive at and depart from **Napoli Centrale** ① *piazza Garibaldi, T081-554 3188*, the city's transport hub. **CTP** ① *T081-700 1111*, and **STP** ① *T081-552 2176*, are the big bus operators.

Four *funicolari* (**cable railways**) connect Napoli's hills (Vomero and Posillipo) with downtown areas: Centrale (via Toledo to piazza Fuga); Montesanto (piazza Montesanto to via Morghen); Chiaia (Parco Margherita to Cimarosa); and Mergellina (via Mergellina to via Manzoni). They are a fun and handy way to get around.

Taking *un tassi* (a **taxi**) is often convenient, and can be an entertaining if hair-raising insight into *Napoletanità*. If the meter isn't switched on, agree to a fixed price before you set off and ask for the regulated price list that should be on view in the back of the cab. Taxis can be hailed at the 90 taxi ranks or by phoning these companies for a €1 booking fee: **Consortaxi** ① *T081-552 5252*; **Consorzio Taxi Vagando** ① *CoTaNa, T081-570 7070, www.taxivagando.it*; or **Radio Free Taxi** ① *T081-551 5151*.

Rail

Italy's hugely extensive, efficient and affordable rail network is the best way to get around the country. It is served by air-conditioned high-speed *Frecciarossa* and *Frecciargento* trains with few stops; new high-speed private slower main line *Frecciabiana*, *Intercity* and *Eurocity* services; and the slower *Regionale* (REG) and *Interregionale* (IR) trains, both of which stop at many more stations. All can be booked at www.trenitalia.com. Register online and you can search months in advance for bargain *Super Economy* tickets. Just print out the ticket and keep a note of the details. **Trenitalia** ① *T89-20-21 from within Italy, T+39 0668-475475 from outside Italy, www.trenitalia.com*, has details of all routes, service issues and latest discount offers.

The **Napoli Centrale** station is on crazy, traffic-ridden piazza Garibaldi. Be especially careful in and around the crowded station, keeping a close eye on your valuables and your wallet, as its frenzied and humid environment can be disorientating and the area is frequented by some dodgy characters and pickpocket squads. The main train line runs north to Rome and south to Salerno and Calabria.

Local railways The **Ferrovia Circumvesuviana** ① *T800-053939, www.vesuviana.it*, runs between Naples (Stazione Circumvesuviana, just off piazza Garibaldi) and the satellite towns southeast of the city, below Vesuvius (including Ercolano and Pompei) and along the Sorrentine Peninsula as far as Sorrento. The Cumana and Circumflegrea networks are now part of the city's metro system, connecting Naples with the Campi Flegrei west of the city.

Road
Bicycle If your thighs are up to it and you are confident on roads populated with fast and crazy drivers, cycling around the rural areas of Campania can be memorable. Arm yourself with a good map: **Edizioni Multigraphic** and **Touring Club Italiano** do excellent road maps, while **Kompass** caters for outdoor enthusiasts seeking wilder climbs. Bikes are allowed on many train services: check out www.trenitalia.com for more information. Naples has a few cycle lanes (*piste ciclabili*) including one along the pedestrianized waterfront. It extends also to Bagnoli but is beset by obstacles and tunnel traffic. Bike hire is available at **Rent a Bike Italy** ① *T346-847 1141, www.rentalbikeitaly.com*, and **Napoli Bike** ① *Riviera di Chiaia, T081-411 934, www.napolibike.com*. The former can also arrange guided excursions around Vesuvius and Campi Flegrei. Luciano Caputo's **Napoli Bike** shop is handily located to enjoy the safest stretch of cycle lane on the waterfront. Friendly cycling group **Cicloverdi** ① *www.cicloverdi.it*, organizes excursions in Naples and all over the Campania region. The **European Cycling Federation** ① *www.ecf.com*, promotes cycling in Europe and offers good advice as well as links to companies that provide biking tours in the region.

Bus/coach With trains so fast, cheap and efficient, it is only in the more rural areas that buses provide a useful service. Check with the local tourist information office to confirm times and pick-up points, as well as to find out where to buy tickets (it's often a nearby newsagent or tobacconist). Travelling around cities by bus is easier as these services are regular. Again you can buy tickets from newsagents, tobacconists (look for a big T sign) and even some cafés. If you intend to make a number of journeys, buy a stash of tickets or a travel card such as **Unico Campania** or **Unico Ischia**, which allow 24 hours of unlimited travel. Always remember to validate your ticket by stamping it in the machine on board the bus. The main bus companies in the region are **ANM** ① *www.anm.it*, which runs buses around Naples and the suburbs, while **SITA** ① *www.sitabus.it*, and **Eavbus** ① *www.eavbus.it*, provide regional services.

Car Having your own vehicle is more of a burden than a bonus in Naples as the traffic is horrendous and car crime is rife. Put it this way: running a car in this city demands some of the highest insurance premiums on the planet! However, if you plan to brave the roads and tour Campania's mountainous interior, having your own transport will allow you to

Driving tips

- *Rimane calmo!* The most important thing is to stay calm so that you can get used to the way Neapolitans drive.
- Try and look into the eyes of the drivers to see their intention. If they are wearing sunglasses, then that's unlucky!
- Neapolitan drivers hoot their horn a lot, like a reflex action. It's a friendly warning.

- The old adage that at traffic lights in Naples, "Green means take care and red means go!" is not as prevalent as it used to be as the *vigilanza stradale* (traffic police) actually dole out fines these days.
- Don't leave valuables or luggage unattended, in your car – ever!

Tassista Francesco Coda

visit more rural destinations that are difficult to reach by bus or train. For those heading into the city and the islands, the most convenient and central car park is **Parcheggio Buono Molo Beverello** ① *piazza Municipio, T335-499658, www.parcheggiobeverello.com, daily 0600-2100*, which is next to the Molo Beverello port.

EU nationals taking their own car into Italy need to have an International Insurance Certificate (also known as a *Carta Verde*) and a valid national or EU licence. Those holding a non-EU licence need to take an International Driving Permit with them.

Speed limits are 130 kph on *autostrade* (motorways), 110 kph on dual carriageways and 50 kph in towns. (Limits are 20 kph lower on motorways and dual carriageways when the road is wet.) When there is fog (*nebbia*) the speed limit is 50 kph. The **A1** links Rome and Naples, passing Capua and Caserta and through the northern suburbs before it becomes the **A3**, which runs eastwards below Vesuvius and towards Salerno. Approaching the city, vehicles use the **Tangenziale di Napoli**, a huge ring road on stilts that sweeps westwards above the city. It has various exits and can be a tad confusing and overwhelming for those not used to the fluid Neapolitan traffic – Uscita 1 (Exit 1) on the Tangenziale is for Capodichino and Naples International airports. For those staying north or west of the city at Capodimonte, Vomero, Fuorigrotta or the Campi Flegrei, it's best to use the Tangenziale to avoid the city's traffic mayhem downtown. Drivers heading to the port or east of the city towards Ercolano, the Sorrentine Peninsula and Amalfi Coast should continue to the intersection near San Giovanni a Teduccio, where the A3 starts.

Autostrade are toll roads, so keep cash in the car as a back-up even though you can use credit cards on the blue and white 'Viacard' gates (avoid the Telepass lanes). The pre-paid Viacard can be bought at service stations, toll gates and Punto Blu outlets along the motorway network. **Autostrade** ① *www.autostrade.it*, provides information on motorways in Italy and **Automobile Club d'Italia** ① *www.aci.it*, provides general driving information. The latter also offers roadside assistance with English-speaking operators on T803-116 (freephone). For the latest traffic and other information (in English) within Italy contact T06-4363 2121, www.autostrade.it/en/autostrade.

ZTL Limited Traffic Zones In recent years controversial limited traffic zones have been set up – restricting circulation to authorized vehicles and residents with a permit only. ZTL are all over the city including in the Centro Antico, Chiaia, Mezzocannone and the Lungomare. Check with your hotel for latest details and parking facilities or consult www. comune.napoli.it. Times and conditions change from week to week and are extended in summer months during major events. Be aware that there are restrictions on driving in many historic city centres, indicated by signs with black letters ZTL (*Zona a Traffico Limitato*) on a yellow background. If you ignore these signs, you are liable for a fine. Parking is usually available outside the Centro Antico for €2-5 an hour depending on the location. City hotels will either provide parking for guests or be able to direct you to the nearest car park.

Since July 2007 on-the-spot fines for minor traffic offences have been in operation; typically they range from €150 to €250 (always get a receipt). Note the following legal requirements: the use of mobile telephones while driving is not permitted; front and rear seatbelts must be worn, if fitted; children under 1.5 m may only travel in the back of the car. Italy has very strict laws on drink driving: the legal limit is 0.5 g per litre of blood compared to the UK's 0.8 g. If your car breaks down on the carriageway, you must display an emergency triangle and wear a reflective jacket in poor visibility. Car hire companies should provide both of these but check the boot when you pick up your car.

Car hire Car hire is available at Naples airport. You are advised to book your hire car before you arrive in the country, especially at busy times of year. Car hire comparison websites and agents are a good place to start a search for the best deals: try www.carrentals.co.uk, www.avis.com, www.europcar.co.uk and www.hertz.co.uk. Check what each hire company requires from you: some companies will ask for an International Driving Licence alongside your normal driving licence; others are content with an EU licence. You will also need a credit card, so, if you book ahead, make sure that the named credit card holder is the same as the person renting and driving the car. Most companies have a lower age limit of 21 years, with a young driver surcharge for those under 25, and require that you've held your licence for at least a year. Confirm the company's insurance and damage waiver policies and keep all your documents with you when you drive.

Sea

There are many operators that provide maritime passenger services to and from the islands (Capri, Ischia and Procida), along the Sorrentine Peninsula (including Sorrento) and along the Amalfi Coast (Amalfi and Positano) towards Salerno. The port terminal (opened in 2008) at **Calata Porta di Massa**, off via Cristoforo Colombo, now handles the bulk of the ferry (*navi/traghetti*) services, whereas nearby **Porto Beverello**, near piazza Municipio, is the place to go for the swifter hydrofoils (*aliscafi*) and catamarans (*catamarani*). The smaller and less hectic quayside at **Mergellina** now handles the bulk of the faster and more comfortable *aliscafi* services to Ischia. In the summer especially, the most comfortable way of reaching Positano, Amalfi and Minori is to take a hydrofoil from the port of Napoli Beverello. Further west in the Campi Flegrei at the port of **Pozzuoli** there are services to and from Ischia (Ischia Porto, Casamicciola and Forio) and Procida (Marina Grande). The main carriers are: **Alilauro** ⓘ *T081-497 2211, www.alilauro.it*, **Caremar** ⓘ *T081-017 1998, www.caremar.it*, **Linee Marittime Artenopee** ⓘ *T081-807 1812, www.consorziolmp.it*, **Medmar** ⓘ *T081-552 2838, www.medmargroup.it*, **Metro del Mare** ⓘ *T199-600700, www.metrodelmare.com*, **NLG** ⓘ *Navigazione Libera del Golfo, T081-552 0763, www.navlib.it*, **Procidalines** ⓘ *T081-896 0328*, **Procidamar** ⓘ *T081-497 2278, www.procida.net*, and **SNAV** ⓘ *T081-761 2348, www.snav.it*.

Where to stay in Naples

Finding decent accommodation in Naples and its environs used to pose the usual dilemma of whether to fork out for a reliable old *albergo* (hotel) or risk it with a small and cheaper B&B-type *pensione*. Over the past 15 years lots of new small hotels, B&Bs and apartment-hotels have sprung up offering comfort, location and style at a reasonable price. New luxury hotels with a dash of contemporary chic are now going head-to-head with well-established hotels, which are having to up their game to attract increasingly demanding and savvy customers. Self-catering is often an economic option and offers flexibility.

Naples' grand old dames along the Santa Lucia waterfront, and smart hotels like **Grand Hotel Parkers** in Vomero, are now up against boutique hotels offering bags of character in the revitalized Centro Antico and swanky Chiaia. Leading the way is **Costantinopoli 104** (see page 54), a *stile-Liberty* palazzo ensconced in a tranquil (for Naples!) courtyard near piazza Bellini, and the arty design-hotel **Micalò** (see page 56) on the riviera di Chiaia. For those on a budget there are lots of new small hotels in the atmospheric old city – such as **Fresh Glamour** (see page 55) and **Piazza Bellini** (see page 55) – offering modern style. B&Bs offer a slice of Neapolitan family life, such as the Raffone family's art-filled **Donna Regina** (see page 55) near the MADRE art gallery and **La Bouganville** (see page 56) in lofty Posillipo.

Naples itself is split into various *rioni* (districts), each offering their own charms, while some are just best avoided. The Centro Antico has lots of atmosphere and fascinating sights but can be a tad hairy after dark, while La Sanità and around piazza Garibaldi are best avoided because of petty crime. Chiaia is a good choice as it's handily located for many of the sights, has swanky shops and bars, and is relatively safe. Posillipo and Vomero are hilltop suburbs with wonderful views of the bay but can feel a little detached from the main action.

Perhaps due to their urban sprawl and history of volcanic events, Campi Flegrei and, on the opposite side of the bay, Vesuvius, Ercolano and Pompeii have less impressive accommodation. However, things are improving and prices are generally much cheaper, except perhaps at Pompeii which has a captive market. Baia's beach and bar scene has spawned the funky **Batis** (see page 73) and family-friendly **Cala Moresca** (see page 73); while right next to ancient Herculaneum is the excellent **Miglio d'Oro Park Hotel** (see page 83), housed in the grand Bourbon-era Villa Aprile.

On the islands, there are truly magical hotels for those with deep pockets. Capri has the new boutique darling **JK Place** (see page 102) while Anacapri's **Caesar Augustus** (see page 102) was King Farouk of Egypt's favourite retreat. Ischia has a glut of spa hotels (with varying standards of cleanliness) as well as the fabulous yet affordable **Albergo Il Monastero** (see page 110), housed in a castle convent. Procida's planning laws have resulted in a dearth of decent hotels, with **La Vigna** (see page 116) a standout choice.

Apartments and agriturismi

For those seeking freedom, whether it's in the city or on the coast, renting an apartment or villa is a great option. Small family-run outfits like **Napoli Residence** (www.napoliresidence.com) and **Amalfi Vacation** (www.amalfivacation.it) can be the easiest to deal with, while large brokers like **Ville in Italia** (www.villeinitalia.com) and **Cuendet** (www.cuendet.com) have hundreds of properties to choose from. Rustic *agriturismi* farm stays offer a taste of the rustic life and home-made food. Examples include **Il Casolare** (see page 73) in the Campi Flegrei and **Bel Vesuvio Inn** (see page 83) on the slopes of Vesuvius, both of which have basic and reasonably priced rooms.

Price codes

Where to stay

€€€€ over €300   €€€ €200-300

€€ €100-200   € under €100

Prices refer to the cost of two people sharing a double room in the high season.

Restaurants

€€€€ over €40   €€€ €30-40

€€ €20-30   € under €20

Prices refer to the average cost of a two-course meal for one person, including drinks and service charge.

Food and drink in Naples → *For menu reader, see page 123.*

Campania is a foodie's heaven. Its fecund volcanic soil and the waters of the Tyrrhenian Sea yield plentiful, tasty and healthy produce and seafood – the term 'Mediterranean diet' was first coined at the University of Salerno. The intense flavours of Campania's vegetables, fruits and seafood need little adornment. It's no coincidence that Graeco-Roman Naples was the natural home of Epicureanism – in its purest philosophical sense – and Bacchanalian revelry.

Neapolitan cuisine

Miseria e nobiltà (poverty and nobility) have shaped *la cucina Napoletana*. While the region's resourceful poor have created two simple world-conquering creations – dried pasta and pizza – 2500 years of foreign influence, especially French and Spanish, with a dash of Arabic, have spawned 'noble' dishes such as *timballi* and *sartù di riso*, as well as rich pastry and ice-cream making traditions.

Pasticcerie

babà a rum-drenched bulbous sponge.

cornetto con crema/con marmellata sweet croissant usually filled with custard or jam; a breakfast favourite accompanied by coffee.

pastiera a large tart made with a filling of sweet ricotta and candied fruit.

sfogliatella meaning 'many leaves' or 'layers', *sfogliatelle* are made of thin layers of pastry and filled with ricotta often infused with orange; *sfogliatella riccia* has flaky pastry while *sfogliatella frolla* is the shortcrust version.

struffoli small deep-fried balls of dough covered in honey.

torta caprese chocolate-and-almond cake from Capri.

zeppole Neapolitan doughnuts or fritters, sometimes with cream but always crusted with sugar and served warm.

Coffee In Naples *caffè* is extra strong with a pre-sugared kick to complete the rush it gives. The *barista* may ask you '*già zuccherato?*' before he makes your caffeine hit, so ask for '*amaro*' (bitter) if you are sweet enough already. A glass of water is served to clear your palate.

espresso/normale/un caffè a standard espresso – a double is a *doppio*.

ristretto an even stronger espresso made with less water.

caffè corretto espresso 'corrected' with a shot of alcohol, usually grappa.
macchiato espresso 'marked' or 'stained' with foamy milk on top.
caffè Americano or lungo espresso made or served with more hot water.
caffè shakerato iced espresso given the cocktail-shaker treatment.
cappuccino a frothy milky coffee seldom drunk after midday.
latte macchiato/caffè latte steamed milk 'marked' or 'stained' with a tiny shot of espresso.
caffè latte shakerato ice-cold *caffé latte* shaken.

Eating out

Breakfast (*colazione*) in Campania may include a *caffè latte* and/or an espresso accompanied by a pastry, usually a horn-shaped *cornetto* with fillings – *alla crema* (pastry cream), *al cioccolato* (chocolate) or *alla marmellata* (marmalade). On holiday and Sundays locals enjoy a long lunch (*pranzo*), perhaps followed by a cheeky siesta at the height of summer. An *aperitivo* is taken in the early evening, usually in a bar, and is served with *stuzzichini* (nibbles). Restaurants tend to serve lunch 1200-1530 and dinner (*cena*) 1900-2300. Traditionally *un ristorante* was posher than *una trattoria*, which in turn was generally more sophisticated than *un'osteria*, which was once just a rustic inn serving wine and simple dishes; however the distintion between each is blurred these days so the title is not a good indicator of quality, price or ambience.

Campania is one of the cheapest regions to eat out and standards are generally excellent. There are wonderful seafood restaurants in magical places and superb-value *pizzerie* are commonplace. The cornucopia of *contorni* (side dishes) on Campanian menus is a great help for vegetarians. Some classic Neapolitan dishes are described on page 125.

Wines of Campania

Where once the Campania region was known for the quantity of richly coloured, alcohol-heavy wine produced, it is now creating quality wines with elegance and subtlety. Here are the best of Campania's DOC wines:

Aglianico del Taburno Rosso
The Aglianico grape, cultivated in the Benevento province, is aged for 2 years; its bold taste goes well with cheese.

Campi Flegrei Falanghina Grown in the volcanic soil, the white Falanghina grape has a lightly aromatic bouquet with fruity notes. Goes well with seafood, especially mussels and crustaceans.

Capri Bianco A small, highly prized production of white wine mixing Falanghina, Greco and Biancolella grape varieties. Best drunk young, its fresh, dry taste is a perfect match for seafood and cheeses like caciocavallo.

Costa d'Amalfi Bianco Falanghina and Biancolella vines grown on the terraces around Ravello, Furore and Tramonti produce a subtle wine that marries well with light seafood dishes and fresh cheeses. *Rosato* and *rosso* versions are also produced.

Fiano di Avellino A venerable white produced in the Avellino province with floral and hazelnut aromas. Goes well with fish and young cheeses.

Greco di Tufo Probably the best-known DOC along with Fiano. The Greco vine is grown in the Irpinia area, whose volcanic soil gives the wine a rich flavour and good acidity. It works well with Neapolitan seafood dishes, artichokes, rice dishes and soups.

Ischia Bianco Generally a mix of Forastera and Biancolella grapes, it has an intense yellow colour, subtle aromas and is a perfect accompaniment to delicate dishes and light antipasti. There is a sparkling *spumante* version.

Ischia Piedirosso The Piedirosso vine's reddish stalks resemble doves' feet, hence the name. With an aroma of violets, and a little tannic, it goes well with *coniglio all'ischiatana* (Ischian-style rabbit).

Taurasi Rosso Wine from the Aglianico vine grown in the Avellino province is aged for 3 years in barrels, giving it complex flavours and aromas; perfect for meat dishes and cheeses.

Vesuvio Lacryma Christi Bianco The white Coda di Volpe grape grown on the slopes of Vesuvius is blended with Falanghina and Greco varities. *Rosso*, *rosato* and *spumante* versions are also produced.

Festivals in Naples

Catholic festivals, many with pagan origins and hundreds celebrating saints' days, dominate the Neapolitan calendar. Neapolitans certainly know how to party and display emotion, so expect full-on fireworks, food, processions and histrionics. Traditional events celebrate the bounty of land and sea, while an eclectic array of cultural and music extravaganzas entertain locals and visitors across the region.

January

Capodanno (New Year) Concert and fireworks in piazza Plebiscito and general mayhem all over.

Festa Nazionale della Befana (6th) Epiphany is celebrated in Italy with Italian children receiving more presents from *la Befana*, a good witch who leaves treats for the good kids and a lump of coal (now some honeycomb candy died black) for naughty ones.

February

Carnevale (14 days before Ash Wed) The 'farewell to meat' festival is an excuse for excess that starts a fortnight before Ash Wed when Lent begins. All over Campania there are float parades, feasts and flamboyant shows throughout. Avellino, Capua and Paestum put on particularly full-on shows with masked revellers.

March

NauticaSud (early Mar) The Mezzogiorno's biggest boat show is held at the Mostra d'Oltremare.

Settimana della Cultura (late Mar) The national week of culture allows visitors to take advantage of free museum entrance, special guided tours and cultural events.

April

Comicon (late Apr) Comic and animation fans descend on Castel Sant'Elmo each spring (www.comicon.it).

Easter *Pasqua* (Easter) in Naples is celebrated with processions and ceremonies, some dating from the Middle Ages and even pagan times. Celebrations at Sant'Anastasia al Vesuvio and Procida are famously flamboyant, with the scoffing of lots of savoury and sweet pies – *il casatiello* and *la pastiera*.

Processione dei Misteri Statues and contemporary depictions of scenes from the Passion of Christ are taken through the streets of Terra Murata, Procida, on Good Friday.

May

Festa di San Costanzo (3rd week of May) Capri's patron saint and protector, who drove away Saracen attacks in the Middle Ages, is honoured with a flower-strewn procession and a host of cultural events.

Maggio dei Monumenti Naples' historic sites can be visited free and some rarely seen sights are opened too. Themed cultural events including lots of concerts and installations in wonderful settings make May a stimulating month to visit.

June

Concerti al Tramonto   A season of concerts (Jun-Sep), classical and jazz, staged by the San Michele Foundation, custodians of Axel Munthe's enchanting Villa San Michele (www.sanmichele.org).

July

Estate a Napoli (till Sep)   A range of cultural events – concerts, theatre and exhibitions – all over the city.

Festa della Madonna del Carmine (15-16th)   On the night before the saint's day, spectacular fireworks light up the Naples sky in a symbolic 'burning' of the campanile of the Chiesa di Madonna del Carmine in piazza Mercato. The following day, Mass is celebrated every hour of the day.

Festa di Sant'Anna (26th)   Ischia's patron is honoured with a flamboyant procession of crazily adorned floats around the Castello Aragonese amid lots of fireworks (www.festadisantanna.it).

Neapolis Festival (late Jul)   The Arena Flegrea in Fuorigrotta stages concerts by established leftfield acts such as Massive Attack, REM and Editors as well as Italian bands like Almamagretta.

August

Ferragosto (15th)   The summer bank holiday, which heralds an exodus of Italians to the beach.

September

Festa di Piedigrotta   The old Piedigrotta festival, involving a Neapolitan song contest and religious procession, is back on the calendar in early Sep although on a smaller scale these days (www.festadipiedigrotta.it).

Festa di San Gennaro (19th)   In and around the Duomo the faithful await the 'miracle of San Gennaro' which is considered a good omen for Naples. After much frenzied imploring and shaking, the reddish matter in the all-important ampoule (supposedly the saint's blood) usually liquefies and there's much relief, rejoicing and pyrotechnics into the evening.

Pizza Village – Pizzafest   Sep brings a celebration of the Neapolitan pizza with lots of competition between the best *pizzaioli* (pizzamakers) as well as much munching, music and general merriment. Recently staged along the lungomare Caracciolo.

Settembrata Anacaprese   Anacapresi come together in late Aug to early Sep for themed events and good-natured competition to see which *quartiere* can deliver the finest food, sweetest song and heartiest laugh.

October

Napoli Film Festival (autumn – dates vary)   Indoor and outdoor screenings in various venues, plus cinematic music events.

Sagra della Castagna   All over Campania during the last weekend of Oct the harvest of sweet chestnuts is celebrated with street parties – at San Cipriano Picentino there's a donkey race (www.lasagradellacastagna.net).

November

Pane e Olio in Frantoio   On the last weekend of Nov, local producers of extra virgin olive oil and bread promote their goods at numerous tastings across Campania (www.cittadellolio.it).

December

Presepi di Natale   Naples and Campania are famous for their nativity scenes (*presepi*). Via San Gregorio Armeno and its *presepi* shops make it a magic place to visit around Christmas and most churches have a tableau replete with Gesù, shepherds and livestock. San Leucio in the province of Caserta has a 'living nativity'.

Essentials A-Z

Customs and immigration
UK and EU citizens do not need a visa but must have a valid passport to enter Italy. A standard tourist visa for those outside the EU is valid for up to 90 days.

Disabled travellers
Italy is beginning to adapt to the needs of disabled travellers but access can still be very difficult due to the age of many historic buildings or the lack of careful planning. For more details and advice, contact a specialist agency before departure, such as **Accessible Italy** (www.accessibleitaly. com) or **Society for Accessible Travel and Hospitality** (www.sath.org).

Electricity
Italy functions on a 220V mains supply. The plugs are the standard European 2-pin variety.

Emergencies
Ambulance T118; **Fire service** T115; **Police** T112 (with English-speaking operators), T113 (*carabinieri*); **Roadside assistance** T803-116.

Etiquette
Facendo la bella figura (projecting a good image) is important to Italians but down in Campania there is a more laid-back, humorous outlook – the locals are famed for flouting rules and dodging barriers. Neapolitan chattiness is one of the infectious aspects of the region. However, as in the rest of Italy, you should check your change, prices and tariffs. Learn the phrase *non è giusto* (it is not right) as a firm word will be needed from time to time. Unfortunately, *La Dolce Vità Italiana* sometimes leaves a bitter taste.

Take note of public notices about conduct: sitting on steps or eating and drinking in certain historic areas is not allowed. Covering arms and legs is necessary for admission into some churches – in rare cases even shorts are not permitted. Punctuality, like queuing (*facendo la coda*), is an alien concept in Italy, so be prepared to wait on occasion – but not necessarily in line or order.

Families
The family is highly regarded in Italy and children are well treated (not to say indulged), particularly in restaurants (although more expensive restaurants may not admit children). Naples is particularly famed for its family-orientated lifestyle and Neapolitans generally welcome children with open arms. There's plenty to do in Naples and Campania besides endless museum visits with seaside attractions aplenty, as well as theme parks and a zoo in Fuorigrotta. Note that lone parents or adults accompanying children of a different surname may sometimes need proof of guardianship before taking children in and out of Italy; contact your Italian embassy for the current details on this (Italian embassy in London, T020-7312 2200).

Health
Comprehensive medical insurance is strongly recommended for all travellers to Italy. EU citizens should also apply for a free **European Health Insurance Card** (www.ehic.org.uk), which replaced the E111 form and offers reduced-cost medical treatment. Late-night pharmacies are identified by a large green cross outside. Out-of-hours pharmacies are listed in most local newspapers. The accident and emergency department of a hospital is the *pronto soccorso*.

Hospitals
Both of these have 24-hr *pronto soccorso* (casualty departments): **Ospedale Cardarelli**, via Cardarelli 9, T081-546318;

Ospedale Fatebenefratelli, via Manzoni 220, T081-769 7220.

Insurance

Comprehensive travel (and medical) insurance is strongly recommended for all travellers to Italy. You should check any exclusions, excess and that your policy covers you for all the activities you want to undertake. Keep details of your insurance documents separately. Scanning them, then emailing yourself a copy is a good way to keep the information safe and accessible. Ensure you are fully insured if hiring a car, or, if you're taking your own vehicle, contact your current insurer to check whether you require an international insurance certificate.

Money

The Italian currency is the euro (€). To change cash or traveller's cheques, look for a *cambio* (exchange office); these tend to give better rates than banks. Banks are open Mon-Fri 0830-1300 with some opening again 1500-1600. ATMs that accept major credit and debit cards can be found in every city and town (look around the main piazzas). Many restaurants, shops, museums and art galleries will take major credit cards but paying directly with debit cards is less common than in the UK, so having a ready supply of cash may be the most convenient option. You should also keep some change handy for toll roads if you're driving.

Campania has always been one of Italy's cheapest regions to visit, although chic spots on Capri and along the Amalfi Coast bump up their prices. Not including entrance fees to the sights and transport costs, the cost of a typical day if you're flirting with frugality, is around €60. If you're going to pad out your day with a bit of largesse by eating at some fancier restaurants then we are talking about €120 per person. Expect to pay for the privilege of consuming sitting down in tourist hotspots Positano and Capri.

Opening hours and holidays

Aperto or *chiuso*? It takes getting used to that shops, churches and some sights close for a long lunch. Shutters start coming down around 1230 and don't open until around 1600 onwards, although in busy city and touristy areas most of the sights and some shops stay open. Many places close on a Sun and/or a Mon (or just the Mon morning). Family-run restaurants or bars may shut for a day during the week. Finally, the Italian holiday month is Aug. This means that shops, bars, restaurants and even some sights can be closed for a fortnight or longer, especially from 15 Aug (**Ferragosto**). They also close for Christmas, New Year and some of Jan too. Aug is definitely not the best month to visit Italy.

Pharmacies

For information on the rota of night-time opening pharmacies (*farmacie di turno*) ask your hotel or telephone T1100 for nearest ones. The newspaper *Il Mattino* and the doors of pharmacies also have lists.

Police

There are 5 different police forces in Italy. The *carabinieri* are a branch of the army and wear military-style uniforms with red stripes on their trousers and white sashes. They handle general crime, drug-related crime and public order offences. The *polizia statale* is the national police force, dressed in blue with a thin purple stripe on their trousers. They are responsible for security on the railways and at airports. The *polizia stradale* handles crime and traffic offences on the motorways and drives blue cars with a white stripe. The *vigili urbani* are local police who wear dark blue (in summer) or black (in winter) uniforms with white hats and direct traffic and issue parking fines in the cities. The *guardia di finanza* wears grey uniforms with grey flat hats or green berets (depending on rank). They are charged with combating counterfeiting, tax evasion and fraud.

In the case of an emergency requiring police attention, dial 113 or approach any member of the police or visit a police station (below). If it's a non-emergency, dial 112 for assistance.

Naples via Medina 5, T081-551 1190.
Pompeii via Sacra 1, T081-856 3511.
Capri via Roma 68, T081-837 4211.
Ischia via Delle Terme, T081-507 4711.
Procida via Libertà 96, T081-896 0086.

Post

The Italian post service (www.poste.it) has a not entirely undeserved reputation for unreliablility, particularly when it comes to handling postcards. Overseas post will require *posta prioritaria* (priority mail, which is actually just ordinary mail). You can buy *francobolli* (stamps) at post offices and *tabacchi* (look for T signs). A stamp for a letter or postcard (up to 20g) costs from €0.75 for EU destinations and €1.60 for transatlantic destinations. For letters over 20g and parcels, there is a maze of prices and options.

Post office

The **Central Post Office** (Ufficio Postale) is housed in the Fascist-era building at piazza Matteotti, T081-551 1456, Mon-Fri 0800-1830, Sat 0800-1230.

Safety

Visitors to Naples, its satellites around Vesuvius, and Salerno should be most wary. Crowded resorts offer opportunities for criminals on the lookout for valuable items.

Naples has a reputation for petty theft and elaborate street scams which is often exaggerated – unfortunately, the stigma has stuck, which combined with its hectic traffic and general sense of chaos tends to frighten many people away. In reality, random acts of violence are less of a problem here than in many cities around the world. As long as you are extra careful (don't flaunt your wealth and valuables), pickpockets and bag

snatchers shouldn't bother you. The use of a money belt to store credit cards, passports and large denominations is advisable – especially when using crowded public transport and visiting chaotic and poor neighbourhoods like Spaccanapoli, the Quartieri Spagnoli and Rione Sanità. Don't leave bags and valuables unattended in your vehicle, and remove everything from the boot at night. Beware of scams, con artists and sellers of fake goods: if someone offers you electrical goods (camcorders and mobiles are current favourites) or a box of cigarettes on the street, just say *no grazie, non mi interessa* (no thanks, I'm not interested) firmly – and walk on.

Telephone

The dialling code for Naples is 081. You need to use these local codes, even when dialling from within the city or region. The prefix for Italy is +39. You no longer need to drop the initial '0' from the area codes when calling from abroad. For directory enquiries call T12.

Time difference

Italy uses Central European Time, GMT+1.

Tipping

It is increasingly common for service to be included in your bill on top of the cover charge. Where this isn't the case (and, sometimes, even when service is included in the bill), tipping is expected wherever there is waiter/waitress service: 50 cents to €1 is fine if you've only had a drink but, for a meal, 10-15% of the total bill is the norm. If you're ordering at the bar, a few spare coins might speed up your coffee and even result in a smile. Taxis may add on extra costs for luggage but an additional tip is always appreciated. Rounding-up prices always goes down well, especially if it means avoiding having to give change – not a favourite Italian habit.

Artecard

The **Campania Artecard** (T800-600601, from mobiles T06-3996 7650, www.campaniartecard.it) enables visitors to see the region's attractions at a discounted price, with public transport thrown in. There are nine different cards covering the region: The **tutta la regione** card allows 'three days all sites' of discounted sightseeing at €27 for adults or €20 for 18-25s with the first two attractions free (visit the pricey ones first) and then 50% off entry to other sights, plus free use of all public transport – including regional trains and certain buses – with a **Unico** travel card. A **seven-day** card costs €30, while an **annual** card is €40 (18-25s €30). Then there's the **three-day Naples and Campi Flegrei** card (€16 adults, 18-25s €10), which gives you the same deal but only within Naples and the Campi Flegrei. The following sights are included in the scheme: Castel Sant' Elmo, Certosa e Museo di San Martino, Città della Scienza, Complesso Museale di Santa Chiara, Museo Archeologico Nazionale, Museo Civico di Castel Nuovo, Museo Nazionale di Capodimonte, Palazzo Reale and all five major attractions in the Campi Flegrei (counted as one admission). Additionally, lots of other sights offer small discounts on presentation of the card. For all the archaeological sites consider the **Archeologia del Golfo artecard** (€30). Artecards are available at major transport hubs, tourist offices, at participating attractions and at some *edicole* (news-stands).

Tourist information

The following official tourist websites are useful places to visit before your trip: www.inaples.it, www.amalfitouristoffice.it, www.capritourism.com, www.infoischiaprocida.it, www.turismoinsalerno.it, www.sorrentotourism.com. If you're travelling by train, also check out www.trenitalia.it. Once you get to Italy, the regional tourist offices have plenty of leaflets and flyers on local sights and attractions and some offices will also help you to book accommodation.

Combined tickets and travel cards

The region of Campania's various **Unico** and **Artecard** (see box, above) combinations offer some free and otherwise discounted entry to many sights, plus savings on public transport. See www.unicocampania.it.

Tourist information offices

The handiest offices are: the EPT Napoli Centrale, T081-268 799; via San Carlo by the Galleria Umberto T081-402 394; and piazza del Gesù, T081-551 2701.

Contents

Footprint features

Naples

Greek-founded Neapolis lies in the most naturally blessed yet deadly bay imaginable, which perhaps explains its inhabitants' lust for life's joys and dark obsessions. Simple pleasures like *la pizza*, *la sfogliatella* and *il bel far niente* (the beauty of doing nothing) are deeply ingrained. In the Centro Antico, beside shiny bronze skulls of a religious cult, the grimy flagstones of the old Graeco-Roman *decumani* buzz and spit with vespas and the clipped vowels of gesticulating *scugnizzi* (Neapolitan 'street kids'). On the Santa Lucia waterfront you gaze out across the shimmering bay towards Vesuvius, the Sorrentine Peninsula, Capri, the islands… Colours and tastes are vivid, the natural fruits of the fertile volcanic soil and ocean. Bright red tomatoes and azure blue seas contrast with shadowy layers accumulated by centuries of history.

Napoletanità (being Neapolitan) is truly a way of life. *Ccà nisciuno è fesso*, they say: nobody is stupid here. Living on their wits the irrepressible Napoletani create Baroque customs and cults. Macabre miracles like San Gennaro's liquefying blood gave Naples the title *L'Urbs Sanguinum*: the City of Blood. It could be applied to today's Camorra clan wars. Fortunately, for the visitor at least, Napoli's life-affirming culture and cuisine, as well as the bay's natural wonders, overshadow the criminal state-within-a-state that infects its troubled suburbs.

hairy after dark

What to see in Naples

One day

Kick off your day at **Bar Gambrinus** and then explore the monumental city, the **Centro Antico**, the **MADRE gallery** and **Museo Archeologico**, eating pizza at **Il Pizzaiolo del Presidente** on via dei Tribunali, drinking an aperitivo in **Chiaia**, **Borgo Marinari** or on via Orazio, and then dining below **Castel dell'Ovo** or at **Rosiello** in Posillipo.

A weekend or more

Spend further days exploring the area's natural and archaeological wonders on day trips or overnighters: **Vesuvius**, **Pompeii** and **Capri** are must-dos. There's plenty more sightseeing and shopping, including incredible art and gardens at **Capodimonte**, the **Certosa di San Martino** and gastronomic goodies aplenty.

Orientation

Central Naples lies between two volcanoes: Vesuvius in the southeast and the Campi Flegrei caldera in the west. All roads converge on piazza Garibaldi and Stazione Centrale, a grimy, chaotic hub that has shaken many a first-timer into hasty retreat. Survive this acrid and anarchic baptism, then Naples reveals and rewards your curiosity.

Heading south to the docks the former ceremonial square piazza Mercato is now a mix of colourful markets and multi-culturalism that feels more Marrakech than Milan. The broad straight line of 19th-century corso Umberto I, and equally traffic-ridden via Foria to the north, frame the captivating street-life of the Centro Antico. The throbbing heart of ancient Neapolis' Greco-Roman gridded lanes and piazzas bubble with mysterious layers, shrines and pizza ovens.

Regal architecture built by a succession of foreign rulers cluster near the reclaimed shore: piazza Municipio's Maschio Angionio castle overlooks the ferry port; beside Palazzo Reale and the Teatro San Carlo opera house is Naples' modern ceremonial expanse piazza Plebiscito; while along the newly pedestrianized waterfront are Castel del' Ovo and the Villa Comunale gardens. Chiaia's swanky shops, galleries and bars stretch to the kitsch neon lights of Mergellina harbour and up to piazza Amedeo.

Running up the hill from main shopping street, via Toldeo, to the snaking corso Vittorio Emanuele are myriad washing lines of working-class Quartieri Spagnoli. Via Toledo passes the Museo Archeologico and the edge of the mean and fascinating Rione Sanità district, then the road climbs to the Bourbon hunting lodge turned world-class gallery at Capodimonte.

Surveying the downtown action is well-to-do district Vomero, with its post-war apartments, *stile-Liberty* villas and two strategic/religious citadels: Castel Sant'Elmo and Certosa di San Martino. In the hills to the west, posh Posillipo's once verdant slopes rise from shoreline villas to stacked apartments up to via Manzoni. Over and beyond lies Fuorigrotta, the Golfo di Pozzuoli and Campi Flegrei's classical ruins, sulphurous spas and beach clubs.

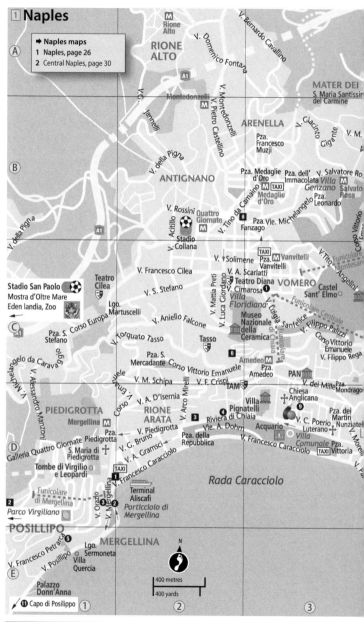

1 Naples

➡ **Naples maps**
1 Naples, page 26
2 Central Naples, page 30

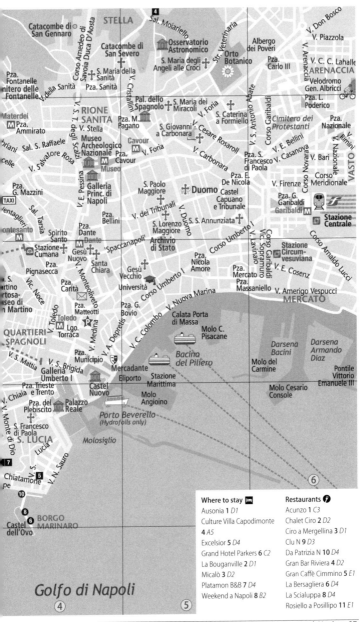

Where to stay 🛏
Ausonia **1** D1
Culture Villa Capodimonte **4** A5
Excelsior **5** D4
Grand Hotel Parkers **6** C2
La Bouganville **2** D1
Micalò **3** D2
Platamon B&B **7** D4
Weekend a Napoli **8** B2

Restaurants 🍴
Acunzo **1** C3
Chalet Ciro **2** D2
Ciro a Mergellina **3** D1
Clu N **9** D3
Da Patrizia N **10** D4
Gran Bar Riviera **4** D2
Gran Caffè Cimmino **5** E1
La Bersagliera **6** D4
La Scialuppa **8** D4
Rosiello a Posillipo **11** E1

Santa Lucia and around → *For listings, see pages 54-66.*

A stone's throw from the waterfront, piazza Plebiscito is the grand focal point of the city. A semicircular colonnade sweeps on either side of the San Francesco di Paola church and a huge pedestrianized space, beloved of football-playing kids, lies in front of the statue and shrapnel-studded Palazzo Reale façade. Grandiose buildings, including the Galleria Umberto I and Teatro San Carlo and smart cafés, surround intimate piazza Trieste e Trento and its elegant, artichoke-adorned fountain. Nearby, the muscular hulk of Castel Nuovo (Maschio Angioino) overlooks muddled piazza Municipio and the port. Buildings cling to the tufa rock of Monte Echia, also known as Pizzofalcone, where Greek settlers founded Parthenope. Santa Lucia is no longer the old fishermen's quarter immortalized in song, although it does have the Borgo Marinari's yachts and restaurants beside the honeycomb-like blocks of the Castel dell'Ovo. The newly pedestrianized waterfront is a wonderful place for a stroll or cycle, and is the focal point of cultural and sports events, as well as the weekend antiques market.

Piazza del Plebiscito and Chiesa San Francesco di Paola
ⓘ *Chiesa T081-764 5133. Mon-Fri 0800-1200, 1530-1800, Sat-Sun 0800-1300. Bus R1-4, C24, E6, 140, 152. Funicolare Centrale: piazza Augusteo.*

Now the traffic has gone and it's no longer used as a car park, the city's largest square and its dramatic architecture is once again the focal point of grand Neapolitan occasions. The Pantheon-aping San Francesco di Paola Church (1817) designed by Pietro Bianchi (1787-1849), with its three wide drum-like domes and sweeping portico, is the backdrop of celebrations, demonstrations, concerts, state visits and quirky contemporary art installations. Begun by the Bonapartist ruler Joachim Murat and finished by Ferdinand of Bourbon, the royal basilica has a circular plan and a rather formal feel, like a severe Palladian mausoleum. Back on the piazza there are equestrian statues of Carlo III and Ferdinando IV by Antonio Canova and Antonio Calì. The Doric colonnades are flanked by lounging lions which draw your eyes to the long façade of the Palazzo Reale, where you can admire eight statues of some of the city's most renowned rulers replete with bulbous breeches, armoury and bullet holes. From left to right, and in chronological order, they are: Roger II, Frederick II, Charles of Anjou, Alfonso of Aragon, Charles V of Hapsburg, Charles III of Bourbon, Joachim Murat and Victor Emmanuel II of Savoy.

Palazzo Reale
ⓘ *Piazza del Plebiscito 1, T081-400547. Thu-Tue 0900-2000, €4, under-18s/over-65s free, discounts with Artecard, guided tour by reservation. Bus R1-4, C24, E6, 140, 152. Funicolare Centrale: piazza Augusteo.*

Chances are your first glimpse of the enormous Royal Palace will be from piazza Plebiscito, where a walk along the 167-m-long façade and its eight regal statues makes for an amusing introduction to Neapolitan history and the city's rulers. Designed by Domenico Fontana (1543-1607), it was built for a planned visit by King Charles III of Spain, who never got around to a sojourn in Naples, let alone sliding down (not advised) the banisters of its **Scalone Monumentale** (Grand Staircase). The **Royal Apartments** are crammed with tapestries, frescoes, paintings, sculpture, period furniture, chandeliers, porcelain and clocks, with pots of gilt and drapes thrown in. Don't miss the **Throne Room**'s chair, which has lions on which to rest divinely chosen elbows and an eagle designed to soar above the sovereign's crown. More fabulously overblown decor can be seen in the **Teatrino**

di Corte (Court Theatre), where there are no prizes for guessing where the king sat; the relatively understated **Studio del Rè** (King's Study); and the **Cappella Palatina** with its grand *presepe* (nativity scene).

You won't find a fustier old library anywhere than the **Biblioteca Nazionale** ⓘ *piazza del Plebiscito 1, Mon-Fri 0830-1930, Sat 0830-1330, free*, frequented by university students and lucky scholars who get to see the priceless papyrus manuscripts rescued from Herculaneum.

Piazza Trieste e Trento and Caffè Gambrinus
ⓘ *Piazza Trieste e Trento. Bus R1-4, C24, E6, 140, 152. Funicolare Centrale: piazza Augusteo.*
Amidst the roundabout traffic and lollypop-wielding *poliziotti* of this piazza near the Galleria Umberto is an alluring fountain with water sprouting from an artichoke, the **Fontana del Carciofo**. Historic **Caffè Gambrinus** (see page 57) on the corner makes a charming espresso stop with its dapper baristas, Neapolitan pastries and grand *fin di secolo* interiors.

Galleria Umberto I
ⓘ *Piazza Trento e Trieste. Entrances on via San Carlo, via Toledo, via Santa Brigida and via Giuseppe Verdi. Bus Bus R1-4, C24, E6, 140, 152. Funicolare Centrale: piazza Augusteo.*
Despite the grime and neglect, the glass and wrought-iron elegance of this 1887-built, *stile-Liberty* arcade will leave you with a sore neck and wide eyes. The cruciform structure is accessed via one of four grand entrances and is worth lingering in to admire its colossal space, ever-changing lighting effects from its curvy skylights, architectural detailing and coloured marble floors. Its rather drab outlets and overpriced cafés do not quite match the swanky smugness of its Milanese twin, the Galleria Emanuele II.

Teatro San Carlo and MeMus
ⓘ *Via San Carlo 93, T081-7972468. MeMus: Mon-Fri 1000-1700, Sat-Sun 1000-1900, €10, under 30s/over 65s and visitors to Palazzo Reale €5. Guided tours Mon-Sat hourly 1030-1630. Bus R1-4, C24, E6, 140, 152. Funicolare Centrale: piazza Augusteo.*
Europe's oldest working opera house was built for King Carlo I in 1737 and its interiors and acoustics still impress. At its height its sumptuous interiors, including Bourbon blue-upholstered seats (now the customary red), and world-famous performances sealed the city's reputation for glamour and worldly pleasures. The present façade was added in 1812 before a fire in 1816 destroyed much of the interior. Among the greats to have graced the stage are Puccini, Rossini, Donizetti, Mascagni, Verdi and Pavarotti, foreign composers Mozart and Haydn, and the smooth castrato falsettos of Farinelli and Velluti. Around the back is the fabulous MeMus museum, dedicated to the historical archive of the opera house. Displays of costumes, documents and multimedia give an insight into Naples' place in operatic history. Guided tours take visitors behind the curtains and among the boxes.

Castel Nuovo (Maschio Angioino)
ⓘ *Piazza Municipio, T081-795 7722. Mon-Sat 0900-1900, €6. Bus C55, R2. Funicolare Centrale: Municipio (under construction)/piazza Augusteo.*
The muscular bulk of the New Castle (or the Maschio Angioino, the Angevin Fortress, as it's known to the locals), with its five cylindrical towers, now stands sentinel over the road and harbour traffic in piazza Municipio and nearby Molo Beverello. Angevin monarch Charles I built it in 1279 and it was remodelled by King Alfonso of Aragon in the 15th century. After hopping over the moat where crocodiles once snapped, you can join tour groups

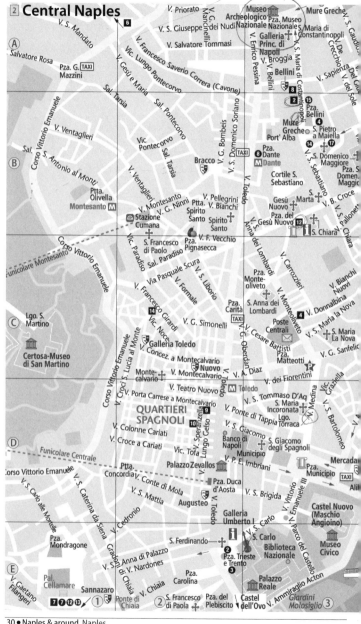

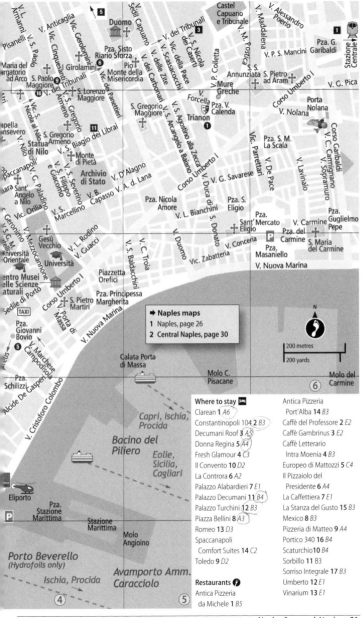

Where to stay 🛏

Clarean 1 *A6*
Constantinopoli 104 2 *B3*
Decumani Roof 3 *A5*
Donna Regina 5 *A4*
Fresh Glamour 4 *C3*
Il Convento 10 *D2*
La Controra 6 *A2*
Palazzo Alabardieri 7 *E1*
Palazzo Decumani 11 *B4*
Palazzo Turchini 12 *B3*
Piazza Bellini 8 *A3*
Romeo 13 *D3*
Spaccanapoli
  Comfort Suites 14 *C2*
Toledo 9 *D2*

Restaurants 🍴

Antica Pizzeria
  da Michele 1 *B5*
Antica Pizzeria
  Port'Alba 14 *B3*
Caffè del Professore 2 *E2*
Caffè Gambrinus 3 *E2*
Caffè Letterario
  Intra Moenia 4 *B3*
Europeo di Mattozzi 5 *C4*
Il Pizzaiolo del
  Presidente 6 *A4*
La Caffettiera 7 *E1*
La Stanza del Gusto 15 *B3*
Mexico 8 *B3*
Pizzeria di Matteo 9 *A4*
Portico 340 16 *B4*
Scaturchio10 *B4*
Sorbillo 11 *B3*
Sorriso Integrale 17 *B3*
Umberto 12 *E1*
Vinarium 13 *E1*

photographing the **Triumphal Arch** (1454-1467), built to commemorate Alfonso's conquest of Naples in 1443. Zoom in on the highest arch to see the four Cardinal Virtues (Prudence, Justice, Temperance and Fortitude) and at its zenith a statue of St Michael. Many of the historical events that took place here are hardly virtuous or saintly; an infamous event involved King Ferrante I, Alfonso's son, who invited some troublemaking barons to a mock wedding, then arrested and condemned them to death. You can stand in the grandiose, octagonal **Sala dei Baroni** (Barons' Hall) where this happened but sadly nothing is left of the Giotto frescoes that once decorated its walls and 28-m-high vaulted dome. More recently, until 2006, it was a council chamber and witnessed modern-day cloak-and-dagger episodes, often involving the Camorra, the local government and mountains of *munezza* (rubbish).

The **Museo Civico** (Civic Museum) here contains Angevin and Aragonese interiors, including 14th- and 15th-century sculptures, some rather dreary 15th- to 19th-century paintings and a mighty bronze door complete with cannonball damage. Don't miss the two chapels: the overblown Baroque **Cappella delle Anime del Purgatorio** and **Capella Palatina** with its tall, stark and handsome Gothic windows and some remnants of Giotto's genius.

Monte Echia and Pizzofalcone
The extinct volcano of Monte Echia was where the Greeks put down their curious odds and gods, and named a colony after the winged siren Parthenope. This lofty perch (renamed Palaeopolis or Old City, when Neapolis – the New City – was founded nearby) is a great place to get your bearings on the city and its history. To reach the summit, also known as Pizzofalcone, head up the hill behind piazza Plebiscito. Some crumbling ancient Greek remains can be seen and nearby is the Baroque **Chiesa di Santa Maria Egiziaca**, designed by Fanzago, and the mighty pink-plastered **Nunziatella** – a former convent turned military academy built by Ferdinando Sanfelice (1675-1748). Don't miss Sanfelice's imposing **Palazzo Serra di Cassano** and its double staircase at via Monte di Dio 14: today it houses the Italian Institute for Philosophical Studies.

Castel dell'Ovo and Borgo Marinari
ⓘ *Borgo Marinari, T081-7956 180. Castle: Mon-Sat 0900-1900, Sun 0900-1400, free. Bus 1, C12, C18, R3-R7, 140.*
The malleable tufa rock of the ancient island of Megaride, with its two islets connected by a natural arch, attracted Greek settlers who established their colony Parthenope here. Today the 'Castle of the Egg' is attached to the once atmospheric Santa Lucia district via a causeway and looks over the Borgo Marinari, the old fishermen's district-turned-swanky restaurant quarter – a relaxing and scenic spot for drinks and dining, and a backdrop to many a Neapolitan wedding photograph. The citadel's strategic position has been put to many uses down the centuries: Roman patrician Lucullus built a villa here, monks of the order of St Basil had a monastery and subsequent incumbents – Frederick II's Hohenstaufen dynasty, Normans, Angevins, Aragonese and Bourbons – put it to various uses including royal palace and prison. Impressive castle spaces can be admired in the Hall of the Columns and Loggiato, while the outside ramparts offer views across the bay and down to the jetties where the Camorra's speedboats ferried contraband in the 1980s. The castle hosts temporary art exhibitions and the **Museo di Etnopreistoria** ⓘ *T081-764343, Sat-Sun 1000-1300 by appointment, free*, containing prehistoric tools and ceramics.

Centro Antico → *For listings, see pages 54-66.*

The ancient heart of the city combines medieval atmosphere, dazzling churches, serene cloisters, eclectic shopping and quirky sights aplenty. Street vendors, boisterous students and scooters rattling along the sticky, pitted flagstones of the dark, narrow Graeco-Roman *decumani* and *cardi* add to the dreamlike spectacle. Most of the main sights and dark delights lie on or just off two of the three original east–west streets of the grid layout of Neapolis: long and straight Spaccanapoli ('Split Naples'), see box, page 34. follows the *decumanus inferior* and consists of via Benedetto Croce, via San Biagio dei Librai and via Vicaria Vecchia, while parallel via dei Tribunali is the *decumanus major*. Three Baroque *guglie* (spires) mark calamitous plagues and earthquakes with swirls and cherubs.

Chiesa del Gesù Nuovo

ⓘ *Piazza del Gesù, T081-551 8613. Mon-Sat 0900-1300, 1600-1900, Sun 0900-1300, free. Bus E1, A, C57. Metro: Dante.*

The austere diamond-pointed stones of the church of Gesù Nuovo's façade hardly hints at the ornamental richness and piety awaiting inside. The Jesuits transformed the battle-hardy 15th-century Palazzo Sanseverino into a sumptuous church with the help of architect Giuseppe Valeriano (1542-1596) and a collection of celebrated Neapolitan artists including Cosimo Fanzago (1591-1678), Andrea Vaccaro (1605-1670) and Francesco Solimena (1657-1747). Its flamboyant frescoes, coloured marble, gilt and stuccowork continue to be a very popular backdrop to Neapolitan worship every day. A side chapel contains votive offerings to San Giuseppe Moscati (1880-1927), the renowned doctor who was canonized in 1987: queues of pious Neapolitans flock here to pray to the saint who dedicated his life to the city's poor and infirm. Two rooms are filled with metallic ex-voto hearts and body parts with imploring messages for miracle cures. Twisted shards of a Second World War bomb that pierced the barrel-vaulted ceiling dangle above these poignant offerings near Moscati's old office, which you can peer into.

Santa Chiara

ⓘ *Via Santa Chiara 49, T081-552 1597, www.santachiara.info. Church: Mon-Fri 0930-1300, 1430-1800, Sat-Sun 0900-1300, free. Cloisters and museum: Mon-Sat 0930-1700, Sun 1000-1300, €3.50 discount students and Artecard. Bus E1, A, C57. Metro: Dante.*

Beyond the robust-looking campanile that towers over bustling Spaccanapoli is one of the most evocative spaces in Naples: cloisters filled with wisteria, citrus trees and vibrant majolica tiles. Before entering this magic world, you can visit the 14th-century Santa Chiara church built for Robert of Anjou's wife Sancia di Maiorca. A Second World War bomb and a devastating fire destroyed the church's 18th-century Baroque flamboyance. The reconstruction recalls the original Provençal-Gothic Franciscan character. Highlights include a Tuscan-style tomb of Robert the Wise behind the high altar and the Coro delle Clarisse (Choir of the Poor Clares) where the nuns stood apart from the public congregation.

The layout of the complex is typically Neapolitan, and a vestige of the Graeco-Roman world, where a cosseted environment lay behind a street façade. A walk amid the cloisters' arcades designed by Domenico Antonio Vaccaro (1678-1745) and the striking tiles with their vivid whirls of blue, green and yellow majolica is uplifting. Hundreds of pastoral scenes created by father and son team Donato and Giuseppe Massa during the 18th century adorn the cloisters' 72 octagonal pillars and benches, while faded frescoes cover the walls under

Spaccanapoli walk

The walk along Spaccanapoli and the parallel via dei Tribunali is captivating and a little hair-raising. These are two of the three main east–west streets (*decumani*) that cut through the heart of the ancient Graeco-Roman city of Neapolis. Leave your preconceptions and valuables behind and go with the crazy Neapolitan flow.

Start at piazza di Gesù with its Guglia dell'Immacolata spire and colourful *palazzi*, then visit the **Gesù Nuovo** church and **Santa Chiara** cloisters before heading into narrow via Benedetto Croce and Spaccanapoli. The streetlife buzz of weaving vespas and animated *napoletani* along these sticky flagstones provide a dizzying spectacle. Behind grimy Renaissance *palazzi* are hidden courtyards, including **Palazzo Filomarino** at No 12, the home of historian and philosopher Benedetto Croce. Passing intriguing outlets and *bancarelle* you come to the *pasticceria* Scaturchio (see page 58) and its sweet offerings, and

then piazza San Domenico Maggiore with its *palazzi*, Baroque obelisk and **Chiesa di San Domenico Maggiore**. A side street to the east of the piazza leads to the mysterious family chapel, the **Cappella di Sansevero**.

Imaginations spiked by strange tales and astonishing sculptures, rejoin Spaccanapoli which is now called via San Biagio dei Librai. There are more intriguing outlets and antique stalls to see. Beside the endearing **Sant'Angelo a Nilo** church, which contains Cardinal Brancaccio's tomb by Donatello, is piazzetta Nilo and **Bar Nilo**, a fine place for a caffeine fix. Next to the lounging **Statua del Nilo** is a humorous mini-chapel dedicated to Diego Maradona. Further east there is the San Nicola a Nilo church, which sits opposite the Palazzo Carafa Santangelo with its equine bust gifted by Lorenzo de' Medici. Drop into the grandest old pawnshop and its adjoining chapel at the **Pio Monte di Pietà** before entering the magical world of **Via San Gregorio**

the arcades. The museum housed within the nuns' old quarters is worth a look for its Roman baths and some interesting artefacts tracing the complex's history.

Chiesa di San Domenico Maggiore

ⓘ *Piazza San Domenico Maggiore, T081-459188. Tue-Thu and Sun 0930-1200, Sat-Sun 0930-1200, 1700-1900, free, Sala del Tesoro €3. Bus C57, R2, E1. Metro: Dante.*

The bulky back-end of the church of San Domenico Maggiore dominates one of the city's most attractive squares and its Baroque monument, the Guglia di San Domenico (1737). The church and monastery were begun by the Angevins (1283-1324) and have been much altered after earthquakes and fires. Enter via a staircase on the piazza or at the true main entrance on the *vicolo* (side street). The interior is 76 m long and contains 14th-century frescoes by Pietro Cavallini, who influenced Giotto, in the Cappella Brancaccio. A copy of Caravaggio's *Flagellation* (1607) by Andrea Vaccaro in the north transept can be compared to the original in the Museo di Capodimonte. Remains of the ancient Chiesa di Sant'Angelo a Morfisa can be seen in the atmospheric crypt. Don't miss the Cappellone del Crocifisso and a reproduction of the 13th-century panel painting through which – legend has it – Christ spoke to the influential theologian Thomas Aquinas. Aquinas, along with many a radical philosopher, studied at the adjoining monastery and original seat of the University of Naples Federico II. Another influential alumnus, Giordano Bruno who

Armeno and its *presepe* nativity-scenes, figurines and fake mossy trees. Serenity and pious relics await at the churches and cloisters of **San Gregorio Armeno**, **San Lorenzo Maggiore** and **San Paolo Maggiore**. If you have 90 minutes free and a head for confined spaces go deep into the city's past at **Napoli Sotterranea** on piazza San Gaetano, the heart of the ancient city of Neapolis.

Reaching via dei Tribunali there is a choice: head east to plunge into oodles of art and pious relics at the **Girolamini**, **Monte della Misericordia** and magnificent **Duomo** or else go west in the open air. If you choose a visit to San Gennaro's congealed blood you can backtrack afterwards, along edgy via Tribunali and end up at the **Intra Moenia** bar beside the old Greek city walls, on leafy and lefty piazza Bellini. Along this stretch of the old *decumanus major* be prepared for the creepy sight of shiny bronze skulls and bones outside the **Purgatorio ad Arco** church, some

fabulous *palazzi* (including Sanfelice's Palazzo Spinelli at No 362) and Roman architectural fragments below the city's oldest campanile, the 10th- to 11th-century **La Pietrasanta**. Along via dei Tribunali are the upper crust of *scugnizz'* (street kids') pizzerias: **Di Matteo**, **Il Pizzaiolo del Presidente** and **Sorbillo**.

Slowly but surely, some of the cracks in the *chiese* and *palazzi* of this UNESCO World Heritage Site, caused by centuries of skirmishes, neglect and earthquakes (including one in 1980 that left thousands homeless), are being patched and properly propped up. Improvements are welcome but thankfully the Centro Antico is unlikely to lose in the near future its edginess and become a sanitized, twee and overly touristy zone. Students, working-class *rigattieri* (rag-and-bone men cum antiquarian dealers), artists and well-to-do diners rub along together here; many congregate in the cafés on piazza Bellini, a leafy haven of Neapolitan esoteric and anti-establishment expression.

promoted the idea of a solar system and an infinite universe, was burnt as a heretic by the Roman Inquisition in 1600.

Capella di Sansevero

ⓘ *Via Francesco de Sanctis 19, T081-551 8470, www.museosansevero.it. Mon, Wed-Sat 1000-1740, Sun 1000-1310, €7, with Artecard €5, concessions €2-5, under 10s free. Bus E1, C57. Metro: Dante.*

Containing some of Italy's most extraordinary sculptures as well as fascinating clues to the life of an infamously mysterious Neapolitan prince, the Sansevero chapel is a must-see. Also known as the Pietatella, it was built as a votive chapel dedicated to Santa Maria della Pietà in what was once the gardens of the Palazzo Sangro di Sansevero in piazza San Domenico Maggiore. Then Raimondo VII Prince of Sansevero remodelled it into a family funerary chapel, commissioning gifted artists including Giuseppe Sanmartino, who created the spine-chillingly lifelike *Cristo Velato* (*Veiled Christ*) as the centrepiece. The darkly furtive imagination of the locals reckoned that after the figure was carved from a single block of marble the alchemist prince mixed up a home-brew to petrify a sheet laid over it – another entertainingly fantastical Neapolitan theory. Beside the main altar is Antonio Corradini's sensuous and immodest masterpiece *La Pudicizia* (*Modesty*), dedicated to the patron's mother, who died at just 23 years. Francesco Queirolo's *Disinganno*

(*Disillusion*, otherwise known as *Freedom from Sin*) depicts a man disentangling himself from a rope net, and honours di Sangro's father who chose to go all monastic after an action-packed life had ensnared him in sin. Mysterious Masonic symbols abound in both the original labyrinthine-patterned floor (still in situ in the mausoleum) and the vibrant frescoed ceiling (by Francesco Maria Russo). Its vibrant hues, including a ghoulish green illuminating the family worthies (saints), were allegedly created by the prince himself. In the vault stand two anatomical figures displaying original skeletons and cardiovascular systems, with a ceramic organ or two thrown in.

Sant'Angelo a Nilo and Statua del Nilo

ⓘ *Piazzetta Nilo, T081-211 0860. Mon-Sat 0830-1300, 1645-1900, Sun 0830-1300, free. Bus E1, C57. Metro: Dante.*

Cardinal Brancaccio instigated the construction of this peachy-hued church in 1384 although much of its exterior was transformed in the early 1500s. Inside is the cardinal's early Renaissance tomb, sculpted in Pisa by Donatello and Michelozzo in the 1420s and brought to Naples by Cosimo de' Medici. The adjoining courtyard, part of the Palazzo Brancaccio, contains the city's first public library (1690).

In piazzetta Nilo an enigmatic ancient Egyptian statue of the Nile river god, with overflowing cornucopia tucked under his arm, lounges atop a Latin-inscribed plinth. The reclining figure was brought to Naples by Alexandrian merchant settlers in Graeco-Roman times, then went missing and reappeared minus its head in the 15th century. A local sculptor produced the present head although the original may have had the head of a beast. Neapolitans still call it *O Cuórpè Napule* (Body of Naples). A vendor used to display his jazz magazines on the statue, which faces a humorous mini-chapel dedicated to that other Neapolitan deity, Diego Maradona, outside **Bar Nilo**.

Cappella del Monte di Pietà

ⓘ *Via Biagio dei Librai 114, T081-580 7111. Sat 0900-1900, Sun 0900-1400, free. Bus R2, E1, C57. Metro: Dante.*

Duck into this refined courtyard to view a 16th-century palazzo, chapel and old pawnshop. Jewellers and moneylenders once rubbed together along this stretch of the via Biagio dei Librai, while the state-run **Pio Monte di Pietà** offered the best deals to impoverished debtors in the form of interest-free loans. It's now owned by the Banco di Napoli. Two sculptures by Bernini, entitled *Charity* and *Security*, flank the entrance and a triangular tympanum frames Naccherino's Pietà and a couple of angels. Inside, the ceilings are filled with colourful frescoes, including the *Misteri del Passione*, painted in 1601-1603 by Belisario Corenzio. The courtyard hosts regular live jazz and classical concerts for a diverse chin-stroking crowd.

Via San Gregorio Armeno

At right-angles to Spaccanapoli, via San Gregorio Armeno's famous *presepi* (nativity scene) shops spill onto the street with bizarre stage sets animated by mains-powered water features, hypnotic mechanized movements of tiny figurines and twinkling lights behind fake plastic shrubberies. You may be charmed and amused by these imaginative visions, but be prepared to part with huge sums for the traditional hand-made figurines made by the area's *figurari* craftsmen. More affordable is the good old-fashioned tat sold alongside caricatures of political figures and celebrities – Northern League firebrand Umberto Bossi gets a witty Neapolitan makeover while Pavarotti is given a more dignified treatment. Napoli's nativity tableau tradition flourished in the 18th century, filling churches, palaces

Fiametta

In 1336 the writer Giovanni Boccaccio (1313-1375) met his Fiammetta (Little Flame) at San Lorenzo Maggiore. So smitten was Boccaccio with Maria d'Aquino, illegitimate daughter of King Robert the Wise in Naples, that her vision inspired the character Fiammetta in *Filocolo, L'Elegia di Madonna* and, most famously, the *Decameron*. In Boccaccio's medieval masterpiece of a hundred tales Fiammetta is one of the wittiest of the 10 storytellers who have fled to the countryside to avoid a bubonic plague-ridden Florence.

and homes, and the **via dei Pastori** (Road of the Shepherds) is still the place for enthusiasts seeking a lovely hand-painted bunch of miniature bananas to pimp their Christmas crib.

Chiesa e Chiostro di San Gregorio Armeno
ⓘ *Church: via San Gregorio Armeno 44; cloisters: piazzetta San Gregorio Armeno 1, T081-552 0186. Daily 0900-1200, free. Bus E1, C52. Metro: Cavour/Museo.*
First sight of this Benedictine convent is of its Baroque red-hued bell tower (1716) that straddles via San Gregorio Armeno, looming over its pastoral scenes and figurines. It is named after the Armenian St Gregory whose remains were brought here in the eighth century by nuns fleeing persecution in Constantinople. Santa Patrizia also came from Byzantium and her congealed blood is said to liquefy here every Tuesday. Amongst the artworks of the sadly neglected yet sumptuous Baroque church interiors are gilt stucco work, vibrant frescoes by Luca Giordano and a carved wooden ceiling. The reclusive nuns that traditionally lived here were daughters of nobles and were not averse to knocking up delicious confections in the refectory including ice-cream desserts and the *sfogliatella* pastry. A walk around the atmospheric cloisters, with their citrus trees and a curvy marble fountain flanked by statues of *Christ* and the *Samaritan* (1733), is often punctuated by the chatter of schoolchildren playing next door.

Chiesa e Scavi di San Lorenzo Maggiore
ⓘ *Piazzetta San Gaetano/via dei Tribunali 316, T081-290580/T081-211 0860 (museum), www.sanlorenzomaggiorenapoli.it. Church daily 0900-1330, free. Excavations and museum Mon-Sat 0930-1730, Sun 0930-1330, €5, concessions, discounts with Artecard €3. Bus CS, R2, E1. Metro: Cavour/Museo.*
Below this Franciscan religious complex located at the intersection of via dei Tribunali and via San Gregorio Armeno are the remains of the Graeco-Roman agora or forum, and a Roman basilica. You can even see part of the old *macellum* (market) in the dimly lit and rather spooky excavations. In the 13th century Charles of Anjou hired a team of French craftsmen to rebuild the complex in Gothic style and after suffering damage in a spate of earthquakes it got the Baroque treatment in the 17th and 18th centuries. More recent restoration (1882-1944) returned much of the church to its Gothic form, although the exuberant 1743 façade built by Ferdinando Sanfelice (1675-1748) and the multicoloured marble-inlaid side chapels by Cosimo Fanzago (1591-1678) remain.

Chiesa di San Paolo Maggiore
ⓘ *Piazza San Gaetano, T081-454048. Mon-Sat 0900-1800, sun 1000-1230, free. Bus R2. Metro: Museo/Cavour.*

The 16th-century church was built over a Roman temple dedicated to Castor and Pollux, Zeus's twin sons. The 1688 earthquake may have destroyed much of the original façade and most of its Corinthian columns, but the replacement Baroque double staircase provides grandstand views of via Tribunali street-life. Highlights of the rather anodyne post-Second World War restoration are Francesco Solimena's (1689-1690) frescoes in the sacristy and a couple of flamboyant chapels with mother-of-pearl, coloured inlaid marble and paintings by Massimo Stanzione (1585-1656).

Napoli Sotterranea
① Piazza San Gaetano 68, T081-296944, www.napolisotterranea.it. Tours in English depart Mon-Fri 1200, 1400, 1600 (also Thu 2100), €10, discounts with Artecard. Bus R2. Metro: Cavour/Museo.
For a sense of the city's multi-layered history take a 90-minute tour with 'Underground Naples' and descend 40 m into the tufa rock labyrinth of Graeco-Roman cisterns. A visit to the dank, cool depths makes a refreshing break on a sweltering day plodding the sticky Centro Antico flagstones – bring a warm top though as it can get chilly. Enthusiastic guides trace the Greek foundations of ancient Neapolis, its aqueducts and the myth of the *monastini* (the little monks) who cleaned the tunnels and entertained the wives. An extra excursion (30 minutes) to a theatre where Nero performed Greek plays is accessed via someone's garage and is now overlooked by a kitchen window. The truly bizarre hotchpotch history of Naples begins to make sense amid the ancient compacted mud and flaking bricks. In the caverns transformed into a Second World War air-raid shelter city you are told that 5 m of 20th-century rubbish is buried under your feet. It's not for claustrophobics but don't miss out on the optional walk by candlelight through a cramped tunnel to a spookily lit cistern. **Napoli Sotterranea** also runs underground tours of the Bourbon-era tunnel near piazza Trieste e Trento and the atmospheric Acquedotto Carmignano, the Graeco-Roman aqueduct that runs under via Chiaia.

Chiesa e Quadreria dei Girolamini
① Church: piazza Girolamini 107; cloisters library and gallery: via Duomo 142, T081-449139, www.girolamini.it. Tue-Thu 0930-1230, Fri-Sat 0930-1230, 1700-1900, free. Bus R2. Metro: Cavour.
The monastery complex was founded by the San Filippo Neri order, of the San Girolamo alla Carità convent in Rome, hence the name 'Church of the Girolamini'. The real highlights here are the two cloisters (a grand space with fragrant orange trees and an intimate one with majolica tiles), the 18th-century, wood-panelled library and the Quadreria (gallery). You can easily spend a relaxing half-hour spotting familiar faces in the chiaroscuro images of saints and sinners on canvas. The church (1619) has paintings by Francesco Solimena and Luca Giordano, sculpture by Pietro Bernini and the tomb of Giambattista Vico, the influential Neapolitan philosopher.

Chiesa e Quadreria del Pio Monte della Misericordia
① Via dei Tribunali 253, T081-446944, www.piomontedellamisericordia.it. Thu-Tue 0900-1430, €6, discounts with Artecard. Bus CS, E1. Metro: Cavour.
Renaissance artworks fill the galleries of this charitable organization and adjoining octagonal church. Beyond the five-arch loggia, the Our Lady of Mercy Church contains the brooding *The Seven Acts of Mercy* (1607) altarpiece by Caravaggio (1571-1610), considered one of his masterpieces and painted during his first exiled stay in Naples. Step next door to view 150 canvasses by 17th- and 18th-century Baroque masters while learning about the

charity set up by seven noble gentlemen in 1601 to help the city's needy and oppressed Christians in the Ottoman empire. Just as uplifting as the displayed works by Vaccaro, Giordano and Ribera is the building itself, and particularly the way that light streams into the cavernous space beneath its dome.

Duomo

ⓘ *Via Duomo 147, T081-449097. Duomo: Mon-Sat 0800-1230, 1630-1900, Sun 0800-1330, 1700-1930, free. Excavations: Mon-Sat 0900-1200, 1630-1900, Sun 0900-1230, €3 (including entry to baptistery). Bus CS, E1. Metro: Cavour.*

Napoli's cathedral is the focus of veneration of the city's patron saint and the thrice-annual public outpouring of Neapolitan piety that is the Miracle of San Gennaro. It was begun by Angevin King Carlo I in the 13th century on the site of the Basilica di Santa Restituta, a Palaeo-Christian structure and the city's oldest surviving basilica. Mosaic floors, Greek flagstones and Roman remnants including ancient pipes inscribed with the name Aurielie Utician can be viewed in the **Scavi del Duomo** (Duomo Excavations). Earthquakes, changes of rule and artistic fashion have erased much of the original French Gothic interior and façade. A richly painted ceiling and Latin-cross structure are supported by 110 granite columns. Beyond the tombs of Angevin kings at the entrance is the lavishly adorned **Cripta di San Gennaro** (also known as Succorpo or the Cappella Carafa), the most apt expression of the Neapolitan Baroque. Above you'll see a fresco cycle by Domenichino depicting the life and miracles of the city's top saint. The highlight of the visit, for pious Neapolitans especially, is the altar tabernacle with its silver bust encasing the skull of San Gennaro and two phials containing his congealed blood. The atmosphere around the venerated relics is always charged with extraordinary emotion. Head to the north transept to see the tomb of Innocent IV, who was pope during the esoteric rule of Fredrick II of Hohenstaufen, founder of the University of Naples. The remains of Prince Andrew of Hungary who was brutally strangled in 1345 in front of his wife, Joan I, are also housed here. The oldest baptistery in Italy, the fifth-century **Capella di San Giovanni in Fonte**, has colourful mosaics depicting biblical scenes including *Christ Saving Peter from the Waters* and the *Miracle of the Fish*. Further chapels include the **Tocco**, with Gothic frescoes (1312), and **Minutolo**, which is paved with majolica and contains the tomb of a cardinal.

Museo del Tesoro di San Gennaro

ⓘ *Via Duomo 149, T081-421609, www.museosangennaro.com. Daily 0900-0730, €7, concessions €5, discounts with Artecard. Bus CS, E1. Metro: Cavour.*

For those seeking more religious relics and ancient bling, head to the Museum of the Treasure of San Gennaro next door to the Duomo, containing seven centuries of shiny treasure donated to the patron saint including lots of golden cherubs and silvery saints.

Santa Maria di Donnaregina Vecchia

ⓘ *Vico Donnaregina 25, T091-441 806. Sun-Fri 0900-1200, Sat by appointment. Bus R2, E1. Metro: Cavour.*

This monastery, founded by an Italo-Graeco order in the eighth century, was totally rebuilt in 1293 under the reign of Carlo III of Anjou. It is built on two levels, to keep the nuns and public separate, with the lower part containing a funeral monument to Maria d'Ungheria by Tino di Camaino (1325-1326) with the upper section containing the largest 14th-century cycle of frescoes in Naples, painted by the Giotto school (1332-1335).

San Gennaro

Little documentary evidence survives about Napoli's patron saint but that doesn't diminish the profound hold that the ancient cult of San Gennaro has on Neapolitans. What we do know is that Gennaro (Januarius) was born in the late third century and became Bishop of Benevento. His martyrdom and subsequent fame came about during Emperor Diocletian's persecution of Christianity (AD 303-311): Gennaro was discovered taking communion to an imprisoned deacon and was decapitated on 19 September 305 near Solfatara, where the Santuario di San Gennaro stands today. According to the legend, a pious lady – Eusebia – collected his blood in two ampoules. A version of the story says that after Constantine allowed freedom of worship, Eusebia presented the ampoules to Gennaro's family, upon which Vesuvius erupted and the blood liquefied. According to another tale, the blood first liquefied in the hands of Bishop Severus when Gennaro's body was brought to Naples. And so the popular belief grew that the liquefaction was a sign that the saint would protect the city from disaster, be it earthquake, famine, plague or even relegation of the SSC Napoli football team to Serie B.

In 1338, around the time the Duomo was being built, the first documented liquefaction happened. The saint's relics were housed in the atmospheric catacombs near Capodimonte, before being moved to Benevento and then finally to the Duomo in 1497 by Archibishop Carafa, who helped popularize the cult by entombing them in the sumptuous Succorpo. Three times a year – on the Saturday preceding the first Sunday in May in a procession to Santa Chiara, on 16 December and on the Saint's Day 19 September – there is a solemn ceremony followed by a frenzy of emotional outpouring by the faithful imploring the miracle. The vigil can last many hours and the fate of the city is believed to depend on the speed of the liquefaction. If the 'miracle' takes a while it's a bad omen for Naples. Many pious Neapolitans may not agree but recent scientific studies posit the idea that the ampoules do not contain solely blood and that liquefaction is due to a bit of kinetic energy. These scientists reckon that the miracle is not unlike the phenomenon of ketchup becoming runny after a good old shake…

Museo Diocesano di Napoli alla Chiesa Santa Maria di Donnaregina Nuova
ⓘ *Largo Donnaregina 7, T081-557 1365, www.museodiocesanonapoli.it. Museum Mon-Sat 0930-1630, Sun 0930-1400, €6. Bus C51, C52. Metro: Cavour.*
At the start of the 17th century Clarissan nuns from the neighbouring Donnaregina monastery commissioned this church with its imposing façade (1640-1650) and rich interiors of colourful marble and artworks by Giordano, de Benedictis and Solimena. The museum here explores Naples' relationship with religious iconography – Maria and San Gennaro especially – as well as Baroque artworks by the likes of Andrea Vaccaro, Mario Stanzione and Aniello Falcone.

Santa Maria delle Anime del Purgatorio ad Arco
ⓘ *Via dei Tribunali 39, T081-211 929, www.purgatorioadarco.com. Church Mon-Fri 0930-1300, Sat 1000-1700; Ipogeo Museum Sat 1000-1230, €3, concessions €2. Bus CS, E1. Metro: Museo/Dante.*

Heading west along the atmospheric via Tribunali, which traces the ancient *decumanus major*, you come across the spine-tingling street-side sight of skulls and crossbones, given a shine by millions of superstitious strokes by devoted Neapolitans, below a brooding 17th-century church façade. A typically dark Neapolitan cult of the dead – where *capuzzelle* (skulls) and souls in purgatory are worshipped – is apparently still practised here in the catacombs below the church. Amid the Baroque interiors is a suitably macabre sculpture of a winged skull (*Teschio alato*) by Cosimo Fanzago (1591-1678).

Piazza Bellini
① *Bus E1, R1, C57. Metro: Dante.*
At the western end of the dark, throbbing via dei Tribunali is this lively and leafy square with a sunken section containing the old Greek city walls, surrounded by handsome university buildings including the peach-coloured former **Sant'Antoniello a Port'Alba** monastery and the Baroque **Palazzo Firrao** by Fanzago. Local artists and students often place an action-painting between the ancient tufa blocks and decorate the grubby statue of composer Vincenzo Bellini (1801-1835) with a traffic cone. There's often a whiff of exotic tobacco amid the flaky grand buildings, palms and orange trees. Despite the slightly edgy vibe added by local *guaglioni (kids)* on scooters, it's a laid-back haven. An array of drinks and snacks are served at the cafés here, their tranquil cobblestoned terraces filled with parasols, potted plants and a friendly mix of arty and alternative types, students and tourists.

Santa Maria la Nova
① *Largo Santa Maria la Nova 1, T081-552 3298. Mon-Fri Free. Guided visits €3.50. Bus R1, R4, C57.*
The church and its adjoining convent were built by Giovan Cola di Franco in 1596 on a site given to the Franciscan order by Carlo I d'Anjou in recompense for having demolished one of their churches to make way for the Castel Nuovo. Beyond the handsome Florentine-style façade the sumptuous interiors include an exquisite marble relief, *The Adoration of the Shepherds* (1524), by Santacroce and a coffered ceiling (1598-1603) with lots of gilt framing some 46 paintings by the likes of Imparato, Corenzio and Curia. The former monastery is now a local governmental building and contains the **Museo ARCA (Museum of Religious Contemporary Art)** and two cloisters with Renaissance frescoes and tombs. In 1609 the exiled artist, Caravaggio, was severely assaulted by three men on a narrow lane behind the church upon leaving inn/brothel Osteria del Cerriglio – an attack that hastened his demise and foreshadowed his death a year later.

Galleria dell'Accademia di Belle Arti
① *Via Costantinopoli 107, T081-441900, www.accademianapoli.it. Tue-Sat 1000-1330, free, Bus E1, Metro: Dante/Museo.*
The former convent building of San Giovanni delle Monache (1673-1732) was turned into the Academy of Arts by Enrico Alvino in 1864. It still attracts students looking to enter the world of art as well as art conservation and restoration. Indeed the Gipsoteca section has many important plaster casts that have inspired its sculpture students. A sweeping staircase with busts set in balustrades sets the classical tone. The gallery exhibits span the 17th to 20th centuries and include works from the influential Posillipo School including idyllic landscapes by Carelli, Gigante and Duclere. Two rooms contain a collection of 20th-century works including Manlio Giarrizzo's Matisse-inspired paintings and some experimental works of the 1960s by Neapolitan artists.

Via Toledo to piazza Cavour → *For listings, see pages 54-66.*

Quartieri Spagnoli
ⓘ *Buses R1, E1, CS, C57. Metro: Toledo.*
The network of streets running up the hill on the western side of via Toledo is known as the Spanish Quarters as the tall tenements were built to house Spanish troops in the 16th century. Despite stories of Camorra shoot-outs and warnings to avoid the area, it's no worse than other districts. The sight of a Rolls Royce with blacked-out windows crawling along a crowded, narrow street can be unnerving though. Just off piazza Carità is via Pignasecca which is well worth exploring for its small shops and market stalls selling fish, fruit and vegetables, as well as bargain homeware and clothing.

Palazzo Zevallos
ⓘ *Via Toledo 185, T081-791 7233, www.palazzozevallos.com. Thu-Tue 1000-1800 (Sat till 2000), €4, concessions €3. Bus R1, R4, C57. Metro: Toledo.*
The main reason for entering this imposing 17th century palazzo with ornate stuccowork and azure ceilings, is to contemplate Caravaggio's last painting *The Martyrdom of St Ursula* (1610). Dark, sparse and with scant background detail – compare with the *Seven Acts of Mercy* (see page 38) – it recounts a fatal moment in a tale from The Golden legend, where a chaste princess Ursula leads 11,000 virgins on a doomed pilgrimage in Germany. Invading Huns behead the virgins before their king comforts and offers to marry Ursula. The painting depicts him firing an arrow at the heart of the unwilling bride-to-be, who looks down serenely at the spurting wound. Behind the martyr a haunted Caravaggio looks into the distance – gasping and contemplating death – the exiled artist was weakened after a savage assaulted in Naples months earlier. The artist would die in July 1610 on the way to seek pardon and influence from the pope and Cardinal Scipione Borghese for a murderous act carried out in Rome, 1606, and death warrant placed by the Knights of Malta. Caravaggio didn't reach Rome – his remains have since been identified at Porto Ercole on the Tuscan coast. You may even find yourself alone before Caravaggio's last known painting – just be careful not to peer too closely as you may set off the alarm. The bank-owned gallery also has serene Neapolitan landscapes by Anton Pitloo and Gaspar van Wittel.

Chiesa Sant'Anna dei Lombardi
ⓘ *Piazza Monteoliveto 44, T081-551 3333. Mon-Fri 0900-1200, Sat 0900-1200, free. Bus R1, R4, C57. Metro: Toledo.*
Just east of via Toledo, not far from piazza Gesù and near a playful Baroque fountain, is this unassuming-looking church containing some of the city's most important Florentine-style Renaissance treasures. It was begun in 1411 and became thereafter the favourite church of the Aragonese rulers, who employed leading artists of the time to decorate its chapels and tombs. In the **Sacrestia Vecchia** (Old Sacristy), Giorgio Vasari's (1511-1574) sumptuous ceiling frescoes and the intricate *intarsia* stalls (1506-1510) by Giovanni di Verona are astonishing. The chapels are no less dazzling with the bas-relief *Nativity* (1475) by Antonio Rossellino in the **Capella Piccolomini** (dedicated to the Duke of Amalfi's wife), and the eight life-size terracotta figures of Guido Mazzoni's *Lamentation of the Dead Christ* (1492) in the **Cappella Orilia** worth seeking out. Bombing in 1943 caused severe damage, and restoration work aimed at bringing the church back to its former glory continues. On the intimate piazza nearby you can relax beside white marble lions and eagles spouting water on the curvy Baroque lip of Cosimo Fanzago's beguiling fountain (1699), with a statue of a young tousle-locked King Carlo II of Aragon looking westwards.

Palazzo delle Poste e Telegrafi

① Piazza Matteotti 3. Mon-Fri 0800-1830, Sat 0800-1230. Bus R1, R4, C57. Metro: Dante.
Fascist urban renewal swept away the old San Giuseppe-Carità quarter and replaced it with bombastic architecture like the brooding Banco di Napoli building on via Toledo and a cluster of civic buildings on piazza Matteotti, including the Central Post Office (1932-1936) by Giuseppe Vaccaro (1896-1979). Its curvilinear façade, clad in a combination of light and dark marble and smooth lines, makes it one of the most alluring (or alienating, depending on your point of view) examples of modernism in Naples. It's also a suitably edifying venue to get yourself acquainted with Neapolitan-style bureaucracy and Italian *Poste*. Up the stairs is the rarely visited **Emeroteca Tucci** *① T081-551 1226*, a fascinating library with newspaper archive and temporary exhibitions. Ring the bell and the friendly staff will chat and show you around.

Piazza Dante

① Via Toledo. Metro: Dante.
The grand piazza on via Toledo is backed by the large semicircular palace **Foro Carolino** topped with 26 statues, designed by Luigi Vanvitelli (1700-1773) in 1757 for Carlo III of Bourbon. After years of neglect it has been scrubbed up, erasing much of the graffiti and mess around the statue of poet Dante Alighieri. It's a meeting place and venue for public gatherings where juggling clowns, food markets and political sideshows vie for attention.

Museo Archeologico Nazionale di Napoli

① Piazza Museo 19, T081-440166, www.napolibeniculturali.it. Wed-Mon 0900-1930, €6.50, under-25s €3.50, under 18s/over 65s free, €4 audioguide in English. Bus C57, 24, R4. Metro: Museo.
Prepare to be blown away by the scale and quality of the National Archaeological Museum of Naples's collection of ancient Greek, Roman and Egyptian artefacts. Formerly a riding school and then a university seat, this enormous building was modified in the 18th century by Bourbon monarchs Carlo III and then Ferdinand IV to house the ever-increasing number of objects discovered at Pompeii, Herculaneum and in the Campi Flegrei. Many of the statuary antiquities of the **Farnese Collection**, begun by a 16th-century pope and ending up in Bourbon Naples through Elisabetta Farnese, can be seen on the ground floor. The imposing presence and beauty of the statues never fails to impress. One of the masterpieces is the *Toro Farnese* (Farnese Bull), a 4-m-high Roman copy of a Greek sculpture from second-century Rhodes depicting five figures, a dog and a bull. Pliny the Elder wrote about the original sculpture in his *Naturalis Historia*, while this colossal version by Apollonius was unearthed at the Baths of Caracalla in Rome. Walking amid the marbled giants and contemplating the lives, myths and journeys surrounding them is electrifying.

You can spend many hours taking in the priceless treasures upstairs so here are a few pieces to look out for. Among the many Roman mosaics is the massive *Alexander and Darius at the Battle of Issus*. As so little Greek painting survived, this Pompeian mosaic is important as it's a copy from the Hellenistic period. There are lots of mosaic animals (the Romans loved their birds, fish, dogs, cats and ducks it seems) as well as skeletons – *La Ruota della Fortuna* (The Wheel of Fortune) has a grinning skull – and paved floors, many with black-and-white geometric patterns. Seek out the *opus vermiculatum* (vermiculated mosaic) *Fauna Marina*, and imagine its colourful crustaceans and marine creatures rippling lifelike below the water of a recessed pool between Pompeian dining couches in the House of the Faun. Similarly alluring are the bronze statues from the Villa dei Papiri, of tousle-haired dancing girls striking a pose and perfectly poised athletes.

Many of the paintings from Pompeii and Herculaneum were based on older Greek works, including the *Sacrificio di Ifigenia* (Sacrifice of Iphigenia) which has a stark quality reminiscent of 20th-century surrealism and characters displaying lots of grief, flailing arms and vacant looks. It was found at the fun-sounding House of the Tragic Poet and is a copy of a lost fourth-century painting by Timanthes that Pliny the Elder raved about. Elsewhere, connoisseurs of ancient hooliganism will get a frisson from the fresco documenting the AD 59 punch-up between the home crowd and Nucerians at the amphitheatre.

You could spend weeks exploring the vast collections of ancient inscriptions, metalwork, furnishings, glassware, coins and gems on the first floor. Seek out the intricate cameo-work on the *Tazza Farnese*, an exquisite bowl from Hellenistic Egypt and on *Il Vaso Blu*, a wine amphora with delicate cupids crushing grapes on cobalt-blue glass, found at Pompeii. A large collection of Egyptian relics, largely amassed by Cardinal Borgia, includes lots of mummies and funerary statuettes.

For those flagging, the sight of the **Gabinetto Segreto** (Secret Cabinet) and its erotic contents should raise eyebrows. At various times during its history the collection of saucy relics was reserved for the eyes of male visitors of 'mature age and proven morality'. Eye-bulging pieces include: painted scenes from Pompeii, advertising *lupanare* (brothel) services; some erotic statues; and an enormous array of average-sized penises belonging to ubiquitous Graeco-Roman fertility god Priapus.

As for the building itself, the central stairway, below a dome and giant compass, is breathtaking but is eclipsed by the cavernous **Salone della Meridiana**, replete with sundial, celestial ceiling frescoes and a chunky Atlas carrying a globe: the *Farnese Atlante* statue. Back down to earth are the up-to-date Neapolitan displays of abandoned masonry dumped in corners that no doubt vex visiting health and safety officers from out of town. Like Naples, it's all very captivating, amusing and hazardous.

Museo d'Arte Contemporanea Donnaregina (MADRE)
ⓘ *Via Settembrini 79, T081-1931 3016, www.museomadre.it. Mon, Wed-Sat 1000-1930, Sun 1000-2000. €3.50, Mon free. Bus CS, E1. Metro: Cavour.*
Napoli's contemporary art gallery, MADRE, is housed in the handsome Donna Regina palace amidst the traffic mayhem near piazza Cavour. Portuguese architect Alvaro Siza has transformed the old palazzo interiors into a series of white cubes: its two main floors of thought-provoking exhibits provide an antidote to Napoli's ancient treasures and religious relics. Standouts from the permanent collection on the first floor are Jeff Koons' bold and brassy *Pop Art*, Richard Long's mud installation, Sol LeWitt's simple yet pulsating wall drawings and the primitive, childlike scratches of Mimmo Paladino. On the second floor there are 100 works from the 1950s to the 1990s including Andy Warhol's *Early Coloured Liz* (Chartreuse), Gilbert & George's in-your-face *Shitty World* and Lucio Fontana's *Attese* series of monochrome canvases and precise slashes. Temporary exhibitions have included Brian Eno's experiments in music and video, and a group show exploring Napoli's relationship with the cross. Take a breather from the mind-blowing art in the two large courtyards and on the roof terrace with views over the city and Paladino's *Cavallo* (horse) sculpture.

San Giovanni a Carbonara
ⓘ *Via San G a Carbonara 5, T081-295873. Daily 0900-1300. Bus CS, E1. Metro: Cavour.*
A double-flighted staircase (1700s) by Sanfelice leads to impressive church interiors that include a towering funerary monument (1428) to Angevin King Ladislao di Durazzo, who had enlarged the original Augustinian structure. Also of note are 15th-century frescoes

by Leonardo da Besozzo and bas-reliefs, statuary, blue tiles and inlaid-marble work in the Renaissance-style Cappella Caracciolo di Vico (1517).

Corso Umberto and around → *For listings, see pages 54-66.*

Corso Umberto I, known as the *rettifilo* (straight line), is the broad, clogged artery running southwest from the monstrous confusion that is piazza Garibaldi to piazza Bovio, centre of the old financial district and stock exchange. To the north is the Università degli Studi di Napoli Federico II and its fascinating museums with their whiff of formaldehyde, dust and scientific finds. The Mercato di Porta Nolana provides pure Neapolitan theatre with its sea of contraband, fish, produce and humanity, while to the south are the nowhere lands of the Mercato district that stretches down to the industrial port area. Between the odd historic attraction, including the Sant'Eligio Maggiore and Santa Maria del Carmine churches, there are grimy outlets and a warren of Camorra-run warehouses for contraband goods.

Mercato di Porta Nolana
ⓘ *Corso Garibaldi, between piazza Garibaldi and Circumvesuviana terminal. Bus 1, 152, 172. Metro: Garibaldi.*
Leave your valuables and preconceptions behind when visiting this general market southwest of Napoli Centrale station. Nicknamed *'sopra le mura'* as it's right under the city walls, it's an exhilarating open-air *teatro napoletano*. Taking in the sights, sounds and smells: wriggling octopuses, shellfish under plastic fountain displays, toothless *fruttivendoli* juggling pineapples while bartering, and contraband goods fallen off the back of Chinese cargo ships. Authorities close the market down temporarily and enforce a clean-up of the contraband and *munezza*.

Piazza Mercato
ⓘ *Bus 1, 152, 172.*
Looking more like a shabby car park and flanked by run-down apartment blocks, at first glance it's hard to believe that piazza Mercato is such an important Neapolitan square. In the 13th century commercial activity thrived around the two Angevin-built churches here, **Sant'Eligio Maggiore** and **Santa Maria del Carmine**. Both have been rebuilt, the latter having a 75-m campanile topped with majolica tiles. Inside there are frescoes by Solimena and a venerated effigy of Madonna Bruna, whose feast day is celebrated with an eardrum-bursting firework display on 16 July. Also worth a gander are the striped towers of the **Porta del Carmine** and remnants of the **Castello del Carmine**, scene of Masaniello's revolt and short-lived republic of 1647.

Centro Musei delle Scienze Naturali
ⓘ *Anthropology, Mineralogy and Zoology at via Mezzocannone 8, Paleontology at largo San Marcellino 10, T081-253 7587, www.musei.unina.it. Mon-Fri 0900-1330, Mon and Thu 1430-1630, €8 for all 4 museums, concessions, students/over 70s free. Bus E1, R2.*
Slightly off the Spaccanapoli trail are the university's Natural Sciences Museums dedicated to animals, minerals, humans and dinosaurs. The bulk of the collection is housed in the Gesù Vecchio, a Jesuit college turned university complex. Fascinating finds include Bolivian mummies, Bourbon King Charles III's Indian elephant skeleton, half-ton Madagascan quartz crystals and *Metaxytherium medium* – that's an extinct relative of the herbivorous sea cow or manatee. Top of the bill goes to the carnosaur, *Allosaurus fragilis*, suspended over a

beautiful majolica floor in the nearby Palaeontology Museum. Those into anatomy should visit the fascinating and gruesome **Museo Anatomico** ⓘ *via L Armanni, T081-566 6010, www.museoanatomico-napoli.it, Mon-Fri 0900-1200 by appointment, free*, near piazza Cavour.

Capodimonte and La Sanità → For listings, see pages 54-66.

North of the city, up on the hill, are the grand open spaces of the Parco di Capodimonte, containing one fancy Bourbon hunting lodge, Palazzo Reale, with its world-class art collection and regal interiors. Nearby on the Miradois Hill stand the three classical pavilions of the Osservatorio Astronomico, while below in the down-at-heel Rione Sanità (birthplace of Antonio de Curtis, the legendary comedian known as Totò) poverty, piety and the macabre mix. Amid the scruffy piazzas are ancient catacombs and cemeteries brimming with mosaics, frescoes and skulls: top billing goes to the catacombs of San Gennaro and San Gaudioso and the Cimitero delle Fontanelle and their spine-chilling chambers that reveal the origins of the Neapolitans' superstitious psyche. Above ground you can escape the traffic of piazza Carlo III at the wonderful Orto Botanico. Nearby, the immense 18th-century poorhouse, the Albergo dei Poveri, is being resurrected after years in purgatory and near ruin.

Palazzo Reale and Museo di Capodimonte
ⓘ *Palazzo Capodimonte, via Miano 2, or accessed via the park from via Capodimonte, T081-749 9111, www.polomusealenapoli.beniculturali.it. Thu-Tue 0830-1930, last entry 1830, €7.50, after 1400 €6.50, concessions €3.75, under 18s/over 65s free. Bus R4,24, C66.*

Art, nature, architecture, history, astronomy, garden design, and fancy porcelain all come together at the world famous Royal Palace and Museum of Capodimonte. The imposing scarlet and grey *palazzo* was commissioned by Carlo III of Bourbon in 1738 and designed by Giovanni Antonio Medrano as a lavish hunting lodge and a gallery for the exceptional Renaissance art collection inherited by Elisabetta Farnese, the king's mother. More fabulous works and furnishings from across Europe have since been added by Bourbon successors, Italy's post-unification royals – the House of Savoy – Joachim Murat's Napoleonic regime and the Italian government, who opened it to the public in 1957. You can easily spend half of a brain-bursting day here just skimming the surface of this world-class collection. The wonderfully lush 124-ha park grounds provide much needed fresh air and views.

After climbing the epic staircase to the *piano nobile*, a series of sumptuous rooms and Royal Apartments contain the **Collezione Farnesiana** (Farnese Collection) as well as Armoury and Porcelain collections. Among the many artistic highlights are: Titian's (1477-1576) erotically charged *Danae*, depicting Jupiter seducing the daughter of the king of Argos; Masaccio's (1401-1428) *Crucifixion*, part of a polyptych from a Pisan church; Bellini's (1432-1516) wintry *Transfiguration*; Bruegel the Elder's (1528-1569) haunting *Misanthrope* with the cheery Flemish proverb, "As the world is deceitful, I am going into mourning;" and El Greco's (1541-1614) *El Soplón*, an atmospheric chiaroscuro piece showing a young man diligently blowing on an ember to light a candle. For a real eyeful of rococo-style Capodimonte porcelain pop into the Salottino della Porcellana, Queen Amalia's parlour (1757) brought here from the Royal Palace at Portici.

The **second floor** galleries provide the most dramatic works and arguably the most rewarding viewing for the visitor by sketching the development of Neapolitan painting, including the city's astounding 17th-century creativity when the city's Baroque painting was famed throughout the world. The rather flat emotion and pious detachment of many earlier works suddenly gives way to brutality and raw human expression in both

Bourbon Court

The 18th-century Bourbon court was so starry-eyed about astronomy that Carlo III set up the first European university department dedicated to its study in 1735. Later in 1791 Ferdinand I commissioned the building of an observatory at the ex-Palazzo degli Studi (which later became the Museo Archeologico), before realizing that the surrounding buildings deep in the Centro Antico blocked sections of the heavens – so the building work was shifted to lofty Capodimonte, which was a more suitable vantage point for a celestial vault.

Caravaggio's influential *Flagellation* and Artemesia Gentileschi's (1593-1652/1653) *Judith Slaying Holofernes*. Billowing clouds, tumbling angels and celestial shafts of light fill Titian's *Annunciation*. Giuseppe Recco's (1634-1695) series of brooding fish-market scenes capture the slimy textures of life wriggling with death. On a more tender note is Niccolò Colantonio's 15th-century Flemish-influenced oil painting *San Gerolamo nello Studio* in which St Jerome removes a thorn from the wounded paw of a lion amid the scattered trappings of study.

On the **third floor**, there is a complete change in atmosphere as more modern, converted spaces under the roof are filled with 19th-century Realists and Impressionists, temporary shows, photography by Mimmo Jodice and contemporary art, including Warhol's colourful pop-art *Vesuvius*.

On the **ground floor** the **Gabinetto dei Disegni e delle Stampe** (Collection of Drawings and Prints) includes absorbing works by Michelangelo (1475-1654), Solimena (1657-1747), Tintoretto (1518-1594), Rembrandt (1606-1669) and Raffaello (1483-1520).

Museo dell'Osservatorio di Capodimonte

ⓘ *Via Moiariello 16, T081-557 5111, www.oacn.inaf.it. By appointment only, free. Bus 24, C66.* On the Miradois Hill to the south of the Palazzo Reale stand three classical pavilions belonging to the Museum of the Capodimonte Observatory. Arcane Neapolitan bureaucracy can make a visit to see the fascinating collection of historic astronomical instruments (lots of shiny old telescopes, intricate time pieces and globes) problematic – don't expect much help unless you phone and make an appointment. However there is ample charm in the tranquil grounds that teem with fruits and flowers, and contain a curious collection of buildings including a contemporary glass pavilion, the handsome neo-classical Specola building and bulbous metallic sheds containing telescopes.

Orto Botanico

ⓘ *Via Foria 223, T081-253 3937, www.ortobotanico.unina.it. Mon-Fri 0900-1400 by appointment only, guided visits Mar-May 0900-1100 by appointment. Free. Bus C55, 3S. Metro: Cavour.*
Escape the traffic fumes on via Foria by taking a walk amid some 9000 species and 25,000 plants at the city's Botanical Gardens, established in 1807 by Joseph Bonaparte. There are some 12 ha to explore and many themed areas, including an arboretum, with rare prickly paperbark trees, a citrus orchard, a section filled with native Mediterranean plants, a palm grove, and ponds bursting with colourful water lilies. Impressive greenhouses imitate temperate, hot-humid and hot-dry climates. The neoclassical Serra Merola, built in 1820, drips with tropical fronds while the Serra Califano contains succulents, cacti and *Cycadales*, the primitive tree fern. A red-hued castle-like building houses a museum that includes

plant fossils and human creations made of plant material – the giant lutes, Amazonian weapons and canoes from Borneo's mangrove swamps are particularly fascinating.

Albergo dei Poveri

ⓘ *Piazza Carlo III. Bus C55, 3S. Metro: Cavour.*

Designed in 1751 by Ferdinando Fuga and Luigi Vanvitelli as a poorhouse for the down-at-heel subjects of Carlo III of Bourbon, this colossal structure covering over 100,000 sq m is undergoing restoration. Originally, five courtyards and a church were planned as part of a massive self-contained village, but the project was never fully realized. Nevertheless, at one time it was the largest building in Europe. Having been put to many uses – including state archive – it fell into almost complete ruin after the 1980 earthquake. So far the 300-m façade has scrubbed up handsomely and it has started to host theatre productions and exhibitions. The city's long-term plans for the building are yet to be set in stone.

Catacombe di San Gennaro

ⓘ *Via Capodimonte 13, T081-741 1071, www.catacombedinapoli.it. Guided tours every hour Mon-Sat 1000-1700, Sun 1000-1300, €8, concessions €5. Bus R4, 178, C63.*

Plonked in the middle of nowhere on the busy road to Capodimonte, the 20th-century **Chiesa dell'Incoronata Madre del Buon Consiglio** (inspired by St Peter's in the Vatican) is the starting point of a descent into the atmospheric Catacombs of San Gennaro. Guided tours go into the dank, spooky depths to peer at second- to 10th-century frescoes, fifth-century mosaics and the tomb of the haloed San Gennaro. Pilgrims used to flock here to venerate Napoli's patron saint and his relics, until they were moved to the city's Duomo.

Catacombe di San Gaudioso

ⓘ *Piazza della Sanità, T081-483328, www.santamariadellasanita.it. Daily tours 1000-1300, €8, concessions €5. Bus R4.*

Under the Church of Santa Maria della Sanità (1603-1613) lie fifth- and sixth-century catacombs with Paleo-Christian frescoes, mosaics and sculpture, including some spine-chilling paintings of skeletons.

Cimitero delle Fontanelle

ⓘ *Chiesa della Maria Santissima del Carmine, via Fontanelle 77, T081-1970 3197. Thu-Tue 1000-1700, free. Metro Mater Dei.*

Nothing prepares you for the bizarre and chilling sight of the thousands of bones and skulls lining the walls of these tufaceous caves dug into the Materdei Hill. Small coffin-like shrines called *teche* attest to the cult of the dead that flourished here: anonymous skeletal remains were adopted by devotees who prayed for the deceased in exchange for favours. Restoration teams found votive slips with imploring messages from devotees in the orbits of skulls.

Chiaia, Mergellina and Posillipo → *For listings, see pages 54-66.*

Heading west from piazza Trieste e Trento, the sticky paving stones of pedestrianized via Chiaia rise and loop around to piazza dei Martiri, with its handsome lion statues representing republican ideals – namely martyrdom at the uprisings of 1799, 1820, 1848 and 1860. The swanky streets to the west are lined with boutiques, bars and restaurants while up on via dei Mille is the PAN arts centre. The Riviera di Chiaia has pockmarked grandeur in its handsome *palazzi* that once peered onto a beach – hence the name Chiaia which derives from the Spanish *playa*. The gentrified air and horses and carts may have been replaced by roaring traffic and a hotch-potch of businesses, yet the Riviera retains some majesty in the Bourbon-built Villa Comunale gardens (with its aquarium, fountains and antiques market) and the well-hidden Villa Pignatelli museum and gardens.

Along the scenic and now partially pedestrianised via Caracciolo you arrive at the marina at Mergellina, a favourite for island escapes and Neapolitan *passeggiate* with ice cream. Posillipo is a well-heeled district, where villas flirt with the coast and sweeping roads named after poets Petrarca (Petrarch), Orazio and Manzoni give giddy views.

Villa Comunale
ⓘ *Riviera di Chiaia. Bus 140, B, C24, R3. Metro: Amedeo/San Pasquale (under construction).*
Sandwiched between Riviera di Chiaia and via Caracciolo is this royal park popular with joggers and families. The Spanish viceroys first laid out a park here in the 1690s but it was Bourbon monarch Ferdinand IV who created the present layout when in 1780 he commissioned architect Carlo Vanvitelli and landscape designer Felice Abate to create the **Passeggio Reale** (Royal Promenade). Its long gravel paths are punctuated with fountains and Baroque statues amid exotic and Mediterranean trees including palms and monkey puzzles. At the end of a broad avenue near piazza Vittoria is the **Fontana della Tasca di Porfido** with its shoreline shells and lounging lions. Its alternative name Fontana delle Paparelle (Fountain of the Ducks) alludes to the fact that ducks once splashed here. Kids' playgrounds, a bandstand and handsome neoclassical buildings are its main attractions these days.

The Villa Comunale houses the Stazione Zoologica Anton Dohrn, established by the German scientist in 1872, which has research labs studying marine environments. On the ground floor is the **Acquario** ⓘ *T081-583111, www.szn.it, Tue-Sun 0900-1700, €2*, Europe's oldest aquarium, containing the slightly unsettling spectacle of 23 huge leaking tanks filled with Mediterranean marine life. Illustrated posters give serving suggestions for each fruit of the sea. Nearby is another elegant edifice (1870), the **Casina Pompeiana** ⓘ *T081-245 1050, Mon-Sat 0900-1900, free*, which once contained views of Pompeii and now hosts art exhibitions and cultural events. Every third and fourth weekend of the month sees the gardens and surrounding streets given over to a fabulous antiques market, the **Fiera Antiquariato** (see Shopping, page 65).

Villa Pignatelli
ⓘ *Riviera di Chiaia, T081-761 2356. Tue-Sun 0830-1400, €2. Bus 140, C9, R3. Metro: Amedeo.*
Peering through the iron gates on the traffic-ridden Riviera di Chiaia, the sight of the Doric columns of Villa Pignatelli (1826) offers a glimpse into how fabulous this road must have once been. Designed by Pietro Valente, pupil of Antonio Niccolini who created the Teatro San Carlo, and built at the behest of Ferdinand Acton of the influential Anglo-Italian family, the villa is set in lush gardens and displays a passing nod to a grandiose Pompeian residence. Subsequent owners, the Rothschilds and Pignatellis, made changes to the villa's interiors and it was eventually bequeathed to Italian state in 1952.

The two museums housed in the villa – the second-floor **Museo Diego Aragona Pignatelli Cortes** and **Museo delle Carozze**, housed in a garden pavillion, contain 16th- to 20th-century paintings and collections of porcelain (with some fine Japanese Edo vases), antiquarian books in the leather-clad library, as well as horse-drawn carriages from Italy, France and Britain. The real draw, however, are the lush gardens with their towering palms.

Palazzo Delle Arti di Napoli (PAN)

ⓘ *Via dei Mille 60, T081-795 8605, www.palazzoartinapoli.net. Wed-Mon 0930-1930, Sun 0930-1430, fee varies show to show (around €3 – often free). Bus C22, C24, C28, Metro: Amedeo.*
Worlds away from the traffic mayhem on via Mille, yet often just as disquieting, are PAN's three floors of contemporary works by up-and-coming artists. Beyond the perkily pink-and-grey façade of the tastefully renovated 18th-century Palazzo Roccella is a relaxing yet vibrant world of temporary themed exhibitions, cultural events and Napoli's leading art documentation centre. PAN's archives and workshops cover such diverse subjects as theatre, photography, architecture, design and comics. Group show *Bellezza Pericolosa* (Dangerous Beauty) explored body image themes. In the courtyard towering apartments rise up the Vomero hill, where 200 years ago it was all *prati* (fields) around the palazzo.

Porticciolo di Mergellina

ⓘ *Bus C16, C24, R3. Metro: Mergellina.*
At the western end of busy via Caracciolo, along the waterfront, the Mergellina marina is an atmospheric slice of Neapolitan life: you can sit down at the breakwater amid canoodling couples watching the ebb and flow of the sea and the comings and goings of hydrofoils, yachts and fishermens' boats, with stunning views of Vesuvius and the bay, and then wander around the neon-lit chalet restaurants, ice-cream parlours and bars near the funicular station. A favourite Neapolitan pastime is to watch the sunset here and then visit one of the local restaurants, such as **Ciro a Mergellina** (see page 59). The marina is served by lots of buses and the Mergellina Funicular, and is a 10-minute walk from the Mergellina metro station.

Tombe di Virgilio e Leopardi and Parco Virgiliano

ⓘ *Via Piedigrotta 20, T081-669390. Daily 0900 till dusk, free. Bus R3, 140. Metro: Mergellina.*
Next to the church of Santa Maria di Piedigrotta, tucked away from the roaring traffic passing through the Mergellina–Fuorigrotta tunnel, is the Parco Virgiliano – not to be confused with the park of the same name in Posillipo (see below). Tombs of the poet **Giacomo Leopardi** (1798-1837) and of Mantova-born poet **Virgil** (19-70 BC) can be seen here, though it's doubtful that the author of the *Aeneid* was actually buried here. Legend has it that Naples-mad Virgil used his magic gaze to create the impressive tunnel, the **Cripta Neapolitana**, nearby. However, Roman bricks and inscriptions suggest that architect Lucius Cocceius Auctus designed this incredible feat of engineering that burrows through tufa rock for 700 m, opening out in the Campi Flegrei. It is undergoing restoration so you can only peer into it.

Parco Virgiliano

ⓘ *Viale Virgilio, Posillipo. Bus C27.*
A series of terraces offer jaw-dropping vistas of the entire Bay of Naples including the Campi Flegrei, Capo Miseno, Capri, Ischia and Procida. Joggers, dog walkers and families enjoy the parkland trees and running track here. On the way, roads via Orazio and via Petrarca have swanky cafés and similarly spectacular views.

Vomero → *For listings, see pages 54-66.*

Up on the hill above the city is the Vomero with its pastel-hued mix of *fin di secolo* palaces and modern apartment blocks, punctuated by some uplifting sights: the parkland and museum of Villa Floridiana and the twin delights of Castel Sant'Elmo and the Certosa di San Martino. Access to the battle-worn castle and fabulous monastery complex give spectacular vistas of the bay. A walk around San Martino's sumptuous interiors, panoramic terraces and spellbinding art collections provides the most fascinating insight into Neapolitan history and the minds that dreamt up this city.

A good tip is to avoid the traffic with a serene funicular ride up to these Vomero sights on one of three lines: Centrale, Chiaia and Montesanto all stop on or near piazza Vanvitelli. It's then a short 10-minute walk westwards to Villa Floridiana or a 15-minute stroll to the castle and monastery. For the adventurous there are two alternative return routes that involve a meandering walk down old steps to the city below. The oldest, dating back to the 1500s, is the **Pedamentina di San Martino**, which starts at the piazza outside the monastery and ends up at the Corso Vittorio Emanuele, towards the western end of the Spaccanapoli. Another staircase is the **Salita del Petraio**, which starts further westwards at via Caccavello, near Castel Sant'Elmo, and follows roughly the route of the Funicolare Centrale, ending up on Corso Vittorio Emanuele at the Suor Orsola Benincasa University complex.

Certosa e Museo Nazionale di San Martino

① Piazzale San Martino 5, T081-229 4541, Thu-Tue 0830-1930, €6, under 18s/over 65s €3, discounts with Artecard. Metro/Funicular: piazza Vanvitelli, then either a 15-min walk to the Certosa or take Bus V1.

This former Carthusian monastery, begun in the 14th century, now houses fabulous artworks and various interesting collections as part of the National Museum of St Martin. It's especially worth a visit for the handsome Baroque cloisters and sublime views across the bay from the terraced gardens. Charles of Anjou, Duke of Calabria, built the main part of the sprawling Gothic complex, including the lavishly decorated church, between 1325 and 1368. From the 16th to the 18th centuries Mannerist-style revetments and Baroque flourishes were added. The original triple-naved interior of the church was modified by Florentine Giovanni Antonio Dosio and then by local architect Giovanni Giacomo di Conforto, who created lots of side chapels adorned with inlaid marble and artworks, including statues by Giuseppe Sanmartino and Cosimo Fanzago and many frescoes by Vaccaro, Giordano, Torelli, Caracciolo and d'Arpino. Seek out Ribera's painting of *Moses*, who is depicted with curious horns of light, and the exquisite inlaid wood panels in the *Sacrestia*. The **Quarto del Priore** was the lavish residence of the prior who governed monastery life and was the sole person allowed contact with lay persons. Its recently restored interiors recreate as it may have looked and contain stunning artworks including the *Madonna con Bambino e San Giovannino* by Gian Lorenzo Bernini (1598-1680), the *Virgin and Child* triptych (1494) by Jean Bourdichon and ceiling frescoes by Micco Spadaro.

Take a breather by walking around the **Chiostro Grande** (Great Cloister), with its Florentine-style gardens, saintly statues and macabre marble skulls by Fanzago. The monks had their cells here. Among the museum collections are historic *presepi* (nativity scenes) and carriages, as well as exhibitions detailing the history of the complex, Naples and Neapolitan theatre. The fascinating section *Immagini e Memorie della Città* is filled with maps and images of Naples made during various periods, including the remarkable *Tavola Strozzi*, a 15th-century view of the city, and *Veduta della Darsena*, a dockside scene by Gaspar Van Wittel painted in 1702. Neapolitan artworks from the 19th century include lots of Arcadian landscapes by artists of the Posillipo School including *Panorama of Naples Viewed from the Conocchia* by Giacinto Gigante.

Castel Sant'Elmo

① Via Tito Angelini 20, T081-229 4401, Wed-Mon 0830-1930, €5, 18-25s €2.50, under 18s/over 65s free. Metro/Funicular: piazza Vanvitelli, then either a 15-min walk to the castle or take Bus V1.

Next to the Certosa di San Martino is the Sant'Elmo Castle. 'Sant'Elmo' derives from the 10th-century St Erasmus Church that stood here and which in typically Neapolitan linguistic fashion has lost some letters. In the 16th century, Spanish Viceroy Pedro Toledo transformed the Angevin construction (1329-1343) into its present star-shaped form. For many centuries it was used as a prison, incarcerating insurgents and outspoken figures including the Renaissance philosopher Tommaso Campanella – author of an outlandish-at-the-time Utopian treatise, *City of the Sun*. Housed within the high prison is the **Museo del Novecento**, a collection of 170 20th-century artworks, mainly by Neapolitan artists.

Villa Floridiana and Museo Nazionale della Ceramica Duca di Martina

① Via Domenico 77, T081-478 8418, www.floridiana.napolibeniculturali.it. Wed-Mon 0830-1400, free. Metro: P. Vanvitelli, Bus C28, C31.

Landscaped royal gardens with some of the best views in town plus the National Ceramics Museum are the refined attractions to be found at Villa Floridiana, a 15-minute walk from Vomero's piazza Vanvitelli. In 1817 Bourbon monarch Ferdinand I gifted the estate and the neoclassical villa to his second wife, Lucia Migliaccio, Duchess of Floridia, and named it in her honour. Connoisseurs of camellias can spot rare varieties in the lush gardens although the fabulous views of the city are likely to divert everyone's attention. Placido de Sangro, the Duke of Martina, was potty about porcelain and ceramics, amassing some 6000 valuable pieces which were donated to the city on the death of his grandson in 1891. As well as the fine examples of Wedgwood, Capodimonte and Ming there are precious objects including tortoiseshell pieces and some 17th- to 19th-century paintings by the likes of Francesco Solimena and Domenico Antonio Vaccaro.

Campania sidetrips → *For listings, see pages 54-66.*

Two outstanding attractions are within an hour's striking distance from Napoli Centrale by train or via the A1 Autostrada: Caserta has an old medieval centre and a Bourbon royal palace to rival Versailles in scale and ambition, while Santa Maria Capua Vetere contains the second-largest Roman amphitheatre, an ancient temple and an archaeological museum.

Reggia di Caserta

① Viale Douhet, T0823-277430, www.reggiadicaserta.beniculturali.it. Wed-Mon, Royal Apartments 0830-1930, last admission 1900. Park 0830 till sunset, last admission 2 hrs before sunset (check website). €14, concessions €7, under 18s/over 65s free, audio guides €5. Bus shuttle to Diana Fountain €1 round trip. The entrance to the palace is opposite the train station.

Out of the scruffy, traffic-ridden modern suburbs of Caserta appears the incongruous sight of a colossal royal palace with a few typically Neapolitan rough edges. The scale of the frontage impresses but nothing prepares you for the expansive gardens and fountains that rise spectacularly up a verdant hill. Carlo III of Bourbon commissioned Baroque behemoth Luigi Vanvitelli to build the palace that was part of his plan for a new administrative centre. He abdicated and returned to Spain in 1759, leaving the project in the hands of his less high-minded son Ferdinand and faithful regent Tanucci. As the ancien regime declined and Italy was unified in 1860 the military occupied the palace;

later it was to play an important role as Allied HQ and venue of official Fascist and Nazi German capitulation in 1943-1945.

The five-storey palace occupies over 45,000 sq m, has two principal façades 247 m long and 36 m high with 243 windows, and took 22 years to build (1752-1774) and another 73 years to garnish with much gilt. Its 1200 rooms and 43 staircases are arranged around four monumental courtyards. The 20-km monumental avenue to Naples was never completed. Amid the sumptuous yet rather garish **Royal Apartments** is the striking throne room containing a frieze with medallions depicting the kings of Naples and a smaller version of Naples' Teatro San Carlo. More uplifting are the expansive gardens, with gravel paths, a long fish pond and lots of fountains including **La Fontana di Eolo** (Fountain of Eolus) with fantastical grottoes, zephyrs and gods. **La Cascata Grande** impressively apes a natural waterfall cutting through a wooded hill and the **Giardino Inglese** (English Gardens), designed by English botanist Andrea Graefer, mixes 2500 sq m of naturalistic parkland scattered with Roman statues from Pompeii and some curious follies with Masonic references that were all the rage when Queen Maria Carolina of Austria commissioned the project in 1786. The Reggia and its grand staircase appeared as the Naboo Royal Palace in the Star Wars prequels, *The Phantom Menace* and *Attack of the Clones*.

Casertavecchia

Built around its sombre 12th-century cathedral is the old hilltop town of Casertavecchia, some 10 km north of Caserta. It retains lots of medieval atmosphere and is a popular place for dining. The **Duomo di San Michele Arcangelo** ① *piazza Vescovado, T082-337 1318, daily 0900-1300, 1530-1800, free,* is built of volcanic tufa stone in a Norman-Arabic style. It has a Moorish *tiburio ottagonale* (octagonal roofed tower) as well as a 13th-century campanile, a façade with strange carved animal sculptures with Lombardic origins, and gracefully stark interiors. There are 18 Roman columns and colourful marble mosaic details on the apse paving and on the elegant pulpit. Also worth seeking out is the Gothic church, **Chiesetta dell'Annunziata**, and the crumbling yet commanding six-pack of tower ruins of the 11th-century **castle**, begun by the Normans in AD 879.

San Leucio

① *Piazza della Seta, strada Statale SS87, T082-330 1817, www.comune.caserta.it/belvedere. Wed-Mon 0930-1800, €6, 6-18s/over 60s €3.*

A few kilometres northwest of Caserta on the SS87 is the model silk workers' community of San Leucio set up by Ferdinando I in 1789, which had liberal laws based on the theories of Neapolitan philosopher and jurist Gaetano Filangieri. It takes its name from the small church on the hill here. As well as superb views from the belvedere, orderly rows of workers' houses and the handsome **Casino Reale** palace with its sumptuously frescoed royal apartments, there's a **Museo della Seta** (Silk Museum) that displays historic fabrics and weaving machines. The privately owned **Stabilimento Serico de Negri** still produces plush fabrics here today.

Santa Maria Capua Vetere

① *Museo Archeologico: via Roberto D'Angio 48, T0823-844206, www.cir.campania. beniculturali.it/museosmcv. All sites opening times Tue-Sun 0900-1600 (Anfiteatro till 1800). €3 to see all sites. Frequent trains from Napoli and Caserta. A1 Autostrada Exit Caserta Nord. From Caserta head westwards along the via Appia (SS7).*

Seven kilometres west of Caserta through nondescript suburbs is Santa Maria Capua Vetere, where the Thracian gladiator Spartacus is said to have launched his rebellion against Rome in 73 BC. There are evocative archaeological sites to investigate including the **Arco di Adriano**, a triumphal arch of the ancient via Appia, and – most famously – the **Anfiteatro Campano** ⓘ *piazza Ottobre, T0823-798864*, started by Hadrian in the first century AD. Despite being looted for its stone and metal, the ruins of this arena, which held around 60,000 spectators, are mightily impressive. Highlights include traces of frescoes and Palaeo-Christian remnants in the passages under the arena, a **Museo dei Gladiatori** displaying suits of armour, and architectural fragments scattered around the picturesque grounds. The **Museo Archaeologico dell'Antica Capua-Mitreo** ⓘ *via Roberto d'Angio 48, T0823-844206*, housed in the Torre di Sant'Erasmo, displays artefacts from the Bronze Age as well as lots of ceramics, artworks, weaponry and trinkets made by Etruscans, Samnites, Greeks and Romans. Ask a member of the museum staff for access to the nearby **Mitreo Temple**, dedicated to a Persian god, which has a fresco depicting the ritual sacrifice of a bull.

Naples listings

For hotel and restaurant price codes and other relevant information, see pages 14-17.

🛏 Where to stay

Lots of B&Bs and mid-range hotels have appeared in the suburbs and deep in the old city in recent years. Many of the big swanky hotels are not happy about the competition, but it's good news for visitors. Generally prices remain lower than the rest of Italy. There are now some very stylish conversions of old apartments, in Chiaia and the Centro Antico especially, while around Santa Lucia lots of well-established hotels live off past glories and business customers, and tend to disappoint. It's best to avoid places on corso Garibaldi and near piazza Garibaldi because of the traffic noise, pollution and crime.

Santa Lucia and around *p28, map p30*
€€€ Palazzo Turchini, via Medina 21/22, T081-551 0606, www.palazzoturchini.it. Located off piazza Municipio in a 1590s building that once formed part of the Royal Conservatory, this well-appointed hotel offers a comfortable, a/c stay within easy reach of the Monumental City, the port and the Centro Antico. Modern interiors with marble and hardwood, giving the place a sleek but warm feel.

Centro Antico and corso Umberto area *p33, map p30*
€€€ Romeo, via Cristoforo Colombo 45, T081-017 5001, www.romeohotel.it. Swanky contemporary glass and steel building near the port, so handy for the ferries. The large lobby area combines minimalism with striking ancient and modern artworks, and runs into a sushi restaurant. There's a rooftop pool, bar, Michelin-starred restaurant, Il **Commandante**, plus a luxury spa, **Dogana del Sale**. Guest rooms and suites have lots of remote control gadgetry and sleek design.
€€ Costantinopoli 104, via Santa Maria di Costantinopoli 104, T081-557 1035, www.costantinopoli104.com. Metro: Museo/Dante. Take one *stile-Liberty* palazzo with a gorgeous palm-fronded garden in the throbbing heart of the Centro Antico then add a pool and attractive interiors to make a very special hotel package. Beyond the art nouveau ironwork and stained-glass windows is an elegant yet homely reception area/lounge and equally alluring breakfast room. The 19 bedrooms mix carefully chosen artworks, luxurious bathrooms and smart furnishings.
€€ Palazzo Decumani, via del Grande Archivio 8, T081-4201379, www.palazzo decumani.com. Excellent-value hotel within a noble residence right in the heart of the Centro Antico. There's an

elegant whitewashed lobby area and cosy bar where cocktails come with friendly chat and quality nibbles including mozzarella, salami and salad. A sweeping staircase leads to a range of rooms with understated decor and smart bathrooms.

€€-€ Piazza Bellini, via Santa Maria di Costantinopoli 101, T081-451732, www.hotelpiazzabellini.com. Metro: Museo/ Dante. Ensconced in the Bohemian heart of Naples, Hotel Piazza Bellini is housed in a handsome historic palazzo with impressive courtyard and statuary. Expect minimalist contemporary interiors with lots of colourful flourishes and public spaces. Many of the 48 rooms feel functional but sterile – like an upmarket hostel that lacks character. Breakfasts are excellent and can be eaten in the courtyard. Good choice with deals for groups and families.

€ Clarean, piazza Garibaldi 49, T081-553 5683, www.clarean.hotelsinnapoli.com. If you need a place close to the station this hotel is a good bet: it's close to the Alibus stop, so it's convenient for an overnight stop or early start. Be aware that it's in the seedy piazza Garibaldi area so not recommended for long stays.

€ Fresh Glamour, via Donnalbina 7, T081-020 2255, www.donnalbina7.it. The Fresh is a great-value find. The unfussy, whitewashed rooms have vibrant 1970s-style fabrics, artworks by local artists and decent bathrooms. You can even have breakfast in bed, which is a real treat in this price bracket. Excellent facilities include free Wi-Fi connection.

Self-catering

Decumani Roof, via dei Tribunali 197, T333-600 9627, www.decumaniroof.net. These smart new flats at the Castel Capuano end of the Decumanus Maggiore have original artworks and stunning rooftop views. However the climb to the tiled terrace is not really suitable for families with young children or the less mobile. A small 1-roomed apartment for 3 people

costs €90-120; a 2-roomed apartment for 4-6 people is €100-180.

Via Toledo to piazza Cavour *p42, map p30*

€€ Il Convento, via Speranzella 137/A, T081-403977, www.hotelilconvento.it. A homely place in a 17th-century palazzo run by a friendly family. Decent facilities include a bar, a/c and free Wi-Fi. It's on an atmospheric and chaotic Spanish Quarter street off via Toledo.

€ Donna Regina, via Luigi Settembrini 80, T081-442 1511, www.discovernaples.net. Despite traffic mayhem and a dodgy old lift, this B&B – within a crumbling 14th-century convent building – has plenty of character and history perfect for the adventurous but not the unwary. Owned by the Raffone family, whose members include sculptors, painters and chefs, the rooms are large and crammed with oddities, antiquarian books and paintings. It's very handy for the MADRE and Museo Archaeologico Nazionale.

€ Spaccanapoli Comfort Suites, via Francesco Girardi 37, T081-417809, www.bbspaccanapoli.com. A great-value choice with spacious modern rooms and suites in an old building in the Quartieri Spagnoli. Expect fabulous service from helpful owners and facilities to match.

€ Toledo, via Montecalvario 15, T081-406800, www.hoteltoledo.com. Just off the bustling shopping street. Its 33 rooms are functional and fairly well soundproofed – when you close the shutters – from the Quartieri Spagnoli streetlife outside. The amiable manager explains that before the 1980 earthquake this old palazzo once housed a brothel. Breakfast can be taken on the leafy roof terrace.

Chiaia, Lungomare and Posillipo *p48, maps p26 and p30*

€€€€ Excelsior, via Partenope 48, T081-7640111, www.excelsior.it. This *belle époque* hotel overlooks the newly pedestrianized waterfront. Many of the spacious suites and rooms have small balconies. Grand public areas near the lobby made an appearance in Rosselini's 1954 film *Viaggio in Italia*. Bountiful breakfasts are taken in the **La Terrazza** rooftop restaurant.

€€ Ausonia, via Caracciolo 11, Mergellina, T081-682278, www.hotelausonianapoli.com. The **Ausonia** is in the perfect spot for those using the Mergellina hydrofoils. The restful rooms have a nautical theme: porthole windows, framed knots and prints of ships give it a slightly kitsch yet charming feel.

€€ Culture Villa Capodimonte, via Moiarello 66, T081-459000, www.villa capodimonte.it. A modern hotel (1990s) near the Museo di Capodimonte, though far from downtown sights. The business-orientated feel may disappoint some. However, on the plus side it's away from the Naples hubbub, with relaxing public areas include a piano bar, rooftop terrace and lush gardens.

€€ Micalò, Riviera di Chiaia 88, Chiaia, T081-761 7131, www.micalo.it. Bus R3, 140, 152. **Micalò**'s Anglo-Italian owners commissioned a talented young architect to create the city's most inspiring boutique hotel in a 17th-century palazzo opposite the Villa Comunale Gardens. Its cool marble floors and curvy walls are sprinkled with interesting objects and artworks by Neapolitan artists. The cavernous guest rooms have huge beds below minimalist-style mezzanine bathrooms. Scrambled eggs and fresh *cornetti* are on the healthy yet hearty breakfast menu which is served in the **Art Bar**.

€€ Palazzo Alabardieri, via Alabardieri 38, Chiaia, T081-415278, www.palazzo alabardieri.it. Chiaia's chic shops, smart restaurants and swanky bars are on the doorstep. Guest rooms are spacious and soundproofed, with traditional furnishings and botanical prints. A reading room filled with lots of armchairs and historic Neapolitan scenes leads to a cream-hued dining room with coved ceiling.

€ La Bouganville, via Manzoni 155, Posillipo, T081-769 2205, www.labouganville.com.

Take a breather from Napoli's traffic mayhem up in this small and tranquil Posillipo B&B run by the helpful host Giuliano. Staying in a Neapolitan home gives you a real taste for the city and Giuliano does not disappoint. The guest rooms open onto a leafy garden. It's near the via Manzoni funicular, so handy for Mergellina and Parco Virgiliano.

€ Platamon B&B, via Chiatamone 55, Chiaia, T081-764 3203, www.bebnaples.com. Just up the road from **Napoli Residence** (see below), Marco Platamon has a small B&B containing 3 largish guest rooms with tiled floors, fresh white walls and some exuberant artworks. Doubles cost €80-100.

Vomero *p50, maps p26 and p30*

€€€€ Grand Hotel Parkers, corso Vittorio Emanuele 135, T081-761 2474, www.grandhotelparkers.it. Bus C16. Metro: Amedeo. The stunning view of the bay from the swanky terrace restaurant **George's** is the biggest draw of this grand old 5-star hotel. English aristocrat George Parker Bidder acquired the hotel in 1889 and it still maintains some *belle époque* elegance despite some uninspiring recent refurbishments. Guest rooms have art nouveau decorative flourishes but lack character somehow. Overall the level of service, style and atmosphere is not quite what you would expect from an historic hotel that once hosted illustrious guests such as Oscar Wilde and Virginia Wolfe.

€€ San Francesco al Monte, corso Vittorio Emanuele 328, T081-423 9111, www.san francescoalmonte.it. Housed in an old monastery, this place commands fabulous views over the city. Public areas and some of the rooms retain vestiges of religious life and there's a chapel too. On the roof is a pool and garden set into the Vomero tufa rock, and the breakfast terrace is wonderful. However, customer service, attention to detail and room cleanliness are lacking.

€€ Weekend a Napoli, via Enrico Alvino 157, T081-578 1010, www.weekendanapoli. com. Switched-on owners Paolo and Patrizia have created a truly comfortable hotel with superb-value accommodation in a quiet residential corner of Vomero. There are various room options available and even a small apartment. Some of the small doubles lack natural light but the suites are spacious and bright, and some have jacuzzi baths.

€ La Controra, piazza Trinità alla Cesarea 231, T081-549 4014, www.lacontrora.com. Metro: Salvator Rosa. Hostel buildings don't often come as grand as this former 17th-century convent near a crumbling old Baroque church. Recent refurbishments have added a smart modern café and landscaped gardens which are venues for DJ sets and art exhibitions. As well as well-maintained mixed dorms there's a selection of en suite doubles and family rooms at very reasonable rates. The rooms have recently been refurbished, and you'll find pieces of contemporary sculpture alongside retro furniture. Prices start at €16 for a bed in a dorm.

ⓘ Restaurants

Santa Lucia and around *p28, maps p26 and p30*

€€€ La Bersagliera, Borgo Marinari 10/11, T081-764 6016. Closed Tue. Opened in 1919 and frequented by Neapolitan geniuses Totò and Eduardo de Filippo, as well as Sophia Loren and the late Luciano Pavarotti, this historic eatery still pulls in the punters. Book a table outside overlooking the harbour or in the elegant dining room and sample seafood specialities including *insalata di polipo* (octopus salad), *frittura di paranza* (fried marine medley) and their home-made *pastiera*.

€€€ La Scialuppa, Borgo Marinari 4, T081-764 5333, www.lascialuppa.it. Closed Mon. Down on the Borgo Marinari, La Scialuppa has bags of nautical character, wonderful views and arguably the best dining experience on the marina. Specialities include *rigatoni al pesce spada* (chunky pasta tubes with swordfish) and *linguine al scialuppa* (linguine, scampi, prawns, tomatoes and parsley).

€ Da Patrizia, Borgo Marinari 24, T081-764 6407. Closed Mon. Among the swanky eateries is the ever-reliable **Patrizia**'s, which has just half a dozen tables on the quayside. It's tiny, popular and only open in the warmer months. Expect classics like *spaghetti alle cozze* (with mussels and tomatoes), *frittura di gamberi e calamari* (lightly fried prawn and squid) and *polipo alla Luciana* (octopus cooked in garlic, wine and its own juices).

Cafés and bars

Caffè del Professore, piazza Trieste e Trento 46, T081-403 0410. Daily 0700-0200. This refined bar near piazza del Plebiscito is famed for its *caffè ai gusti di nocciola e cioccolata* (coffee flavoured with hazelnut and chocolate) and delicious *sfogliatelle*.

Caffè Gambrinus, via Chiaia 1, T081-417582, www.caffegambrinus.com. Daily 0800-0130. Take in the handsome *stile-Liberty* (Italian art nouveau) interiors of this historic café, with its dazzling display of mirrors, gilt and chandeliers, while watching the entertaining interaction of the dapper baristas and Neapolitan clientele. Prop up the long marble bar or pay for the privilege of sitting in an elegant corner or on the terrace, sipping espresso and munching on a few of their excellent pastries: it's famed for *babà al rhum*, *coda d'aragosta* (*sfogliatella* in the shape of a lobster's tail) and the creamy topped cake *Il Vesuvio*. Fancy cocktails are accompanied by *stuzzicherie* (savoury nibbles). Among the illustrious guests who have chatted and chomped here are Oscar Wilde, Benedetto Croce and Lucifer Box (Mark Gatiss's dashing fictional secret agent in *The Vesuvius Club*).

Centro Antico *p33, map p30*

€€€ La Stanza del Gusto, via Costantinopoli 100, T081-401 578, www.lastanzadelgusto.com. Closed Sun evening and Mon. Vibrant and informal restaurant run by the ever-creative Mario Avallone whose inventive dishes and artistic outlook make **La Stanza** a special place.

Expect the freshest produce in dishes such as aubergine *capanata* with roast octopus. Exquisite experiments with seaweed and seafood go into Mario's *Oceano* dish. The melon and aniseed sorbet cleans the palate. Superb wine and drink selection.

€€ Sorriso Integrale, Vico san Pietro a Majella 6 (piazza Bellini), T081-455 026, www.sorrisointegrale.com. A well-established vegetarian restaurant that brings eastern culinary influences to fabulous organic Campanian produce. Owner Bruno Zarzaca also helps run London's first vegetarian Italian restaurant, **Amico Bio**.

€ Antica Pizzeria da Michele, via Cesare Sersale 1/3, T081-553 9204. Closed Sun. Pizza purists flock to this no-nonsense pizzeria for just 2 classic varieties, the *Margherita* and *marinara*. Thin crusts with wonderful charred bubbles are the order of the day. Pick up a ticket and join the queue that disappears almost as quickly as you can say *pizza pizza ca' pummorala 'ncoppa* (pizza pizza with tomatoes on top).

€ Il Pizzaiolo del Presidente, via dei Tribunali 120/121, T081-210903, www.il pizzaiolodelpresidente.it. Closed Sun. The 'President's Pizza Maker', the late Ernesto Cacciali, handed Bill Clinton a *pizza-piegata* during the G7 summit in 1994 and, on the back of his fame, the fly *pizzaiolo* opened this no-frills pizzeria, just up from his old place **Di Matteo**. Take a seat at the paper-clothed tables in the cosy basement and order from a couple of dozen pizza varieties including their famed *pizza fritta* (fried pizza).

€ Pizzeria di Matteo, via dei Tribunali 94, T081-455262. Closed Sun. Metro: Dante. It's one of the city's top pizzerias – President Clinton dropped in during the G7 summit of 1994. As well as making a tasty *Margherita* that spills over your plate, they do an excellent *ripieno al forno* – a folded *pizza calzone* with a choice of fillings.

€ Sorbillo, via dei Tribunali 32, T081-446643. Closed Sun. Step into the flagstone ground floor of this historic pizzeria opened in 1935 and you sense a friendly, youthful

vibe. Red-shirted Neapolitan waitresses glide around while boss Gino Sorbillo conducts the *pizzaioli* music behind the counter. The huge rectangular and very thin-based pizzas spill over the plates: *passata di pomodoro* makes the *Margherita* swimmingly delicious while 2 pizzas named after the founding grandparents, Luigi and Carolina, retain an elastic, charred base reminiscent of naan bread.

Cafés and bars

Caffè Letterario Intra Moenia, piazza Bellini 70, T081-290988, www.intramoenia.it. Daily 1000-0200. Art, music and books combine in this boho bar popular with students, academics and creative types who sit at the tables on leafy piazza Bellini or browse through the fascinating collection of books and prints inside.

Portico 340, via Tribunali 340, T081-27030. Minimalist, contemporary haven under the porticoes, in the gritty Centro Antico. Attracts an arty crowd: artworks and books abound, accompanied by good cocktails and light snacks.

Scaturchio, piazza San Domenico Maggiore 19, T081-551 6944, www.scaturchio.it. Closed Tue. Opened in 1921, this Neapolitan institution is famed for its pastries and cakes including *sfogliatelle*, the papal-approved *pastiera* cake (Pope John Paul II was a big fan apparently) and *lo zefiro* (orange-flavoured *semifreddo* cake).

Via Toledo to piazza Cavour *p42, map p30*

€ Antica Pizzeria Port'Alba, via Porta Alba 18, T081-459713. 1400-1600, 1800-0100. Metro: Dante. One of the oldest pizzerias (allegedly opened in 1738 as an open-air pizzeria stand, with interiors and tables added in 1830), **Port'Alba** serves all the classics as well as various pasta and seafood dishes, at very reasonable prices. The crust here is a little thicker and it's much pricier than your average *pizza Napoletana* to sit down. Opt for the takeaway stand outside.

Cafés and bars

Mexico, piazza Dante 86, T081-549 9330. Mon-Sat 0730-2030. Café connoisseurs from near and far flock to the Passalacqua family's bars on piazza Dante and piazza Garibaldi to sample coffee made with roasted arabica beans, which you can buy here. A must visit for the *caffè*, barista banter and kitsch 1970s decor. Pick up a 250 g yellow/brown tin of their iconic *Mekico caffè* on the way out.

Corso Umberto and around *p45, map p30*

€€ Europeo di Mattozzi, via Marchese Campodisola 4, T081-552 1323. Mon-Sat 1200-1530, Thu-Sat 1930-2300. Bus R1, R2, R4. Opened in the 1930s, this elegant establishment on piazza Bovio serves fine food amid colourful ceramics and old prints. Perennial favourites include *polpo in casseruola* (octopus casserole), *pasta e patate con provala* (pasta and potatoes with smoky melted cheese) and *baba* for dessert.

Chiaia, Lungomare and Posillipo *p48, maps p26 and p30*

€€€€ Rosiello a Posillipo, via Santo Strato 10, Posillipo, T081-769 1288. Closed Wed. It may be pricey and a bit out of the way in Posillipo (catch the 140 bus from Mergellina or, better still, take a cab), but the wonderful terrace views of Capri and Vesuvius and their gorgeous food and wine make **Rosiello** a very special place to dine. Vegetarians can enjoy the flavoursome *parmigiana di melanzane* and carnivores can savour the *braciole* (rolls of beef) served with a tomato ragout. The bianco, rosso and rosato wines are produced at their **Varriale** vineyard.

€€ Ciro a Mergellina, via Mergellina 18/21, Mergellina, T081-681780. Closed Mon. Close to the Mergellina *lungomare* this Neapolitan favourite does classic Neapolitan dishes including seafood and pizzas. The dining experience in this open-plan 1960s chalet is enhanced by the entertaining, dapper waiters. You can order your *Margherita* topped with either *pomodorini*

di Vesuvio (the tasty tomatoes grown below Vesuvius) or *passata*. Their *ripieno al forno* – baked *calzone* style – is very filling and their *insalate di mare* (seafood salad) is a popular antipasto choice with the locals. For something a bit different try the delicious *polipo affogato* – a huge octopus cooked simply in its own brick-red juices.

€€ Umberto, via Alabardieri 30/31, piazza dei Martiri, Chiaia, T081-418555. Closed Mon lunch. The di Porzio family have run this elegant restaurant-pizzeria for 3 generations. The spacious rooms have interesting artworks for sale and often host cultural events. Expect slightly smaller pizzas here but excellent quality, pressed tablecloths and friendly service from dapper waiters. Their Pizza DOC is topped with San Marzano tomatoes and the best buffalo mozzarella. As well as classic fishy *frittura* and meaty *ragù alla Genovese* with pennolini pasta, they do delicious *contorni* (side dishes) like *mozzarella in carozza* (in a breaded carriage), *zucchini alla scapece* (marinated courgettes) and tasty *friarelli* (bitter broccoli-like shoots).

€ Clu, via Carlo Poerio 47, T081-764 1576. Smart contemporary bar-restaurant that offers a buffet breakfast 0800-1000 for €5, lunch for €8, and an abundance of *aperitivo* snacks in the early evening. Buy a drink (a glass of wine costs from €6) take a plate and tuck in. It also stages cultural events and DJ sets frequented by Chiaia's well-heeled. A stylish place that offers great value and atmosphere.

€ Vinarium, Vico Santa Maria Cappella Vecchia 7, Chiaia, T081-764 4114. Closed Sun lunch. There's a bar and *enoteca* serving fabulous wine at the front of this busy place in Chiaia. It's great for lunch and late-night diners and drinkers. A sheet with the day's choices includes hearty pasta dishes, abundant salads and seafood. A combination of that classic Neapolitan wedge of carbohydrate, *pasta frittata*, followed by a baked fish, and a tempting *semifreddo* cake served with hot chocolate sauce, is great fuel for a trawl around Naples.

Cafés and bars

Chalet Ciro, via Mergellina 11, Mergellina, T081-669928. Open 24 hrs. **Ciro** has been pulling in the punters to sample their yummy dollops of *gelato* on the Mergellina waterfront since the 1950s. Choose from hundreds of *coni*, *coppe*, *semifreddi* and *sorbetti* combinations and flavours, including the fantabulous *pizza al gelato* (ice-cream pizza) and the exotic fruit-filled *coppa Tarzan*.

Gran Bar Riviera, Riviera di Chiaia 183, Chiaia, T081-665026. Open 24 hrs. Day and night this café is filled with Neapolitans enjoying its refreshments, pastries, ice cream and cakes. Their famous *buondì notte* combo of nutella and *semifreddo zabaglione* is a treat well worth trying.

Gran Caffè Cimmino, via Petrarca 147, Posillipo, T081-575 7697. Daily 0700-0100. There are wonderful views from the scenic via Petrarca – a favourite of tour buses and loved-up couples – this fabulous place has the *sfogliatelle* and famed *babà alla frutta* to match.

La Caffettiera, piazza dei Martiri 25, Chiaia, T081-764 4243. Daily 0700-2230. This popular café, with refined interiors and outside tables, looks onto the lions in piazza dei Martiri. Great little pizzas, savoury cakes and lots of sweet pastry treats.

Vomero *p50, map p26*

€€ Acunzo, via D Cimarosa 64, T081-578 5362. Closed Sun. Open since 1964 and often full – for good reason. **Acunzo** serves great pizzas (try their *pizza pulcinella* piled with mince, *prosciutto*, mozzarella, ricotta and mushrooms) as well as tasty fried foods from their traditional Neapolitan *friggitoria* cookbook.

⚙ Entertainment

Nightlife

Be Bop Bar, via Ferrigni 34, Chiaia, T081-245 1321. Daily 1800-0200, usually later at weekends, free. Metro: Amedeo. Less posy and packed than many of Chiaia's swanky *locali*, **Be Bop Bar** attracts a wider age range of punters who come for the relaxed atmosphere and eclectic tunes.

Enoteca Belledonne, Vico Belledonne a Chiaia 18, Chiaia, T081-403162. Daily 1200-0200. Metro: Amedeo. Locals cram into and gather outside this popular wine bar to quaff the quality *vino* and to nibble on tasty *stuzzichini* snacks before moving on. It's a buzzing spot for an *aperitivo*.

Rootz Klub, vicolo delle Quercia 26, T335-547 7299, www.kinkyjam.com. Daily 2200-0300. After 15 years of the **Kinky Bar**, the reggae, dub and wacky baccy moved to bigger premises and a new name. The Caribbean feel is enhanced by top live acts including Mad Professor and Mr Dennis Alcapone.

Perditempo, via San Pietro a Maiella 8, T081-444958. Daily 1000 till late, free. Metro: Dante. A favourite "waste of time" of the Neapolitan band Almamegretta, the **Perditempo** is a kind of cultural centre cum bar that combines a bookshop, record store and venue for leftfield events including live music acts.

S'Move Light Bar, Vico dei Sospiri 10A, Chiaia, T081-764 5813. Daily 1000-0300. Metro: Amedeo. Opened in 1992, **S'Move**'s stylish 3 floors serve food and drink throughout the day while by night it hosts mainly house music DJs.

Superfly, via Cisterna dell'Olio 12, T347-127 2178. Tue-Sun 1700-0300. Chilled-out lounge and jazz tunes combine with the sleek contemporary decor, making this tiny place a Parthenopean poseurs' paradise. It's worth popping in for a daiquiri or mojito in the evening when the crowd spills out onto the Centro Antico street.

Cinema

Foreign films in their original language are rarely shown in Italy and Naples is no exception. Warner Village shows the mainstream flicks whereas **Amedeo** (via Martucci, T081-680266), **Academy Astra** (via Mezzocannone, T081-552 0713) and **Modernissimo** screen art-house films.

Modernissimo, via Cisterno dell'Olio 23, T081-580 0254, www.modernissimo.it. The recently refurbished 4-screen Modernissimo in the Centro Antico is the most stylish venue, screening art-house films and hosting left-field 'Videodrome' programmes including MaiGay, which explores sexuality and gender.

Warner Village Metropolitan, via Chiaia 149, T081-4290 8225, www.warnervillage.it. Mainstream Italian films and the latest Hollywood blockbusters dubbed into Italian are screened here.

Gay and lesbian

Although conservative and strongly family orientated, Naples has always been a city with many influences and a free-thinking, open and tolerant core lies at the heart of *Napoletanità*. There may not be exclusively gay venues but there are many club nights. Outlying areas of Naples may have more traditional values but the university quarter and piazza Bellini is the centre of many of the leftfield scenes and is a meeting place for the gay community, with **Caffè Letterario Intra Moenia** (see page 58) being particularly popular.

ArciGay Circolo Atinoo & ArciLesbica Circolo le Maree, Vico San Gerolamino 19, T081-552 8815, www.arcigaynapoli.org, www.arcilesbica.it/napoli. The city's main gay and lesbian organizations organize cultural events, parties and political demonstrations. They welcome visitors to their offices in the Centro Antico.

Depot, via della Veterinaria 72, T081-780 9578. Leather vests and bare chests are all the rage at this the self-styled leather cruising bar.

Evaluna, piazza Bellini 72, T081-292372. A relaxing meeting place and cultural centre that specializes in womens' books, arty gifts, courses and esoteric tours of the city.

Sputnik Club, via Santa Teresa degli Scalzi 154 bis, T081-1981 3222. An intimate internet and gay bar that opens till the wee early hours every day.

Music
Classical and opera

As well as grandiose operatic and classical productions at the Teatro San Carlo, various organizations stage chamber music concerts across the city, including the Associazione Alessandro Scarlatti, named after Naples' most famous composer.

Associazione Alessandro Scarlatti, piazza dei Martiri 58, Chiaia, T081-406011, www. associazionescarlatti.it. Check out this well-established (1918) organization's website for details of their programme of chamber concerts held at various venues including Villa Pignatelli, Castel Sant'Elmo and the Chiesa di San Domenico Maggiore.

Centro di Musica Antica Pietà de' Turchini, via Santa Caterina da Siena 38, T081-402395, www.turchini.it. Baroque music concerts are staged in the former Conservatorio della Solitaria, in the Convent and Church of Santa Caterina da Siena.

Chiesa Anglicana, 15 via San Pasquale a Chiaia, Chiaia, T081-411842. The neo-Gothic Christ Church hosts choral concerts, organ recitals and renditions of Handel's *Messiah* at Christmas.

Chiesa Evangelica Luterana, via Carlo Poerio 5, Chiaia, T081-663207, www.lutero. org. Established by the Franco-German evangelical community in the 1820s, this Lutheran church off piazza dei Martiri hosts ecclesiastical concerts.

Conservatorio di Musica San Pietro a Majella, via San Pietro a Majella 35, T081-564 4411. Students and teachers often play amid the grand surroundings of this famous conservatory in the heart of ancient Naples.

Teatro di San Carlo, via San Carlo 98f, T081-797 2331, www.teatrosancarlo.it. Founded in 1737, this prestigious opera house attracts discerning audiences to its lavish ballet and opera productions and large-scale classical concerts staged in the grandest of settings. Tickets start at around €30. See also page 62.

Contemporary and jazz

Around Midnight Jazz Club, via Bonito 32A, T081-742 3278. Tue-Sun 2200 till late. Vomero's historic jazz club serves food and hosts mainstream jazz and blues gigs 6 nights a week.

Doria 83, via G Doria 83, T081-556 6960, www.myspace.com/doria_83. Alternative live acts, from the mellow indie of Lara Martelli to electro 'parteno-pop' outfit Plastic Penguin, play at this popular venue in Vomero.

Officina 99, via Gianturco 101, T081-734 9091, www.officina99.org. Metro: Gianturco. Ska, rock,dub, hip hop, folk and industrial sounds can be heard at this social centre that produced the 1990s rap group 99 Posse.

Theatre and dance

Naples has grand theatres and fiercely independent ensembles, and every night there is something different to see from mainstream TV spin-offs to edgy and experimental works. The productions are mainly in Italian and often in dialect. Contemporary dance productions appear occasionally on many of the city's theatre programmes while the most lavish ballet productions are staged at the **Teatro San Carlo** (see Music, page 61). **Napoli Danza** (www.napolidanza.com) promotes contemporary dance and runs an annual festival featuring dance videos.

Bellini, via Conte di Ruvo 14, T081-549 1266, www.teatrobellini.it. Metro: Dante. Epic musicals, classic dramas and occasional concerts are staged at this grand theatre in the Centro Antico.

Elicantropo, Vico Gerolimini 3, T081-296640, www.teatroelicantropo.com. Metro: Cavour. Experimental theatre and contemporary dance get a run-out at this tiny space near the Duomo.

Mercandante, piazza Municipio 1, T081-551 3396, www.teatrostabilenapoli.it. Innovative writers including the acclaimed musicologist Roberto de Simone and Roberto Saviano, creator of the internationally acclaimed book-turned-play-turned-film *Gommora*,

are amongst the talent to have recently staged productions at this famous theatre opened in 1779.

Nuovo Teatro Nuovo, via Montecalvario 16, T081-497 6267, www.teatronuovonapoli.it. Plays by celebrated playwrights such as Shakespeare, Goldoni, Ionesco and Pinter fill the programme of this innovative theatre.

Sancarluccio, via san Pasquale 49, Chiaia, T081-405000, www.teatrosancarluccio. com. Opened in 1972, Teatro Sancarluccio mounts avant-garde productions from Italy and elsewhere – it provided the debut performance of comic actor Massimo Troisi in *La Smorfia*.

Sannazaro, via Chiaia 157, T081-411723, www.teatrosannazaro.it. Although comic productions have always been the mainstay at Sannazaro, one-off events including Burlesque cabaret and unplugged concerts are staged at this elegant theatre.

○ Shopping

Being a port city with 2500 years of history, crafts and trading behind it, you can get just about anything in Naples. In the Centro Antico, particularly on Spaccanapoli and via dei Tribunali, there are lots of interesting independent outlets, *bancarelle* (stalls) and *rigattieri* (bric-a-brac sellers) peddling everything from pasta to fading gouaches, *corni collaudati* (charmed horns for the superstitious) and marble busts. Via San Gregorio Armeno is the world-famous home of skilled artisans who make *presepi* (nativity scenes) and figurines. Port'Alba, off piazza Dante, is renowned for its second-hand and specialist bookshops and stalls. Via Santa Maria di Costantinopoli and via Domenico Morelli are famed for their *antiquariati* (antique dealers), who stock anything from Capodimonte porcelain and Posillipo School paintings to period furniture and historic prints. The main shopping drag is via Toledo, part of which is pedestrianized these days – it's good for window shopping while you do the evening *passeggiata*.

A good introduction to Neapolitan market life can be found in the nearby Quartieri Spagnoli, around via Pignasecca and Montesanto, where you'll find food, clothing and household goods – perfect for the budding barista or for anyone after Italian spoons and kitchenware. For a more full-on experience head to Mercato di Porta Nolana and piazza Mercato which have just about everything, legal and otherwise. For food, the market at Porta Capuana (aka Mercato dei Vergini) is entertaining, edgy and teeming with tasty produce. The Mercato dei Fiori (flower market) is at Maschio Angioino while the Fiera Antiquaria is an antiques market held once or twice a month in and around the Villa Comunale.

Chiaia (via Chiaia, piazza dei Martiri, via della Cavalarizza and via dei Mille) is the best place to go if you are after swanky fashion, designer labels and interiors shops. The best clothing sales are held here in Jan. On a larger scale, out of town towards Nola is a shopping centre full of designer labels and world famous brands – the rotund Renzo Piano-designed Vulcano Buono resembles Vesuvius, has ample parking and is also reached via a free shuttle bus run by City Sightseeing Napoli (see page 65) from piazza Vittoria and piazza Fanzago. Shop hours are generally 1000-1300 and 1600-1930, closing Sun.

Art and antiques
Not surprisingly, given its rich history and artistic heritage, there are lots of *antiquariati* (antique dealers) in Naples, with clusters of antique shops along via Domenico Morelli in Chiaia and all over the Centro Antico, especially on via Santa Maria di Costantinopoli.
Antiquariato Florida, via Domenico Morelli 13, Chiaia, T081-764 3440. Closed Sun. It's pricey but well worth a look around to see the neoclassical paintings and interesting portraits, as well as handsome period furniture and the occasional Parisian chandelier.

Ieffam, via Alabardieri 28, T081-341 9537. Closed Sun. A dealer in 20th-century antiques with design classics and quirky artworks, including Flos lamps, Eames chairs and one-off sculptures.
Il Rigattiere, via dei Tribunali 281 and 87, T081-299155. Closed Sun. Brigida d'Amato, the spiky and spirited owner of these bric-a-brac shops, is passionate about her city and is happy to tell you about her cornucopia of dusty treasures, which often appear as props in films and on stage.
Quagliozza Salvatore, via S Biagio dei Librai 11, T081-551 7100. Mon-Sat 1000-1330, 1630-1930. Antiques and ephemera addicts love the eclectic items often displayed on church steps along Spaccanapoli and this *rigattiere* (second-hand dealer cum rag-and-bone man) is crammed with intriguing oddities from the recent and distant past.

Books
Being the home to an illustrious and influential university, Naples has lots of interesting bookshops. Just off piazza Dante, via Port'Alba is famed for its second-hand and specialist outlets and stalls.
Feltrinelli, via Santa Caterina a Chiaia 23 (piazza dei Martiri), T081-240 5411, www.lafeltrinelli.it. Daily. The nationwide chain's flagship Naples shop has it all covered including an English-language section and stacks of CDs, DVDs magazines and stationery. There's even a café, which hosts regular cultural events including appearances by musicians such as Almamegretta and Daniele Sepe.
Intra Moenia, piazza Bellini and via Benedetto Croce 38, T081-290 988. Daily. The arty café-shop (see page 58) and its right-on sister shop **Edizioni Intra Moenia** stock lots of Napoli-themed black-and-white postcards, excellent books of photojournalism as well as unusual prints and books, many with an historical, political or cultural slant.
Libreria Neapolis, via San Gregorio Armeno 4, T081-551 4337. Closed Sun. All things to do

with Naples and its culture, and the south of Italy, fill the pages of the publications in this interesting little bookshop in the midst of via San Gregorio Armeno's nativity scene frenzy. **Treves**, via Toledo 249-250, T081-415211. Closed Sun. Along via Toledo, this venerable *libreria* (opened in 1861) has a vast selection of books including Neapolitan philosophical tomes and travel guides, some in English.

Chocolates

Gay Odin, via Toledo 427, T081-551 3491, www.gayodin.it. **Gay Odin**'s chocolates are as flamboyant as its famous name, which first hit the street in the 1920s: *Vesuvio* is laced with rum and *la foresta* is the poshest, crumbliest and flakiest chocolate log ever tasted. There are 8 other outlets in Naples, including one at via Benedetto Croce 61.

Clothing

If you're after the designer labels like Armani, Prada and Bulgari then head to the Chiaia area and these streets: via Chiaia, via della Cavalerrizza, via Poerio, via Filangeri and via dei Mille. Before entering some designer-label shops in and around piazza dei Martiri you may be vetted before they buzz you in.

Department stores

Coin, via Scarlatti 86/100, T081-578 0111, www.coin.it. Daily. Italy's ubiquitous department store is always good for a browse. There are usually bargain accessories to be found, while the excellent kitchen department stocks plenty of stylish gadgets and cutlery.

Doll repairs

Ospedale delle Bambole, via San Biagio dei Librai 81, T081-563 4744, www.ospedale dellebambole.it. Closed Sat. You might not be in possession of a doll requiring emergency treatment, but don't let that put you off a visit to the Dolls Hospital, a magical shop crammed with old dolls and doll parts.

Food and drink

Augustus, via Toledo 147, T081-551 3540. Closed Sun. As well as wonderful pastries, Augustus has lots of ready prepared snacks and meals including *pizze*, *arancini*, *parmigiane di melanzane* and *pasta al forno*.

Charcuterie Esposito, via Benedetto Croce 43, T081-551 6981. Daily. Should you need some Neapolitan delicacies like mozzarella or even unusual pasta shapes to take home, this place on Spaccanapoli is full of gastronomic goodies.

Enoteca 2000, via Tribunali 33, T081-211 0079, www.professionevino.it. Metro: Dante. This is a good spot in the Centro Antico to pick up wines and spirits at very reasonable prices.

Gastronomia LUISE, piazza dei Martiri 68, Chiaia, T081-551 6944. Mon-Sat 0830-1400, 1630-2000. Metro: Amedeo. This posh deli is packed with local specialities and has a tiny bar manned by one barista.

Mercadante, corso Vittorio Emanuele, 643/644, T081-680 964. Closed Sun. With over 2000 wine labels from all over the world and especially strong on southern Italian and Tuscan wines, **Mercadante** have now added a wine bar to their wine shop, so you can sit down, quaff and snack on quality cheeses, *salume* and chocolate while you're selecting your *etichette* (wine labels).

Homeware

Bonetti, piazzetta Carolina 16/17, T081-764 5433. Closed Sun. Rows of shiny *caffetiere* in the shop window beckon you into this place near piazza Plebiscito. Pick up and feel the quality of their Italian kitchen products including weighty pans, elegant glassware and stylish espresso cups.

Spina, via Pignasecca 62, T081-552 4818. Daily. If you fancy recreating your very own Italian bar at home or need new kit for the kitchen, this shop in the Quartieri Spagnoli, established in 1870, is a must-visit.

Markets

Naples has some fantastic markets including the ever-entertaining **Mercato di Porta Nolana** (see page 45) which has just about everything legal and otherwise. For food, the markets at Porta Capuana (sometimes called **Mercato dei Vergini**) and via Pignasecca (off via Toledo) are superb. Under the towers of the Castel Nuovo there is the daily **Mercato dei Fiori** (flower market) – get there at the crack of dawn for the freshest petals. The **Fiera Antiquaria** (www.fieraantiquaria poletana.it), the antiques market, is held in and around the Villa Comunale from 0800 to 1400, generally on the 3rd and 4th Sun of each month and preceding Sat – check the website for the latest details.

Multimedia and music

Fnac, via Luca Giordano 59, T081-220 1000. Daily. Time wasters will enjoy browsing through the multimedia gadgets, cameras, music and DVDs here. You could find a Morricone soundtrack, Fellini flick or Mina album to enhance your life.

Outdoor equipment

Arbiter, via Toledo 268, T081-416463. Mon-Sat 0930-2000. Metro: Dante. According to vulcanologist guide Roberto Addeo and walking expert Giovanni Visetti, **Arbiter** is the best shop for outdoor equipment in Campania.

Souvenirs

Via San Gregorio Armeno is the world-famous home of skilled artisans who make *presepi* (nativity scenes) and figurines. For those wanting to pimp their crib there are dizzying lines of miniature shepherds, animals and fake moss-and-bark trees. These shops also do a roaring trade in caricature figures of the famous. On Spaccanapoli the curious trappings of Neapolitan superstition are sold everywhere: horns of many sizes and charts to help you live by *la smorfia* – an amusing yet, to many, deadly serious system of using images seen in dreams to win the *lotto*. Via Costantinopoli used to be full of craftsmen and now has only a few overpriced antique shops. **Giuseppe Ferrigno**, via San Gregorio Armeno 8, T081-552 3148. Closed Sun. Only traditional materials – including terracotta, wood and silk – go into the making of these hand-crafted *presepi* figurines. After the death of world-renowned *maestro del pastore* Giuseppe Ferrigno in 2008 at the age of 73, his son Marco continues the family tradition begun in 1836.

Wellbeing

Farmaceutica di Santa Maria Novella, via Manzoni 153, T081-769 2082. Closed Sun. This branch of the 800-year-old Florentine pharmacy is famed for its herby perfumes and almond hand cream.

⚙ What to do

Cookery courses

CucinAmica, via Solimena 80, T081-589 3973, www.cucinamica.it. Metro: Vanvitelli. Carmela Capote, biologist by profession and gluten-free specialist, runs courses teaching both the basics of Neapolitan cuisine and Italian haute cuisine from her Vomero villa. **La Cucina di Posillipo Dream**, via Manzoni, 214/O, T081-575 6000, www.posillipo dream.it. Funicolare di Mergellina: Manzoni. Enterprising cook Giovanna Raffone runs personalized cookery courses from her B&B kitchen in Posillipo, where you can learn how to make *frittura di mare* (fried seafood medley) and survey stunning views over the Campi Flegrei.

Cultural

City Sightseeing Napoli, T081-551 7279, www.napoli.city-sightseeing.it. €22 adults, 6-15s €11, family ticket for 2 adults and 3 children €66 valid for all city routes. 3 open-top city bus tours departing from piazza Municipio allow you to hop on and off at various sights. Headphone commentary is available in 8 languages. Line A visits the principal artistic attractions

(11 stops including piazza del Gesù and the Museo di Capodimonte) and lasts 75 mins. Line B tours 12 panoramic spots in 75 mins including Posillipo and the Castel dell'Ovo. Line C includes San Martino and the Vomero sights, the streets of the Centro Antico, and Chiaia's piazza dei Martiri.

Gaiola, Discesa Gaiola 27-27, T081-240 3235, www.gaiola.org. Bus 140. Tours from €5, snorkelling from €15, diving from €40. The Parco Sommerso di Gaiola is a protected stretch of Posillipo coastline studied by marine biologists. The friendly Gaiola study group runs fascinating tours of the area and its ruined Roman structures – including the Villa Pausilypon – by land and sea. Other excursions are snorkelling, diving and birdwatching in and around the Pausilypon archaeological site, Marechiaro, the island of Nisida, the Grotta di Seiano and the Baia di Trentaremi.

Itinera, corso Vittorio Emanuele 663, T081-664545/T339-755 1747, www.itinera napoli.com. Metro: CV Emanuele. Friendly, English-speaking Francesca Del Vecchio organizes tours around the city and beyond, including trips around the Campi Flegrei sights (see page 67).

Museo Aperto Napoli (MAN), via Pietro Coletta 89, T081-563 6062, www.museoapertonapoli.it. Bus: R2, C57. **MAN** hires out audio guides to 81 Neapolitan monuments and has created 4 signposted routes around the city's sights. Drop in for information and to use their luggage-deposit service.

Cycling
Napoli Bike, Riviera di Chiaia 201, Chiaia, T081-411934, www.napolibike.com. Metro: Amedeo. Next to Villa Pignatelli Luciano **Caputo** rents out mountain bikes for €10 half-day, €15 per day. On weekdays cycling in Naples is a pretty scary proposition unless you can get your bike out of town by car. A good place to cycle is the Parco Virgiliano

in Posillipo. Otherwise, a couple of hours in the Villa Comunale gardens opposite the shop and then along the *lungomare*, via Posillipo, to Marechiaro is an option.

Football
Having won 2 *scudetti* in the late-1980s with Diego Maradona, SSC Napoli endured financial problems and relegation before remerging as Scudetto contenders in recent years. The 60,000-capacity San Paolo stadium had a roof added for the 1990 World Cup Finals, for which it staged the infamous semi-final between Italy and Argentina, in which Maradona called on Napoli fans to support his nation. Tickets to see SSC Napoli play are available from the stadium in Fuorigrotta and in agencies around town.

Kayaking
Kayak Napoli, T331 9874271, www.kayak napoli.com. Bus 140. Various kayaking trips around the coast of Posillipo exploring the swanky villas, archaeology and wildlife – including a moonlit excursion.

Swimming
The sea on the *lungomare* adjacent to the Villa Comunale gardens has been cleaned up of late although it hardly looks enticing. There are fabulous swimming spots outside the city though – mainly on the Amalfi Coast and the Islands. 2 public baths with irregular opening hours provide the safest city swimming: **Piscina Collana** (via Rossini 8, Vomero, T081-560 0907) and **Piscina Scandone** (via Giochi del Mediterraneo, Fuorigrotta, T081-570 2636).

Tennis
Tennis Club Napoli, viale Dohrn, Villa Comunale, Chiaia, T081-761 4656, www.tennisclubnapoli.it. The poshest club in town hosts prestigious tournaments and hires out its clay courts.

Campi Flegrei

A few miles west of Naples, just over the Posillipo hill, are the Campi Flegrei – the Phlegrean (Fiery) Fields. Its Arcadian landscapes may be a tad scruffy these days and don't offer quite the same epic drama as described by Virgil in the *Aeneid*. However, exploring this bubbling volcanic landscape and its colourful Graeco-Roman past, you get the feeling that the Roman poets and chroniclers like Petronius, author of the *Satyricon*, had the juiciest material to inspire their mythical tales and saucy prose. Campi Flegrei's palaces of pleasure witnessed dastardly deeds including the pact that sealed Julius Caesar's fate on the Ides of March.

Dozens of craters lie within the Campi Flegrei caldera system, including steamy Solfatara and eerily beautiful Averno, which the ancients believed to be the entrance to Hades: the Hell that inspired Dante's *Divine Comedy*. Roman Puteoli (modern-day Pozzuoli) was the empire's most important port and has an amphitheatre; Baia has Roman spas above and below the waves; and amid the atmospheric ruins at Cuma there are fantastical stories of an immortal prophetess, the Cumean Sybil.

Through ancient tunnels you emerge at SSC Napoli Stadio San Paolo and traffic-ridden Fuorigrotta, with its curiously Neapolitan theme parks and the monumental Fascist-era Mostra d'Oltremare, venue of concerts and trade fairs. Ancient and modern mix again at Bagnoli, where the incredible Serino aqueduct passes rusty chimneys and new leisure developments.

Arriving in the Campi Flegrei → For listings, see pages 73-75.

Getting there and around
The Campi Flegrei are 20 minutes by rail or 30 minutes by road from Naples. The bus/ train station is at piazza Vincenzo Oriani, Pozzuoli, **SEPSA** ① *T0800-001616, www.sepsa.it.* ▶▶ *See Transport, page 75.*

By road Two tunnels emerge at Fuorigrotta. The more scenic Discesa Coroglio descends from Capo Posillipo to Bagnoli, while the inland A56 Tangenziale di Napoli (Naples circular) heads towards Cuma.

By bus SEPSA bus route 152 from piazza Garibaldi in Naples is cheap but tortuous. The open-topped **Archeobus**, also run by SEPSA, is a circular 90-minute route that starts and ends at piazza della Repubblica in Pozzuoli, visiting the main archaeological sites (with Artecard). Buses depart on the hour Friday to Sunday and public holidays 0900-1900, but check in advance as they are notoriously unreliable. **City Sightseeing Napoli** runs a similar service, *Retour Campi Felgrei,* starting at piazza Municipio, Naples (see page 65).

By metro/train The Metropolitana Linea 2 is handy for Solfatara, Bagnoli and Agnano. The Ferrovia Cumana and Circumflegrea railway lines run from Montesanto station in Naples and are excellent for travelling to and from Pozzuoli and Baia but it's quite a hike (a bus is available) to the ruins from the station at Cuma.

Tourist information
Contact the main **Campi Flegrei tourist office** ① *via Matteotti 1, Pozzuoli, T081-526 6639, www.icampiflegrei.it, daily 0900-1530; also at via Risorgimento 29, Baia, T081-868 7541.*

Fuorigrotta and Bagnoli → For listings, see pages 73-75.

First impressions are not great. Traffic, pollution and heavy industry have taken their toll on an area once famed for its lavish roman spa resorts and villas. Fuorigrotta ('beyond the grotto') is accessed via a tunnel that burrows through the hill of Posillipo. For many years politicians have talked up plans to resurrect Bagnoli from industrial ruin. Once a beauty and bathing spot, it was blighted by Second World War bombing and, more recently, the enormous Eternit/Italsider steel and chemical works, the largest in southern Italy. Parts of the rusty *cantieri* have been transformed into an aquarium, sports complex, media park and environmental study centre. Pontile Nord, a spectacular pier, now juts 900 into the sea. Corruption, scandal, pollution and, most notably, a fire that flattened the Città della Scienza in 2013 have stalled regeneration. The islet crater of Nisida, where Lucullus and Brutus had villas, is now the home of a juvenile prison and NATO. Within two nearby dead volcanoes, Agnano and Astroni, are a racecourse and a WWF nature reserve.

Mostra d'Oltremare
① *Viale Kennedy 54, T081-725 8022, www.mostradoltremare.it. Metro: Campi Flegrei.*
Built by the Fascist government in 1940 and redeveloped in the 1990s, the Oltremare Exhibition Centre stages trade shows and festivals including **Pizzafest** (see page 18). There are lots of modern structures in typically bombastic and fantastical Fascist style,

---

What to see in the Campi Flegrei

One day
Head straight to **Pozzuoli** to see the **Anfiteatro Flavio** and **Solfatara**, followed by **Baia**'s archaeological sites and **Cuma**'s ruins.

A weekend or more
Linger for longer at **Pozzuoli** and **Baia**, taking in the **Rione Terra** and **Parco Archeologico di Baia** by boat, then visit **Piscina Mirabilis** at Miseno followed by lunch at one of Bacoli's beachside restaurants. **Cuma** and add excursions to the **Astroni** reserve and Bagnoli's changing post-industrial landscape. **Fuorigrotta**'s theme parks, Fascist-era **Mostra d'Oltremare** and an **SSC Napoli** fixture at **Stadio San Paolo** will excite some. Move on to **Procida** and **Ischia** from the port at **Pozzuoli**.

including a couple of theatres, pavilions – including the Padiglione America Latina, home to occasional art exhibitions – as well as the monumental Fontana dell'Esedra, whose colossal fountain columns are often lit up in lots of juicy colours. The 6000-seater Arena Flegrea hosts concerts during the annual **Neapolis Festival** (see page 18).

Edenlandia
① *Via JF Kennedy 76, T081-239 1348, www.edenlandia.it. Mon-Fri 1500-2000, Sat-Sun and holidays 1030-1200, €3, children under 110 cm free, €2 per ride or €12 for a bracelet that allows unlimited rides. Ferrovia Cumana: Edenlandia-Zoo.*
In contrast to the region's cultural and historical sights, Edenlandia provides an entertaining insight into Neapolitan family life. Dodgems, carousels, a flight simulator, video arcades, tenpin bowling, water flumes and family-friendly restaurants keep the hordes happy.

Zoo di Napoli
① *Via JF Kennedy 76, T081-610 7123, www.lozoodinapoli.it. Apr-Oct 0930-1800, Nov-Mar 0930-1700, €6, children under 80 cm free. Ferrovia Cumana: Edenlandia-Zoo.*
Naples' zoo nearly joined the extinct list many times but was saved again by investors in 2013. You can see exotic animals including Indian elephants, lions, tigers, leopards, deer, llamas, buffalo and bears as well as many bird species including pelicans and pink flamingos. There's also a *fattoria* (farm) where you can pet ponies, cuddle rabbits and feed goats.

Riserva Cratere degli Astroni
① *Via Agnano agli Astroni, Pianura, T081-588 3720. Daily 1000-1600. Ferrovia Circumflegrea to Pianura, then bus C14; if driving, take the Agnano exit off the A56 Tangenziale, then it's 1 km to Pianura.*
Lush woods interspersed with lakes, streams and a network of paths make up the 300-ha WWF Astroni Nature Reserve. You wouldn't know it but the former Bourbon royal hunting grounds and its three hills – Imperatrice, Pagliaroni and Rotondella – sit within a long-dead volcano that last erupted 4000 years ago. You can hire bikes and explore the landscape which is teeming with rare plants, handsome trees such as red oak, lots of birdlife ranging from blackcaps to geese and heron, as well as mammals including wolves, dormice and rodents. One of the Astroni's loudest residents is the greater spotted woodpecker, which is the symbol of the park.

Pozzuoli, Baia, Bacoli and Cuma → *For listings, see pages 73-75.*

The busy port town of Pozzuoli (Roman Puteoli) is beset by volcanic ups and downs, and awash with ancient ruins including the Anfiteatro Flavio. The curving bay has ancient, grimy charm. After years of neglect following an earthquake in 1980, the childhood home of Sophia Loren has recently attracted investment and is now on the up, economically. Further west are Baia and Bacoli, where there's the Museo Archeologico dei Campi Flegrei and the remnants of once-lavish Roman villas, gardens and thermal baths that can be seen under the sea. There are dead volcanic craters turned into eerie lakes (Averno, Lucrino, Fusaro and Miseno), incredible feats of Roman engineering (Piscina Mirabilis, Cento Camerelle and Arco Felice) and – perhaps topping them all for atmosphere – the picturesque Graeco-Roman ruins at Scavi di Cuma. Some bonkers mythology and the juiciest history imaginable, which spawned *Satyricon* and satire, add to the bubbling pot of wonders here. For tourist information, consult the **Pozzuoli AACST office** ① *Largo Matteotti 1, T081 5261481, www.infocampiflegrei.it.* ▸▸ *See Transport, page 75.*

Serapeo (Tempio di Serapide)
① *Via Serapide, Pozzuoli, T081-526 6007. Open daily but can be viewed from the street. Metro/Ferrovia Cumana: Pozzuoli.*
Not far from the Cumana station lie the sunken remains of a Roman *macellum* (market), complete with the imprints of 36 shops, dating back to the first and second centuries AD. The site is usually referred to as the Temple of Serapis, named after the discovery of a statue of the Egyptian deity much venerated under Emperor Vespasian. The architectural fragments, including marble columns, are sometimes submerged after a deluge. Tiny holes created by marine molluscs tell us that the site once lay under the sea. This is prime evidence of the bradyseism – the gradual subsiding and lifting of the earth's surface – that has affected the Campi Flegrei over the centuries.

Towards the port area is archaeological site **Rione Terra** (Largo Sedile di Porto) – closed to the public at the time of writing. Excavations in the 1990s uncovered *decumanus* (the main east–west high street), underground Roman streets filled with shops and fountains on this tufa outcrop, currently 33 m above the sea. Incredible artefacts found here can be seen at the Museo Archeologico dei Campi Flegrei at Baia.

Anfiteatro Flavio
① *Via Terracciano 75, Pozzuoli, T081-526 6007. Wed-Mon 0900 to 1 hr before sunset, €4, 18-24s €2, under 18s/over 65s free. Metro/Ferrovia Cumana to Pozzuoli, then a 10-min walk up hill or bus 152 or P9.*
Built between AD 67 and 79 during Vespasian's reign, the Flavian amphitheatre's impressive 40,000-capacity structure looms out of busy roads and a scruffy modern backdrop. It measures 147 m by 117 m, making it the third largest Roman amphitheatre. A strange scene unfolds while exploring the overgrown grounds, which are strewn with toppled columns and ancient fragments – including the odd oversized marble foot. An open corridor offers glimpses of the gladiatorial arena, and a rectangular ditch at its heart once housed wild beasts which were hoisted into the melee. In late antiquity the nearby Solfatara volcano spewed ash and other volcanic debris into the amphitheatre, preserving the underground chambers' architectural features. It has staged many a drama: San Gennaro, patron saint of Naples, was imprisoned here in AD 305 alongside other Christian martyrs; notorious exhibitionist Nero lanced a bull here; and some scholars believe that the arena used to be flooded for mock sea battles.

Fiery Fields legends

- The soothsayer Sibyl cast spells at her Cumaean bolthole.
- Caligula built a 5-km bridge of boats from Baiae to Puteoli, and rode across it on horseback.
- Cleopatra, who according to some was no oil painting, bathed at Baiae.
- Hellish Lake Avernus was the entrance to Hades, the mythical underworld.
- Claudius was poisoned with a dodgy mushroom.

Solfatara

ⓘ *Via Solfatara 161, Pozzuoli, T081-526 2341, www.solfatara.it. Daily 0830 to 1 hr before sunset, €7, Artecarde €5.60, 4-12s €4.50, under 4s free. Metro/Ferrovia Cumana to Pozzuoli, then bus P9 or an 800-m walk up hill. Bus 152.*

Northwest of Pozzuoli, this 4000-year-old sulphurous volcanic crater splutters, hisses and froths sulphurous geysers and mud. Recent seismic studies have found increased activity in the Campi Flegrei area but the good news is that Solfatara, the most currently active of the volcanoes of the Phlegrean Fields, hasn't erupted since the 12th century and its energy is on the wane. Bocca Grande (Big Mouth) jettisons water vapour at 70°C and the hollow-sounding ground is stained with luridly red arsenic and yellow sulphur deposits. Hydrogen sulphide vapours with the whiff of rotten eggs did not deter ancient spa-goers and Grand Tourists from bathing in and drinking from the mineral-rich springs and fumaroles. The otherworldly, scalding landscape (don't wear rubber soles or flip-flops!) combined with hissing and gurgling noises, and foul smells make it all very disorientating but thrilling. A well purportedly produces medicinal water, and you can peer into ancient *sudutoria* (steam grottoes) aptly named Purgatory and Hell.

Parco Archeologico di Baia

ⓘ *Via delle Terme Romane, Baia, T081-868 7592. Tue-Sun 0900 to 1 hr before sunset, €4 valid for 2 days including entrance to Museo Archeologico di Baia, Anfiteatro Flavio, the Serapeo and Scavi di Cuma. Ferrovia Cumana to Baia then take the stairs on piazza de Gasperi to the entrance.*

The most fashionable and decadent of all the Roman resorts, Baia can be explored on the slopes behind Baia station. Bulbous domed baths of Diana, Venus, Sosandra and Mercury, and the ruins of a first century BC imperial Roman palace built by Ottaviano make up part of this sprawling site, part of which is under the sea (see **Baia Sommersa**, page 74). Learned Holy Roman Emperor Frederick II reopened many of the establishments in the 1400s as did the Spanish viceroys in the 18th century. Alas, the land has since subsided and most of the hot water emerges elsewhere. For eerie and muddy echoes of the ancient past dust off your best Latin dialect and pour water over yourself below the world's oldest large-scale dome within the Tempio di Mercurio, part of the old spa complex. More strange acoustics can be experienced underneath the arches of the Cryptoporticus, a large cistern that fed the baths.

Museo Archeologico dei Campi Flegrei

ⓘ *Via Castello 45, Baia, T081-523 3797.Tue-Sun 0900 to 1 hr before sunset, €4, 18-25s €2, under 18s/over 65s free. Ferrovia Cumana to Baia, then a 15-min walk or local bus up the hill.*

The 15th-century Aragonese castle housing the Campi Flegrei Archaeological Museum commands fabulous views over the Baia promontory and archaeological area. Highlights of the collection include the Ninfeo di Punta Epitaffio, a recreated Nympheum with statues found in the sea; the Sacello degli Augustali (a shrine dedicated to the emperor's cult, found at Misenum); and the Sala dei Gessi with its plaster-casts of celebrated Greek statues used as models by a sculptor's studio during the first to second centuries AD. In between there are lots of salvaged mosaic floors, ceramics, jewellery and coins.

Piscina Mirabilis
ⓘ *Via A Greco 10, Bacoli, T081-523 3199. Generally open Mon-Fri 0900 to dusk. Ferrovia Cumana to Baia, then bus.*
You wouldn't believe it from the messy Bacoli neighbourhood and its exterior but within this hump of tufa and weeds is a subterranean structure with cathedral-like wonders. The largest known Roman freshwater reservoir impresses with its scale, acoustics, atmosphere and bare facts: it's 15 m high, 72 m long and 25 m wide. Only mossy dribbles penetrate its vaulted ceilings and a few puddles gather amid its 48 cruciform pillars, yet it once contained around 12,000 cu m of water to feed the area's villas, spas and the Imperial fleet at Portus Julius. The water came from the Apennines near Avellino, some 160 km away, travelling along the Aqua Augusta (Serino Aqueduct) and serving Pompeii, Pozzuoli and Naples along the way.

Cento Camerelle
ⓘ *Via Cento Camerelle 165, Bacoli, T081-523 3199. Generally 0900 to 1 hr before sunset. Ferrovia Cumana to Baia, then bus.*
The remains of a once lavish two-storey Roman villa belonging to Ortensio Ortalo, dating from the Republican era and the first century AD, contains atmospheric vaulted passageways and cisterns hewn out of the tufa rock.

Bacoli and Capo Miseno
Bacoli has a curving bay and beach that attracts families and weekend hedonists who enjoy the smart bars and clubs along here. At the head of the promontory is Capo Miseno (Roman Misenum), with its 78-m-high cliffs and a 19th-century lighthouse overlooking Lake Miseno. Misenum became the home of the Roman fleet and its admirals, including Pliny the Elder, when the original Portus Julius at Lake Lucrino, Baia silted up. The Miliscola beach here is popular with Neapolitans.

Scavi di Cuma
ⓘ *Via Licola, Cuma, T081-854 3060. Daily 0900 to 1 hr before sunset, €4, 18-25s €2, under 18s/over 65s free. Ferrovia Cumana to Baia, then bus; or Circumflegrea to Fusaro, then bus.*
The ancient Greeks settled here in 730 BC, making Cumae the first colony of Magna Graecia. Its picturesque ruins spark the imagination with its ancient myths. A couple of hours are enough to explore the parkland, with its crumbling remains and a creepy cavern. Fabulous views of the coastline and architectural fragments belonging to an acropolis (two large temples dedicated to Apollo and Jupiter that were transformed into churches in the fifth and sixth centuries) can be seen atop a hill – it's a breathtaking spot for a picnic. These basilicas were toppled by 10th-century Saracen raiders. Most of what you see dates from Roman and early Christian times.

The biggest draw is the 130-m-long trapezoidal tunnel, the Antro della Sibilla (Cave of the Sibyl). Hewn out of tufa rock, the gallery has an otherworldly ambience that Virgil described in the *Aeneid*, although in truth the structure probably had a funerary or military use. It contains a three-room chamber from where, according to legend, the Cumaean Sibyl helped Aeneas descend into the underworld.

Campi Flegrei listings

For hotel and restaurant price codes and other relevant information, see pages 14-17.

Where to stay

The Campi Flegrei is not renowned for its excellent hotels but things are changing, slowly. Remember, you can get here from nearby Naples quite easily so the area can be visited on day trips and may include a foray to the nearby islands of Procida and Ischia.

Pozzuoli, Baia, Bacoli and Cuma *p70*

€€ Cala Moresca, via Faro 44, Bacoli, T081-523 5595, www.calamoresca.it. Located on a hill above Miseno, this hotel is set amid gardens with a large pool, tennis court and a kids' playground. There's also a gym and access to a private beach. Many of the 27 functional rooms and 9 mini-apartments have balconies with views towards Procida and Ischia.

€€ Villa Giulia, via Cuma Licola 178, Pozzuoli, T081-854 0163, www.villagiulia. info. If you have the use of a vehicle this is a great base. The neighbourhood may not be beautiful but within the high walls of this historic townhouse garden there are citrus trees, a pool and a Neapolitan summer kitchen, where you can make a proper pizza. There are doubles and 5 apartments of various sizes. Breakfasts not the best.

€ Batis, via Lucullo 101, Baia, T081-868 8763, www.batis.it. There's a youthful vibe at Batis and well-priced, attractive rooms – some have mezzanine bedroom areas. It makes a good, sociable base from which to explore Baia's archaeological sites as the spa ruins are nearby and there's a self-styled 'art lounge' bar that hosts latino dance nights and live music.

€ Hotel Relais Villa Oteri, via Lungolago, 174, Bacoli, T081-523 4985, www.villaoteri.it. Villa Oteri provides elegance and a great location at a very affordable price. Close to Bacoli's beach and bars, it has 9 well-turned-out rooms and a restaurant, and offers discounted entry to the **Stufe di Nerone** spa up the road. Discounts are also available for the use of a nearby pool and beach facilities.

Self-catering

Averno Damiani Camping, Hotel & Apartments, via Montenuovo Licola Patria 85, Pozzuoli, T081-804 2666, www.averno.it. It's not a luxury Imperial complex but you get good-value accommodation and lots of activities and facilities here, including a spa, gym, *campo di calcetto* (5-a-side football pitch), swimming pools, go-karting, restaurant and a disco. There are pitches for tents and caravans, as well as hotel rooms (€85-105) and apartments with kitchenettes (€100-150).

Il Casolare, via Pietro Fabris 12/14, Bacoli, T081-523 5193, www.sibilla.net/ilcasolare. Agriturismo goes boho in this rustic 19th-century *masseria* (grand farmhouse). Colourful artworks and knick-knacks give the place an earthy and eccentric feel. 4 functional rooms (€55-65) provide good value, especially for families. Tobia Costagliola and his friendly troupe create tasty dishes using their homegrown produce.

Restaurants

Pozzuoli, Baia, Bacoli and Cuma *p70*

€€€ Il Tempio, via Serapide 13, Pozzuoli, T081-526 6519. Closed Mon. Next to the Temple of Serapis, this pricey place is famed for its freshly caught *pescato del giorno* (catch of the day) creations.

€€ La Villetta, via Lungolago 58, Bacoli, T081-523 2662. A ristorante-pizzeria that regularly features in Italian restaurant guides for its well-prepared Neapolitan fare: featuring pizza, seafood, grilled vegetables and meat dishes. It overlooks Lake Miseno, has a leafy courtyard and is close to Bacoli's bars and nightspots.

€€ Lucullo, via Montegrillo 8, Baia di Bacoli, T081-868 7606. Closed Mon. Francesca di Vecchio, Naples resident and local tour guide, reckons **Lucullo** is "in one of the most beautiful spots – on a pier by the sea at Bacoli". Indeed the varnished wood-filled interior is reminiscent of a yacht. After eating their sublime seafood, there are often some poptastico piano bar acts to enjoy.

Cafés and bars
Buono, corso Umberto I 43, Pozzuoli, T081-526 0472. Closed Mon. Good for a savoury or sweet morning *merenda* (snack) at the bar or on the terrace overlooking Pozzuoli's *lungomare*. As well as *pizzette* (mini pizzas) and pastries like *sfogliatelle*, they do delicious ice cream.

Enoteca Partenopea, viale Augusto 2, Fuorigrotta, T081-593 7982. Closed Sun. Southern Italian specialities, including wines from Irpinia, swordfish purée, mozzarella and Campanian *salame* fill this wine bar-deli near the Stadio San Paolo.

Monkey Café, via Lucollo 2, Bacoli, T081-868 7082. Popular with the Bacoli *ragazzi*, they serve all sorts of *spuntini* snacks including panini, brioche and roast meats.

🎭 Entertainment

Pozzuoli, Baia, Bacoli and Cuma *p70*
Music
Arena Flegrea, viale Kennedy 54, Fuorigrotta, T081-725 8000. The 6000-seater venue stages concerts throughout the year including the **Neapolis Festival** (www.neapolis.it) each Jul.

Nightlife
Arenile, via Coroglio 10, Bagnoli, T081-019 9156, www.arenilereload.com. A chic beach club overlooking the *pontile nord*, popular with sunbathers by day and clubbers by night, featuring emerging bands and top DJs. Also hosts Napoli jazz festival gigs in Aug.
Kestè d'Inner, corso Umberto I 51, Pozzuoli, T081 526 4072, www.keste.it.

Opened in 2008, this stylish arts club hosts contemporary art exhibitions, gastronomic evenings and eclectic musical events.
Nabilah, via Spiaggia Roma 15, Bacoli, T081-868 9433, www.nabilah.it. During the summer, the swankiest beachside bar-club in Italy attracts top DJs like Gilles Peterson.
Turistico Beach Club, via Miliscola 21, Bacoli, T081-523 5228, www.lidoturistico.com. Raucous, hands-in-the-air house music on at weekends followed by laid-back tunes after Mass, on the *domenica*.

🛍 Shopping

Pozzuoli *p70*
Food and drink
Daber, via Anfiteatro 1, Pozzuoli, T081-526 7443. A handy *supermercato* for picnic supplies near the train station and amphitheatre.
Dolci Qualità, via Carlo Rosini 45, Pozzuoli, T081-526528, www.dolciqualita.com. Campanian wine including Per' 'e Palummo (red) and Falanghina DOC (white), as well as Miele d'Acacia – honey produced in the Campi Flegrei/Castelvolturno area.
Il Mercato Ittico, Pozzuoli. Pozzuoli's wholesale fish market, one of the biggest in Italy, is next to the Temple of Serapis. The area generally has excellent fishmongers.

🏛 What to do

Pozzuoli, Baia, Bacoli and Cuma *p70*
Boat trips
Baia Sommersa, Porto di Baia, T349-497 4183, www.baiasommersa.it. Glass-bottomed boat *Cymba* does tours of the underwater archaeological area, including Roman villas and Portus Julius, Sat and Sun at 1000, 1200 and 1500 (€10, 4-12s €9, 0-3s free).

Cultural
Itinera, corso Vittorio Emanuele 663, Napoli, T081-664545, www.itineranapoli.com. Friendly English-speaking Francesca Del

Vecchio organizes a host of tours around the Campi Flegrei and beyond. From €35 per hr.

Diving
Baia Sommersa, Porto di Baia, T349-497 4183, www.baiasommersa.it. Scuba-diving and snorkelling amid the molluscs and mosaics of the underwater archaeological area of Portus Julius, including submerged Roman villas, one of which belonged to Lucius Piso, Julius Caesar's father-in-law.

Football
SSC Napoli, Stadio San Paolo, piazzale V Tecchio, Fuorigrotta, www.sscnapoli.it. Metro: Campi Flegrei/Mostra. Tickets to see SSC Napoli play cost around €30 and are available from the stadium and in agencies around town. The *tribuna laterale*, along the touchline, offers good views of the action.

Swimming
Piscina Scandone, via Giochi del Mediterraneo, Fuorigrotta, T081-570 2636. Metro: Campi Flegrei/Mostra. Olympic-size pool, diving areas and regular *pallanuoto* (water polo) matches can be enjoyed at this pool in Fuorigrotta.

Wellbeing
Terme Stufe di Nerone, via Stufe di Nerone 45, Bacoli, T081-868 8006, www.termestufe dinerone.it. Daily from 0800. Metro/Ferrovia Cumana: Lucrino. This spa complex, near Emperor Nero's sprawling villa, is not the most luxurious but it is very popular and offers 52°C natural steam, outdoor pools and mud treatments. Its steamy reputation would make Nero blush.

⊖ Transport

Fuorigrotta *p68*
Frequent **Ferrovia Cumana** train services to **Napoli Montesanto** (6 mins), **Bagnoli** (7 mins), **Pozzuoli** (17 mins), **Fusaro** (27 mins). Bus Linea 1 to **Napoli piazza Garibaldi** (24 mins) and **Solfatara** (34 mins).

Bagnoli *p68*
Frequent **Ferrovia Cumana** train services to **Napoli Montesanto** (13 mins), **Fuorigrotta** (7 mins), **Pozzuoli** (9 mins), **Fusaro** (20 mins).

Pozzuoli *p70*
Frequent **Ferrovia Cumana** train services to **Napoli Montesanto** (22 mins), **Fuorigrotta** (16 mins), **Bagnoli** (9 mins), **Fusaro** (11 mins). **Caremar** (T081-017 1998, www.caremar.it), **Medmar** (T081-333 4411, www.medmargroup.it) and **Procidalines** (T081-896 0328) run hydrofoil and ferry services to and from the **Porto di Pozzuoli**, **Ischia** (50 mins) and **Procida** (15 mins).

ⓘ Directory

Pozzuoli *p70*
Accident and emergency Ospedale Santa Maria delle Grazie, Pozzuoli, T081-855 2111. **ATM** Banco di Napoli, piazza della Repubblica, Pozzuoli, T081-526 1386. **Pharmacy** Farmacia Carella, via Terracciano 69, Pozzuoli, T081-526 1162.

Ercolano and Vesuvius

You can squeeze two stupefying sights and a whole lot of history and geology into a day here. In AD 79 the good, the bad and the scholarly (most Romans were squat and ugly according to the Ercolano guides) of Herculaneum were seared by the instant karma of a 482°C pyroclastic surge that roared down Vesuvius at 400 kph. The depth and heat of the blistering debris that swept into the elegant resort helped preserve organic matter including wooden beams supporting roofs, papyrus scrolls of Greek wisdom, and boats filled with the skeletons of those fleeing for their lives. Herculaneum's intimate scale means you need only a few hours to see the wonders of this Roman time capsule.

Grand Tourists were carried to Vesuvius's summit on sedan chairs or aboard the famous funicular railway, whereas today you are likely to use less stylish transport to reach the lip of the volcano. Scientists estimate there to be 400 sq km of molten rock 8 km under the well-monitored volcano, and the authorities reassure Neapolitans that there should be ample warning to evacuate the 600,000 people living in the Zona Rossa (Red Zone) nearest the volcano. Imagine living on the slopes with the threat of a Plinian eruption: some scientists have controversially posited that an event like the cataclysmic Avellino eruption nearly four millennia ago is not out of the question.

Arriving in Ercolano and Vesuvius

Getting there and around

Reaching Ercolano by train is easy but ascending Vesuvius is less straightforward: the Eavbus services are the most reliable way. To get there by road take the A3 Napoli–Salerno Autostrada and exit at Ercolano. **Eavbus** ① *T800-053939, www.eavbus.it,* runs various services around Vesuvius and Ercolano, connecting with Naples and satellite towns around the bay. Alternatively take an infrequent public bus or a small minibus outside Ercolano station. Note, however, that these minibuses are cramped and do not allow much time at the summit. Ercolano's bus station is on piazzale stazione 1. **ANM Autobus** ① *T081-763 1111.* By train, from Naples or Sorrento, take the Ferrovia Circumvesuviana Railway to Ercolano from the Stazione Vesuviana (corso Garibaldi; Metro: Garibaldi); there are stations as far as Sorrento. Ercolano's train station, Circumvesuviana Ercolano, is on piazzale Stazione 1, T800-053939, T081-772 2444, www.vesuviana.it. ►► *See Transport, page 85.*

Tourist information

Tourist information office ① *via IV Novembre 82, Ercolano, T081-788 1243.* For information about Herculaneum, check out www.pompeiisites.org. **Parco Nazionale del Vesuvio** ① *via Palazzo del Principe, Ottaviano, T081-865 3911, www.parconazionaledelvesuvio.it,* has information about the park and guided walks in the area, including night time visits to the crater. **Vesuvius Information Point** ① *Contrada Osservatorio, T081-777 8069.*

Herculaneum → *For listings, see pages 83-85.*

① *Ercolano Scavi (Herculaneum excavations), corso Resina, Ercolano, information T081-732 4338, ticket office T081-777 7008, www.pompeiisites.org. Apr-Oct daily 0830-1930, Nov-Mar daily 0830-1700, last entry 90 mins before closing time, closed 1 Jan, 1 May, 25 Dec. €11, 18-25s €5.50, under 18s/over 65s free. You can visit all 5 archaeological sites – Herculaneum, Pompeii, Oplontis, Stabiae and Boscoreale – within 3 days by buying a* biglietto cumulativo *(combined ticket) for €20, 18-25s €10, under 18s free. The entrance to the site is a 5-min walk downhill from Ercolano station.*

Herculaneum was a well-to-do Roman town of around 5000 residents, with elegant seaside villas, many of which were buried to a depth of over 15 m by the huge pyroclastic flows of the AD 79 eruption. In 1709 Emmanuel de Lorraine, Prince d'Elbeuf, came across the back of the Roman theatre while digging a well and shortly afterwards the first haphazard excavations began. The nature of the volcanic deluge resulted in fewer roofs collapsing here than in Pompeii, and the searing heat carbonized organic materials, meaning that extraordinary architectural details, bodies and objects are still being discovered. Around 300 skeletons were found huddled together in boathouses along with fine jewellery in the 1980s, and it's reckoned that archaeologists have only brushed the surface of the so-called Villa dei Papiri (see page 80) and its fascinating library of Graeco-Roman scrolls. Indeed some hope that papyri will be revealed containing the lost works of Greek writers such as Epicurus, Aristotle and Euripides.

The broad sloping path that curves around and descends into the archaeological site allows you to appreciate the enormity of the AD 79 eruption and the vast amount of debris that buried the town. It also provides an overview of the Roman grid layout of the streets and blocks. The roads orientated north–south are the *cardi* while the east–west routes are called *decumani*. These define the six rectangular *caseggiati* (blocks or sections) of the city, known as *insulae*.

Insulae II and III

The first building on Cardo III Inferiore is the **Casa di Aristide** (House of Aristides) where fleeing victims' skeletons were found. One of Herculaneum's finest villas (discovered in 1828) is next door, the **Casa d'Argo** (House of Argus), named after a painting depicting the myth of Argus, which sadly was stolen. Opposite is the back entrance to the **Casa dell'Albergo** (House of the Inn), not an inn at all but a sprawling villa that was undergoing refurbishment at the time of the eruption. The only private *thermae* (thermal baths) were found here, while a carbonized pear tree trunk was found in the garden.

Herculaneum

Abitazioni/Houses

1. Casa di Aristide
2. Casa d'Argo
3. Casa dell'Albergo
4. Casa dello Scheletro
5. Casa dell'Erma di Bronzo
6. Casa del Tramezzo di Legno
7. Casa dell'Atrio a Mosaico
8. Casa dell'Alcova
9. Casa dei Cervi
10. Casa Sannitica
11. Casa del Gran Portale
12. Casa di Nettuno ed Anfitrite
13. Casa del Bicentenario
14. Casa del Salone Nero
15. Casa del Rilievo di Telefo
16. Casa della Gemma
17. Casa di Galba
18. Casa del Genio
19. Casa del Colonnato Tuscanico
20. Casa dei Due Atri
21. Casa a Graticcio
22. Casa dell'Atrio Corinzio
23. Casa del Mobilio Carbonizzato
24. Casa del Sacello
25. Casa del Telaio
26. Casa della Stoffa

Garden of thermal delights

Roman plumbing meets idle pleasures at the Terme Urbane (see page 80). A large *praefurnium* (furnace/boiler room) heated the baths and water was drawn from an 8-m-deep well. The men's baths have an *apodyterium* (dressing room) with basins for washing and niches for storing clothes. To the left is a round *frigidarium* (cool plunge pool) with a blue vaulted ceiling painted with fish and pierced by a skylight. The temperature rises in the *tepidarium* and *caldarium*. Roman plumbing prowess and engineering ingenuity are displayed in the exposed pipes and smoke vents.

On Cardo IV Superiore is the entrance to the women's baths. It has a magnificently decorated *apodyterium* with mosaic floors depicting Triton swimming with dolphins, a cuttlefish, an octopus and a cherub with a whip. On to the *tepidarium* with its mosaic floor, and then the *caldarium* with white and red marble benches. Check out the grooves in the vaulted ceiling, designed for channelling condensation.

After a stint in the baths the patrons would relax in the porticoed garden, perhaps exercising in the outdoor *palaestra* (gym) or shooting *pila* (a ball game) in the *sphaeristerium*, a covered hall.

No prizes for guessing what was found in the **Casa dello Scheletro** (House of the Skeleton). The less palatial **Casa dell'Erma di Bronzo** (House of the Bronze Herm) has a bronze sculpture of the owner and a Tuscan-style atrium. On Cardo IV the **Casa del Tramezzo di Legno** (House of the Wooden Partition) is a grand Roman dwelling named after the wooden partition that closes the *tablinium* (main room). Seek out the mosaic paving, corniced façade and dog's-head spouts on the compluviate roof that channels rainwater to a sunken pool. There were shops, including one used by a *lanarius* (fabric maker), known as the Bottega del Lanarius (Store with a Clothes Press) – you can see the instrument inside.

Insulae IV and V

You get a feel for the might of tectonic forces at work when you see the geometric mosaic flooring rippled by the eruption in the **Casa dell'Atrio a Mosaico** (House of the Mosaic Atrium). Next door, the **Casa dell'Alcova** (House of the Alcove) has a lavish room with paintings and wooden couches.

The **Casa dei Cervi** (House of the Deer) was an opulent waterfront residence named after two marble groups of deer being savaged by dogs in the garden (the originals are in the Archaeological Museum in Naples). A drunken Hercules relieves himself nearby.

The **Casa Sannitica** (Samnite House) has the layout of a pre-Roman dwelling, with an imposing portal of Corinthian capitals and a graceful open gallery with Ionic columns and fabulous frescoes. Just as grand is the elegant façade of neighbouring **Casa del Gran Portale** (House of the Great Portal) with its two pilasters, demi-columns and carved capitals with winged Greek-style Victories.

Under the **Casa di Nettuno ed Anfitrite** (House of Neptune and Amphitrite) is a well-preserved wine store with intact wooden fittings, counter and shelves for amphorae. Along the east wall is the remarkably vivid Neptune and Amphitrite glass wall mosaic. The much-photographed *nymphaeum* has elaborate decoration depicting hunting scenes and attractive motifs, all topped with a head of Silenus (best mate of wine god Dionysus). On the *decumanus maximus* is the **Casa del Bicentenario** (House of the Bicentenary), found in 1938 by archaeologist Amedeo Maiuri, 200 years after Charles III began the official digs.

Insula VI

The **Terme Urbane** (Thermal Baths) date back to the first century AD, during the reign of Augustus. Separate baths and entrances for men and women are on Cardi III and IV respectively. Unusual red and black interiors mark out the **Casa del Salone Nero** (House of the Black Hall). Worth checking out are the two large panels depicting Jupiter, Hercules, Juno, Minerva and the Etruscan god Acheloo in the **Sacello degli Augusti** (College of the Augustali), the seat of the cult of Emperor Augustus.

Insulae Orientalis I and II

Head eastwards to the **Palaestra**, the public sports centre, with its monumental vestibule, a lower terrace with porticoes, a long pool for breeding fish and part of a cruciform swimming pool. Seek out the mythical five-headed serpent, Hydra, entwined around a tree trunk. The 18th-century Bourbon excavation tunnels run beneath the avenue here, offering an insight into the scale of the excavations.

Moving to the southeast corner of the excavations is the three-storey **Casa del Rilievo di Telefo** (House of the Relief of the Telephus), Herculaneum's largest villa, named after a bas-relief depicting the myth of Telephus – the son of the god Hercules – founder of the city. Don't overlook the circular plaster cast copies of the original marble *oscilla* (discs depicting satyrs to ward off evil) hung between the red-hued columns. Also on Cardo V is the **Casa della Gemma** (House of the Gem), named after an engraved stone found here, where there are large frescoed panels and refined graffiti in the toilets recording the visit of a renowned physician.

Suburban district

On the western fringes of the south terrace are the **Sacelli** (sacred areas) which have two temples – one dedicated to Venus and the other to four gods: Neptune, Minerva, Mercury and, most fittingly, Vulcan. The **Terme Suburbane** (Suburban Baths) has a *frigidarium* with white marble flooring and a *tepidarium* with a stuccoed wall depicting warriors. There's an extraordinary impression made by a *labrum* (washing tub) on the volcanic material that immersed the *caldarium*. Nearby is a half disrobed and handless statue of the senator M Nonius Balbus, an ally of Octavian (who reigned as Augustus from 27 BC to AD 14).

A theatre is buried nearby, accessed via 18th-century tunnels dug by Prince d'Elbeuf's speculative excavators – its *scaenae frons* (monumental stage backdrop) was unceremoniously stripped of its lavish decoration and statuary. This area was right on the beach: boat storehouses and warehouses line the old shoreline. In the early 1980s, 300 human skeletons and then a 9-m-long Roman boat containing an oarsman, soldier, swords and a pouch of coins were found here. In 2008 work began on recreating the beach.

Villa dei Papiri

ⓘ *Northwest of main excavation. The villa is currently not open to the public.*

Historians believe that this most opulent villa, where a priceless library of papyrus scrolls was discovered, belonged to Lucius Calpurnius Piso Caesoninus, father-in-law of Julius Caesar. In the 1750s engineers dug into the multi-storey villa when excavating a well. The scale and beauty of the residence is mind-blowing: covering almost 3000 sq m, the villa had a 250-m-long shoreline frontage, rooms filled with exquisite art and statuary, a porticoed garden and terraced grounds brimming with vineyards, orchards and fountains. The Archaeological Museum in Naples houses a collection of marble and bronze busts from the villa.

Museo Archeologico Virtuale (MAV)

ⓘ *Via IV Novembre, Ercolano, T081-1980 6511, www.museomav.com. Tue-Sun 0900-1630, €7.50, under 18s/over 65s/students/teachers/Artecard €6, 3D virtual show €5, €11.50 combined.*

Opened in July 2008, this €10 million museum near the ruins takes visitors on a virtual journey around the villas and public spaces of ancient Herculaneum. There are lots of interactive multimedia displays to explore as well as some intriguing sights, smells and temperature fluctuations thrown in to get you into the Roman mood. A new immersive 3D show, *Eruption of Vesuvius*, allows you to imagine the force of the eruption.

Ville Vesuviane including Villa Campolieto

ⓘ *Corso Resina 283, Ercolano, T081-732 2134/081-1924 4532, www.villevesuviane.net. Tue-Sun 1000-1300, free. A 5-min walk heading east from the entrance to Herculaneum.*

In the 1700s, sumptuous aristocratic residences were built along the coast from San Giovanni a Teduccio to Torre Annunziata. The celebrated stretch of road from Resina to Torre del Greco known as the *Miglio d'Oro* (Golden Mile) has many a classical pile but alas most are privately owned or in disrepair. Collectively they are known as as the Ville Vesuviane. In Ercolano you can visit the **Villa Campolieto**, home of the Ente per le Ville Vesuviane that overlooks the restoration and preservation of these mansions – 122 of them – and organizes guided tours, by appointment, of many villas including **Villa Favorita**. Opportunities to hobnob with the Bourbon descendants are best during the annual events: **Emozioni Vesuviane** (late April to June), the **Festival delle Ville Vesuviane** (when classical concerts are held at mansions built by the likes of Vaccaro and Vanvitelli) and **Natale nelle Ville** at Christmas. The royal palace **Reggia di Portici** ⓘ *via Università 100, Portici, T081-775 5109*, and its **Villa d'Elbeuf** by Sanfelice are also open by appointment.

Parco Nazionale del Vesuvio → *For listings, see pages 83-85.*

ⓘ *Park headquarters Ente Parco Nazionale del Vesuvio, piazza Municipio 880040, San Sebastiano al Vesuvio, T081-771 0911, www.vesuviopark.it; visitor centre at summit T081-777 5720/T081-739 1123. For those wanting to combine visits to Pompeii and Vesuvius in a day, City Sighteesing Napoli/Eavbus run a bus service (T081-551 3109, www.unicocampania. it, €10 return). Busvia (T3409-352616, www.busviadelvesuvio.com, €20 including entrance to park) runs a tour that includes a 2-bus trip from Pompei Villa dei Misteri Circumvesuviana train station. There's a 4WD scenic drive to the summit and a walk along the AltoTirone Nature Reserve along the dusty Via Matrone: suitable for those fit and keen to walk over rough ground. Be aware that the buses sometimes get oversubscribed so you may have to stand onboard. Eavbus also operates a bus to and from Vesuvius from Naples Stazione Marittima Mergellina (stops at Castel dell'Ovo, Molo Beverello and piazza Garibaldi Hotel Terminus. For latest timetables: www.eavbus.it. Compagnia Trasporti Vesuviani has a small office outside Ercolano Scavi station and runs regular minibuses (often cramped, so don't bring luggage) to the national park car park for €20 return. The minibus departs for the volcano when full and waits for about 1 hr at the car park, so there's not that long to enjoy the visit. The park path is open daily from 0900 and closing times vary throughout the year – last admission is about 90 mins before sunset. €10, under 18s/students €8, under 8s accompanied by an adult free.*

Tectonic timebomb

When the Eurasian and African tectonic plates met it was murder: the superheated earth's crust spilled magma into the Bay of Naples, forming the Campanian Volcanic Arc and the volcanoes of Sicily. Vesuvius's Gran Cono (Large Cone) is 1281 m high, 200 m deep and has a diameter of 600 m. It sits within the caldera of Monte Somma, the remains of a larger and higher (1149 m) crater that formed some 18,000 years ago and subsequently collapsed. Between Monte Somma and the Gran Cono is the Valle del Gigante (Valley of the Giant), which is in turn divided between the Valle del Inferno (Valley of Hell) to the east and the Atrio del Cavallo (Hall of the Horse) in the west.

Vesuvius's violent eruptions are called 'explosive' or 'Plinian' eruptions – they propel ash and smoke high into the atmosphere in the shape of an umbrella pine tree, and include the event of AD 79, witnessed and described by the Plinys. The last such explosion in 1631 killed some 4000 people. Recent findings of Bronze Age footsteps and buried skeletons as far away as Afragola and Avellino paint a disquieting picture of the 1780 BC eruption*, dubbed "a first Pompeii". On that occasion a sonic boom accompanied the propulsion of molten rock, cinders and ash at 100,000 tons per second some 30 km into the stratosphere. Northeasterly winds carried pumice and weighty lapilli rocks as far as Nola and Avellino, where over several hours it reached up to 3 m in height. After 12 hours the column collapsed and caused a blistering pyroclastic surge that laid waste to everything in its path – it deposited 20 m of debris some 5 km away.

Alarmingly, the volcano has been dormant for more than 60 years now, the longest period of inactivity in nearly 500 years: the longer the wait, the more the pressure builds below. There have been many 'effusive' eruptions (these spew lava) over the past 25,000 years, including the last eruption in 1944 which killed 26 people. The question is: will the next eruption be effusive or Plinian?

*A fascinating piece by Stephen S Hall in the National Geographic (Sep 2007) describes this eruption and the controversial theories of vulcanologists Mastrolorenzo, Petrone, Pappalardo and Sheridan.

Summit walk

The route to the summit of Vesuvius involves motor transport to the entrance car park followed by a walk over volcanic rocks. All vehicles, bar the jeeps driven by official guides, stop at the car park at 1017 m. The climb to the summit is around 250 m over rough ground, which combined with the heat of a summer's day or high winds can make for an uncomfortable walk for even the fittest person. The Vesuvius National Park authority looks after the protected area around the volcano and their nature trail (Trail 5 of nine routes, see page 85) incorporates part of the ascent to the summit and halfway around the crater. Upon reaching the visitors centre you pay an admission charge to enter the park and go to the crater's rim.

The views along the steep, wide gravelly path and around the mountain are incredible. Inside the crater (out of bounds unless accompanied by a guide, see page 85) fumaroles steam amid luridly coloured rock crystals and silver-grey pumice. The 200-m chasm to the floor of the crater adds to the dizzying spectacle. A rusty, makeshift handwritten sign points the way to Pompeii down below. A souvenir stall-cum-bar sells assorted tat, snacks, postcards, refreshments and Lacryma Christi wine.

Osservatorio Vesuviano

ⓘ *Via Diocleziano 328, T081-610 8483, www.ov.ingv.it. Sat-Sun 0900-1400, free.*
Built by Bourbon monarch Ferdinand II in the 1840s, the neoclassical Vesuvian Observatory has an exhibition exploring volcanology, with lots of video, observatory instruments and interesting collections of volcanic rock. Eyes are fixed nervously on the instruments that record the seismic and geochemical activity across 300 sq km – they are monitored closely from the surveillance centre in Fuorigrotta.

Trekking in Vesuvius National Park ⓘ *For national park headquarters, visitor centre and transport options to the summit, see page 81. For further information and maps contact the park wardens or official guides, T081-777 5720, T337-942249 (mobile), www.guidevesuvio.it.*
Within the Vesuvius National Park there are nine colour-coded trails, varying in difficulty. Trail 4 (orange) is a seven-hour round trip and covers over 8 km of rough terrain including the **Tirone Alto Forestry Nature Reserve**, established in 1972. On the trail you can hear and see lizards, martens, cuckoos, foxes and hares. Trail 9 (grey) *Il Fiume di Lava* (the Lava Flow) is a much easier 90-minute circular track that starts and ends at via Osservatorio. Amid the 1944 lava flows is a unique yellow lichen species, *stereocaulon vesuvianum*, that thrives on mineral-rich magma and whose very mention can set a botanist's heart pounding.

Ercolano and Vesuvius listings

For hotel and restaurant price codes and other relevant information, see pages 14-17.

⊖ Where to stay

Ercolano and Vesuvius *p76*
€€ Bel Vesuvio Inn, via Panoramica 40, San Sebastiano al Vesuvio, T081-771 1243, www.agriturismobelvesuvioinn.it. This attractive 18th-century farmhouse with modern comforts is set amid vineyards on the slopes of Vesuvius. It's especially good for nature lovers and families as there are farmyard animals, a playground, horse riding, local walking trails and a *bocce* area where you can enjoy Italian boules. Meals are served on a large terrace and feature local produce including *piennolo* tomatoes, apricot jam, cheeses, chicken and *salume*.
€€ La Murena B&B, via Osservatorio 10, Ercolano, T081-777 9819. This small B&B is a good base for exploring Vesuvius National Park and visiting the Vesuvian Observatory and Herculaneum. The accommodation includes suites and an apartment with a kitchen and a terrace for alfresco dining, while the wonderful grounds are a great place to eat breakfast and relax. There's also the option of renting the entire house for €260 per night.
€€ Miglio d'Oro Park Hotel, corso Resina 296, 80056 Ercolano, T081-739 9999, www.migliodoroparkhotel.it. The 18th-century Villa Aprile is within easy reach of Herculaneum, with awe-inspiring views of Vesuvius and a new pool. Its fountains and garden follies reveal the whimsical tastes of its first owner, the Count of Imola and Forlì, Gerolamo Riario Sforza. It's all very modern with some crazy artworks spanning various cubed spaces around a lounge bar. A smart glass-and-chrome lift whisks you to the guest rooms, which range from a reasonably priced Classic to the spacious Suite – all have fabulous bathrooms (some with jacuzzi baths, others with jet showers), a/c, internet and satellite TV.
€ Andris Hotel, via San Vito 130, Ercolano, T081-777 7220, www.diiserniagroup.it. Top-value modern hotel, with helpful staff, simply furnished rooms in a quiet location and bay/Vesuvius views. Great family room sleeping 4 for around €100.

🍴 Restaurants

Ercolano and Vesuvius *p76*
€€€ Casa Rossa al Vesuvio, via Vesuvio 30, Ercolano, T081-777 9763. Wed-Mon 1230-1500, 1900-2300. The sister restaurant of the renowned **Casa Rossa 1888** in Torre del Greco, the 'Pink House' is all about elegant Neapolitan dining. The house specialities include Parthenopean pasta dishes like *vermicelli ai frutti di mare* and *paccheri al ragù di mare*. They also do pizza and have a selection of the very best Lacryma Christi del Vesuvio wine.

€€€ Viva lo Re, corso Resina 261, Ercolano, T081-739 0207, www.vivalore. it. Tue-Sat 0930-0100, Sun 0930-1600. This *osteria-enoteca* run by suave Maurizio Focone has handsome wooden interiors lined with hundreds of bottles of wine. Some may find the presentation of the food a tad pretentious (it comes on fancy flat, angular plates) but the food itself is expertly prepared. *Piatti del giorno* are written on a board and often include a plate of *pesce crudo* (raw seafood), grilled cuttlefish with bitterly delicious *friarelli* (a type of broccoli and an acquired taste) and chunky steaks. They also have 3 stylish rooms overlooking Villa Campolieto.

€€ La Lanterna, via Colonnello Aliperta 8, Somma Vesuviana, T081-899 1843. Tue-Sun 1200-1500, 1930-2300. After a day on the slopes of Vesuvius, vulcanologist guide Roberto Addeo enjoys coming here to try their various *baccalà* dishes: the imported Norwegian stockfish (*stucco* or *stoccafisso*) is a traditional ingredient in Somma Vesuviana cuisine. Their classic pasta dish is the much imitated *paccheri con lo stucco* and they also make pizzas including *pizza al baccalà*, which is best eaten outside under the garden pergola.

Cafés and bars
L'Angolo degli Scavi, via IV Novembre 1, Ercolano. Daily 0730-2100. Just over the road from the Scavi entrance, on the 'Corner of

the Excavations', this small and often busy bar is convenient but the prices are geared to tourists. You are better off walking further up via IV Novembre to one of the many bars used by the locals.

🎭 Entertainment

Ercolano and Vesuvius *p76*
Sciuscià Club, via Viulio 2, Ercolano, T081-771 9898, www.sciusciaclub.it. Commercial house music and latino pumps out under the vaulted ceilings, and there's a garden where you can sample Neapolitan classics. Check in advance for the latest programme.

🛍 Shopping

Ercolano and Vesuvius *p76*
Food and drink
F/lli de Luca Bossa, via IV Novembre 4/6, Ercolano. Daily 0800-1300, 1600-2100. This tiny *alimentari* near the entrance to the Scavi is where the locals come for their supplies. As well as decent bread and snacks like *taralli di finochietto*, you can pick up a bottle of Valdobbiadene prosecco for just €7 and a large bottle of water for €1.50 here.

Markets
Mercato di Resina, piazza Pugliano, Ercolano. Daily 0730-1300. Famous since the Second World War, when impoverished locals peddled objects and clothes stolen from the Allied forces, colourful Resina second-hand market often throws up a quirky clothing item. Just take care of con artists offering dodgy electronics goods and cigarettes.

🎯 What to do

Ercolano and Vesuvius *p76*
Cultural
Itinera, corso Vittorio Emanuele 663, Naples, T081-664545/339-7551747 (mobile), www.itineranapoli.com. Metro to corso V Emanuele. Friendly, English-speaking Francesca del Vecchio organizes a host of

tours along the Bay of Naples including trips around the Vesuvian sights. A 2-hr guided tour around Pompeii or Herculanuem costs €130 (for up to 4 people) while a 4-hr tour of Pompeii or Herculanuem, plus Vesuvius, costs €160.

L'Ultima Notte di Ercolano, T081-8631581, www.tappetovolante.org. €25 – check for latest programme. This is a tour under the stars with a theatrical performance thrown in – 40 costumed actors perform Domenico Maria Corrado's musical version of Virgil's *Aeneid* amid Ercolano's ancient baths and villas. Check out their latest theatrical events on the website.

Walking and outdoor activities

Adventurous types will relish a trek in the otherworldly volcanic landscape of Vesuvius National Park or a scramble into the crater itself, accompanied by an expert guide. You can combine a trip to Herculaneum with a trip to the summit, perhaps followed by a trek along one of the designated trails around the park. Sturdy walking boots with ankle support, outdoor kit (from mid-Oct to May especially) and food supplies are essential. **Vesuvio Trekking**, T333-866 4497, www.vesuviotrekking.com. Roberto Addeo is one of the vulcanological guides who take people around the Vesuvius National Park. The guided walk around the crater costs €10. Roberto can be contacted on his mobile T338-441 0102 or via email at vesuviotrek@libero.it.

Vesuvio Wild Eco Campus, via Cifelli, Trecase, www.vesuviowild.it, T081-247 4698/T334-170 7752. Rope work, climbing, mountain biking, geocaching and survival courses organized by outdoor enthusiasts in the Tirone Alto Vesuvio forest.

⊖ Transport

Ercolano *p76*
Ercolano Scavi
Frequent Circumvesuviana train services to **Napoli** (20 mins), **Pompei Scavi** (20 mins), **Torre Annunziata-Oplonti** (15 mins), **Castellammare di Stabia** (30 mins) and **Sorrento** (50 mins).

Parco Nazionale del Vesuvio *p81*
Eavbus from piazza Garibaldi in Naples (65 mins), piazza Anfiteatro in Pompei (90 mins) or Ercolano Circumvesuviana station (35 mins).

❶ Directory

Ercolano and Vesuvius *p76*
Medical services Ospedale Maresca, via Montedoro 2, Torre del Greco, T081-849 0191. Corso Italia 9, Ercolano, T081-739 0021 (daily 0900-1300, 1600-2000). **Money** Banca Monte dei Paschi di Siena, at piazza Longo B40, T081-863 6511. **Post office** Via Panoramica 298, Ercolano, T081-739 5385 (Mon-Fri 0800-1330, Sat 0900-1230).

Pompeii and around

Around 20,000 people lived in Pompeii when Vesuvius spewed and spat ash, pumice and wave upon wave of scorching pyroclastic debris on the town in AD 79, sealing a bubble of Roman life for 2000 years. Built on a lava plateau the city was ruled by Oscans, Etruscans and Samnites – Italic tribes – as well as by Greek colonists, before the Roman Empire ceded it. Walking around Pompeian streets – houses, baths and shops among its graffiti, artworks and artefacts of horror – is a spellbinding experience that warrants a couple of days' exploration.

Mind-boggling time-travel explorations of AD 79's victims continue at the dreamlike, epicurean gardens of Villa Oplontis, where Nero's colourful second wife Poppaea Sabina sojourned. At Boscoreale, further up the slopes of Vesuvius, visitors can discover life on a Roman farm and vineyard. Four villas were found at Roman Stabiae and more artefacts will be unearthed in the coming years as part of a US$200 million archaeological project.

Shoddy management and millions of visitors have taken their toll on the area's ancient treasures. The government has now declared a state of emergency with new emphasis placed on protecting the excavations. Bureaucratic inertia and headline-hitting collapses at the House of the Gladiators and Domus di Diomede now threaten Pompeii's UNESCO Patrimony of Humanity status.

Arriving in Pompeii

Getting there and around

To get here by road, take the A3 Autostrada and exit at Pompei Ovest then follow signs to Pompei Scavi; Torre Annunziata and follow signs for Boscoreale; Torre Annunziata Sud then signs for Scavi di Oplonti, Castellammare di Stabia and the SS145. **SITA** ① *T081-552 2176, www.sitabus.it*, runs various buses from piazza Garibaldi in Naples to Pompei and along the Amalfi coast. By train, from Naples or Sorrento: take the Ferrovia **Circumvesuviana Railway** ① *T800-053939, www.vesuviana.it*, which departs regularly from the Stazione Vesuviana (corso Garibaldi; Metro: Garibaldi) and along the coast from the Sorrento station – it stops at Pompei, Boscoreale, Torre Annunziata-Oplonti Villa di Poppea and Castellammare di Stabia. The Circumvesuviana railway is also the cheapest and most convenient way of getting to and around the archaeological sites. If you'd prefer to visit the area using a tour guide, **Itinera** ① *T081-664545, www.itineranapoli.com*, runs tours around the sites. ➠ *See Transport, page 96.*

Tourist information

Tourist information office ① *Ufficio AASCT, piazza Esedra 12, T081-536 3293.*

Pompeii → *For listings, see pages 95-96.*

① *Pompei Scavi, via Villa dei Misteri 2, Pompei, information T081-857 5347, ticket office T081-536 5154, www.pompeiisites.org. Apr-Oct 0830-1930 (last entry 1800), Nov-Mar 0830-1700 (last entry 1530), closed 1 Jan, 1 May, 25 Dec, €11, EU citizens 18-24/school teachers €5.50, EU citizens under 18/over 65 free. You can visit all 5 archaeological sites – Herculaneum, Pompeii, Oplontis, Stabiae and Boscoreale – within 3 days by buying a biglietto cumulativo (combined ticket) for €20, 18-25s €10, under 18s free. Porta Marina entrance is just over the road from the Scavi-Villa dei Misteri station. The piazza Anfiteatro entrance is nearest the town and Pompei Santuario train station.*

Fascination in the beauty and sophistication of Pompeii's everyday objects, buildings and society is tempered with the horror of its devastation. Thousands stayed behind after the first deluge of volcanic debris: some perhaps to save their possessions from looting, some no doubt just unable to flee. Roofs collapsed under the weight of ash and pumice, crushing many before the massive pyroclastic surges engulfed everyone and everything. Haunting casts of human and animal victims created by archaeologist Giuseppe Fiorelli, who poured plaster into cavities left by bodies in the ash, freeze the mortal positions of the incinerated victims.

Pompeii covers 67 ha, 44 ha of which have been excavated. Its walls are punctuated by seven gates: Marina, Ercolano, Vesuvio, Nola, Sarno, Nocera and Stabia. Many of its older Greek-influenced buildings and irregular sixth-century BC street plan are around the Foro Triangolare (Triangular Forum) area. The later grid layout, with rectangular *insulae* (urban blocks), *decumani* (east–west streets) and *cardi* (north–south streets) date from the fourth century BC onwards.

Orientation

The vast scale of the Pompeii ruins makes it worthwhile having a planned route around the site (bear in mind that some villas may be closed). However, the heat of the sun and stamina will also play a part in your day out – bring lots of sun protection, water and energy snacks. Set out early in the morning if you can and plan a rest for the hottest part of

Pompeii

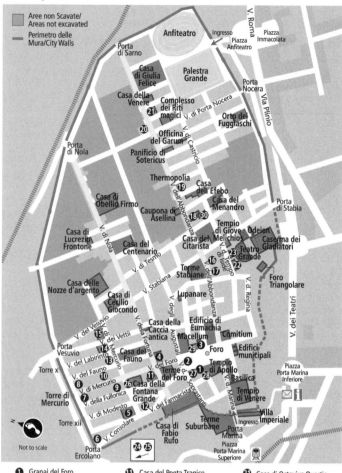

Aree non Scavate/
Areas not excavated

Perimetro delle
Mura/City Walls

Anfiteatro
Ingresso
Piazza Immacolata
Piazza Anfiteatro
V. Roma
Porta di Sarno
Porta Nocera
V. di Pcompeo
Casa di Giulia Felice
Palestra Grande
Casa della Venere
Complesso dei Riti magici
V. di Porta Nocera
Orto dei Fugglaschi
Officina del Garum
Porta di Nola
Panificio di Sotericus
V. di Castricio
Thermopolia
Casa dell'Efebo
Casa del Menandro
Porta di Stabia
Casa di Obellio Firmo
Caupona di Asellina
Tempio di Giove Melichio
Odeion
Caserma dei Gladiatori
Casa di Lucrezio Frontone
Casa del Centenario
Casa del Citarista
Teatro Grande
V. di Nola
V. di Tesmo
V. Stabiana
Terme Stabiane
V. dell'Abbondanza
Foro Triangolare
Casa delle Nozze d'argento
Lupanare
V. degli Augustali
V. d. Regina
V. dei Teatri
Casa di Cecilio Giocondo
Casa della Caccia antica
Edificio di Eumachia
Macellum
V. del Vesuvio
V. dei Vettii
V. della Fortuna
Comitium
Porta Vesuvio
Casa del Fauno
Foro
Edifici municipali
V. del Labirinto
Terme del Foro
Tempio di Apollo
Piazza Porta Marina Inferiore
Torre x
V. di Mercurio
Casa della Fontana Grande
Tempio di Giove
Basilica
Torre di Mercurio
V. della Fullonica
V. di Modesto
V. del Farmacista
Tempio di Venere
Villa Imperiale
Torre xii
V. Consolare
Casa di Fabio Rufo
Terme Suburbane
Porta Marina
Porta Ercolano
Piazza Porta Marina Superiore

N Not to scale

1. Granai del Foro
2. Tempio di Giove
3. Tempio di Vespasiano
4. Tempio della Fortuna Augusta
5. Casa di Sallustio
6. Casa del Chirurgo
7. Casa di Apollo
8. Casa di Meleagro
9. Casa di Adone
10. Casa dei Dioscuri
11. Casa del Poeta Tragico
12. Pistrinum
13. Casa del Labrinto
14. Casa di Vettii
15. Casa degli Amorini Dorati
16. Orto Botanico
17. Quadrivio di Holconio
18. Fullonica di Stefano
19. Bottega del Fruttivendolo Felix
20. Casa del Moralista
21. Casa di Octavius Quartio
22. Palestra Sannitica
23. Tempio di Iside
24. Villa di Diomede
25. Villa dei Misteri
26. Casa della Fontana Piccola
27. Latrina del Foro
28. Mensa Ponderaria
29. Santuario dei Lari Pubblici
30. Casa dei Ceii

Controversial Roman deities

Dionysus/Bacchus The god of wine, fruits and ecstasy is associated with a popular cult, initially worshipped by women. The Bay of Naples was the natural home of wild Bacchanalian rites, where tales spread of untamed shenanigans and mysterious rituals that led to Bacchanalia being outlawed by the Roman Senate in 186 BC.

Isis Egyptian goddess and the idealized mother and wife, Isis was a focus of magic and mysterious cults especially amongst slaves and Graeco-Roman bigwigs. Emperor Augustus (27 BC-AD 14) was so threatened by the cult that he outlawed it and promoted state-sponsored gods.

Persephone/Proserpina Springtime goddess and Greek Queen of the Underworld who chomped on pomegranate seeds with Hades.

Priapus Son of Aphrodite and Dionysus and god of fertility – his phallus is all over Pompeii, on walls, doorknobs and candle holders.

Vulcan Fire god worshipped on 23 August (the Vulcanalia) outside city walls when fish were flung into the flames. Little did they know that Vulcan would appear from the seemingly serene mountain bearing juicy grapes above them.

---

the day in a cool spot – the trees around the amphitheatre provide welcome shade. Expect lots of walking on uneven ancient surfaces: pace yourself and mind your step.

The description below divides the sprawling 44 ha area into mini-itineraries that roughly follow the classic route from Porta Marina, opposite the Circumvesuviana station, ending up at the amphitheatre. To take in all these sights, and the suburban villas and baths, requires a couple of full days, so pick out the most interesting ones to visit.

Here is a five-hour route that starts at the Porta Marina and ends at the amphitheatre: around the Forum, Casa del Fauno, Casa di Vettii, Casa degli Amorini Dorati, Lupanare, Terme Stabiane, the Theatre district, the western section of via dell' Abbondanza, Palestra Grande and the Anfiteatro.

Forum On entering through Porta Marina you come to the **Tempio di Venere** (Temple of Venus), dedicated to the city of Pompeii's guardian goddess, then the **Basilica**, seat of the law courts, before the Roman **Foro** (Forum) opens out to your left. The Forum was the centre of the city's public life, covering 17,400 sq m and containing governmental buildings and temples.

Starting clockwise, the **Tempio di Apollo** (Temple of Apollo) was erected on the site of an earlier building constructed by the southern Italian Samnites in the fifth century BC. Seek out the bronze statue of Artemis shooting arrows here. The **Granai del Foro** (the *holitorium* or grainstore) houses archaeological finds and some poignant plastercasts of some of the victims of the AD 79 eruption (other examples can be seen at the Garden of the Fugitives and the Stabian Baths). At the north end, flanked by two triumphal arches, is the **Tempio di Giove** (Temple of Jupiter), which became the Roman Capitolium – the raised podium once had statues of Jupiter, Juno and Minerva.

The Forum is still the meeting place of a motley flock, nowadays consisting of tour parties, snoozing stray dogs and Italian school kids who hop on the empty plinths and strike poses. There is little shade but it's worth lingering here by the patch of grass to view the architectural fragments backdropped by Vesuvius. On the east side you'll find the **Macellum** (market), the **Sacrarium** (more venerated deities) and the **Edificio di Eumachia**

(Building of Eumachia), the headquarters of the wool fullers, who cleaned (with a brew of urine and potash) and thickened woollen cloth. Exquisite marble decoration depicts birds and insects amid acanthus leaves here, while the marble altar of the **Tempio di Vespasiano** (Temple of Vespasian) has bas-reliefs of a sacrificed bull. Municipal elections were held at the Comitium.

North of the Forum The **Terme del Foro** (Forum Thermal Baths), built around 80 BC, have rich architectural details including a stuccoed *tepidarium* (warm water baths) and terracotta *telamones* (male figures supporting the ceiling). At the junction of via del Foro and via della Fortuna is the **Tempio della Fortuna Augusta** (Temple of Fortuna Augusta) whose once-magnificent Corinthian columns, double staircase and towering marble-faced entrance were built in honour of an imperial cult by Marcus Tullius, a military man, imperial knight and ally of Augustus.

Towards Porta Ercolano On the way to Porta Ercolano and the suburban villas (which is a fabulous detour for those with extra time and stamina, see page 93) is the area first excavated by archaeologists – it may have consequently faded and been damaged but has a striking atmosphere and views. On via Consolare is the mighty old **Casa di Sallustio** (House of the Sallust) dating from the third century BC. It was split into various commercial uses, becoming an inn with a *thermopolium* (restaurant) after the AD 62 earthquake, and suffered the indignity of a 1943 US air attack. Beyond the grand frontage of *opus quadratum* pillars of tufa stone, are cavernous interiors, a clever *viridarium* (garden) with an Ionic portico and a luxuriant *trompe l'œil* garden scene painted on the back wall. The nearby **Casa del Chirurgo** (House of the Surgeon) is a colossal building where grisly looking surgical instruments were found.

Via del Mercurio Starting at the **Torre del Mercurio** (Tower of Mercury) and heading south on via del Mercurio, there are some grandiose dwellings. The **Casa di Apollo** (House of Apollo) has a mosaic of Achilles at Skyros, the **Casa di Meleagro** (House of Meleager) contains a fountain, fish pond and a simple fridge, while the **Casa di Adone** (House of Adonis) is named after a painting of a wounded Adonis tended by Venus and some cupids. The grandest though is the **Casa dei Dioscuri** (House of Castor and Pollux) with its imposing colonnade and mythological paintings of Apollo and Daphne, Adonis and Scylla. Paintings of the Dioscuri (the Divine twins Castor and Pollux) that adorned the entrance, and of Perseus and Andromeda, are in the Archaeological Museum in Naples.

Further along is the **Casa della Fontana Piccola** (House of the Little Fountain), with its *trompe l'œil* effects and a cute cherub grasping a goose, while neighbouring **Casa della Fontana Grande** (House of the Large Fountain) has a mosaic fountain and tragicomic masks. More mosaics and theatricality fill the **Casa del Poeta Tragico** (House of the Tragic Poet), where a much-reproduced mosaic in the floor of the vestibule warns visitors to '*Cave Canem*' ('Beware of the dog').

House of the Faun Crowds gather around the copy of the statuette of a dancing faun at the **Casa del Fauno** (House of the Faun), a large house covering over 3000 sq m. Its best finds include the *tesserae* mosaic of Alexander the Great tussling with Darius at the Battle of Issus, now at the Archaeological Museum in Naples. Around the corner on vicolo Storto is the best-preserved *pistrinum* (bakery), whose millstones and bulbous ovens were owned by one Popidius Priscus.

Casa di Vettii and around vicolo di Mercurio On vicolo del Labrinto at the **Casa del Labrinto** (House of the Labyrinth) there's a mosaic maze depicting Theseus slaying the Minotaur, while the must-see **Casa di Vettii** (House of the Vetti) has lavish paintings in the Fourth Style (the most intricate decorative style that was all the rage around the time of the AD 62 earthquake), peppered with mythology and mischievousness. Owned by the Vettii family of freedmen, who prospered around the time of the AD 62 earthquake (look out for the electoral slogans on the south wall) and commissioned quality restoration after the quake, it is much visited and consequently damaged by footfall. It has been undergoing restoration in recent years.

The Vettii's conversation pieces include a modestly endowed and demi-proud Priapus, and a witty frieze lined with endearing cherubs (or psyches) busy peddling gold and perfume, lobbing stones at a target and topsy-turvy chariot racing. Look out for the cherub cracking the whip astride a crab. The sumptuous *triclinium* (dining room) and *oecus* (living area) have a compendium of mythology and include lots of romantic couples (Perseus and Andromeda, Dionysius and Ariadne, Poseidon and Amymone) and Hellenistic scenes, including Ixion bound to a spinning wheel, punishment for leering at Zeus's wife. Statues of Bacchus and cupids clutching grapes and a goose were rigged up to a sophisticated system of fountain jets in the *peristyle* (porticoed garden). Other highlights include erotic paintings in the servants' quarters (some scholars guess that it was a private brothel) and the frescoed *lararium* (shrine) with household *lares* (gods) and a snake.

Historians reckon the well-to-do Poppaea family owned the **Casa degli Amorini Dorati** (House of Gilded Cherubs), at the junction with via del Vesuvio, renowned for its marble relief bacchanalian scenes, Egyptian gods and gold cupids.

Around Porta di Nola On via di Nola is the extensive **Casa del Centenario** (House of the Centenary), excavated in 1879, 18 centuries after Vesuvius's eruption. A certain A Rustius Verus owned and enjoyed its baths with Egyptian flourishes, a *nymphaeum* and garden fountain portraying a young satyr pouring wine. In the servants' atrium – now in the Archaeological Museum in Naples – was a celebrated scene showing Bacchus with a cape of grapes among birds, snakes, a panther and a vine-strewn Vesuvius.

Eastern section of via dell'Abbondanza Starting at the Forum, Pompeii's wide high street slopes down to Porta di Sarno and is lined with shops, workshops and hostelries. The inscriptions along the way offer insights into the commercial, political and sexual lives of the people of Pompeii: stepping stones would have been handy to hop over water and detritus; while deep ruts attest to the busy cart traffic that would have rumbled along here. Imagine the onslaught of movement, sound and pongs, with Vesuvius brooding in the corner of your left eye.

Terme Stabiane Entering the Stabian Baths, along the via dell'Abbondanza, the men's *tepidarium* is a whirl of intricate stucco work and camera shutters. In the footsteps of ancient bathers, you enter the antechamber (dressing room) with its *clipei* (shields) decorated with nymphs and cupids, then the *tepidarium* and circular *frigidarium* with its plunge pool and twinkling, lapis lazuli dome. The niches held towels and massage ointments. Bathers would then brave the *calidarium*'s 40°C steam and hot baths, followed by a massage in the *tepidarium*. Patrons would relax with a drink under the porticoes of the *palaestra*. According to some scholars, women paid almost double to enter their baths, which are adjacent to the mens' and were accessed on the vicolo del Lupanare.

Side-trip to the Lupanare Expect a lot of eye-bulging images advertising personal services in the compact brothel quarters of the **Lupanare** (named after the howl of a *lupa*: she-wolf) on the vicolo del Lupanare. Among the tiny cubicles are pieces of Latin graffiti, including: "Long live lovers, death to those who do not know how to love! Double death to those who hinder love!"

Western section of via dell'Abbondanza Upon reaching the **Nuovi Scavi** (new excavations begun in 1911 yet largely untouched to the north), there are a number of small businesses such as the **Fullonica di Stefano** (Stefano's Laundry), **Thermopolia** (inns serving hot food and drink), and the **Bottega del Fruttivendolo Felix** (Shop of Felix the Fruit Merchant), with its amusing Bacchic scenes. There are lots of middle-class dwellings along here. The **Casa del Moralista** (House of the Moralist) has a fine loggia and gardens, and the **Casa di Octavio Quartio** (House of Octavius Quartius) has scenes from *The Iliad* and a long marble pool shaded by a pergola. Don't miss the huge **Casa di Giulia Felice** (Villa of Julia Felix) with its extensive gardens and baths.

Towards Porta di Stabia On via Stabia is the main entrance to the sprawling **Casa del Citarista** (House of the Lyre Player), which has a copy of a statue of a wild boar and snarling dogs. Victims were crushed by a shaky peristyle at the **Casa del Menandro** (House of the Menander) along nearby vico Meridionale. It was excavated by celebrated archaeologist Amadeo Maiuri in 1930-1931 and is important for its lavish furnishings, decoration and jewellery, including cluster earrings of gold globes and green semi-precious gems strung on golden thread. Don't miss the painting of the poet Menander and exquisite mosaic flooring in the private *thermae* depicting a bunch of acanthus with a bird and sea creatures including dolphins. A multi-coloured mosaic in the *oecus* shows pygmies punting along the Nile. It's reckoned that the villa was owned by the magistrate and friend of the Empress Poppaea (who liked a milky bath), Nero's second wife.

Theatre district Hellenistic influences between the sixth and second centuries BC feature in the layout and history of the theatre district. The monumental **Foro Triangulare** (Triangular Forum), with its Ionic portico leading to a Doric colonnade and temple, was a venue for religious and athletics events, while the **Palestra Sannitica** (Samnite Palaestra) had a statue of Doryphorous. The **Tempio di Giove Melichios** (Temple of Jupiter Meilichios) was dedicated to a Greek cult as well as Jupiter, Juno and Minerva. Greek-aping turns into the capers of the Egyptian cult of Isis at the **Tempio di Iside** (Temple of Isis) where small bones were found on the main altar. Picture the scene: shaven-headed priests in black robes and men with dog-faced masks performing weird rituals.

The **Teatro Grande** (Large Theatre) had a two-storey Greek-style *scaenae frons* at the back of the stage, with doorways for the thesps and niches with honorary statues, all framed with entablatures and columns. Next door is the **Odeion** (Odeon), a small covered theatre built around 80 BC. The **Caserma dei Gladiatori** (Gladiatorial Barracks) has the Quadriporticus, a large square surrounded by a portico.

Around the amphitheatre and Porta Nocera Welcome shade is provided by the tunnel entrances, porticoes and surrounding trees around the amphitheatre and Great Palaestra. The **Anfiteatro** (Amphitheatre) is an elliptical structure begun around 70 BC and completed around the turn of the new millennium. It's the oldest surviving Roman amphitheatre and an incredible arena to explore, making a fitting climax to a day in

Pompeii. Gladiatorial battles were watched by around 20,000 spectators, seated in three tiers, or *cavea* (sections for different social classes). Roman chronicles and inscriptions found outside the arena, where spectators gathered to eat and chant at the popular inns, attest to the popularity of star gladiators: Felix was the "bear fighter", Thracian Celadus was dubbed "a heart-throb" and Oceanus was the "barmaid's choice". Boisterous rivalry spilled over into hooliganism in AD 59 when Pompeians clashed with rivals from Nuceria. In 1823 tons of volcanic debris was cleared from the site but it was not until the 20th century, under the archaeological eye of Amedeo Maiuri, that it was properly excavated.

The **Palestra Grande** (Great Palaestra) was built under the reign of the state-strengthening Emperor Augustus as a place where the *collegia iuventum* (youngsters) could train body and mind, primarily in preparation for Roman army service. It has a sloping pool that was continually fed water by a lead pipe, and the 141 x 107 m area is enclosed on three sides by a handsome portico. Stucco reliefs found here depict Dionysus as a wrestler and an athlete resting on an exercise hoop. Rows of plane trees have been planted recently to recreate the layout of AD 79.

In 1961, 13 victims of the eruption were revealed near the Porta Nocera, at the **Orto dei Fuggiaschi** (Garden of the Fugitives).

Suburban villas and baths

Outside the city walls, at Porta Marina, erotic artworks were recently exposed in the **Terme Suburbane** (Suburban Baths). Built in the first century BC, the multi-storey complex was the only unisex baths in Pompeii and probably had a brothel on the top floor. It has mosaics and stuccoed cherubs. Nearby, the **Villa Imperiale** has frescoed rooms splashed in Pompeian red.

The via dei Sepolcri, outside Porta Ercolano, is lined with tombs and leads to two opulent residences. The **Villa di Diomede** (Villa of Diomedes) had the largest garden in Pompeii. During the excavations in the late 1700s, 18 skeletons of unlucky souls who tried to escape were found in the vaulted cellar. The **Villa dei Misteri** (Villa of Mysteries) has a colourful history: this sumptuous pile was turned into a large winery but it's the Dionysian Cycle in the so-called Hall of Mysteries – nine scenes from a ritual dedicated to the Greek god of wine and revelry, Dionysus – that really captures the imagination. Although outlawed by Rome, the cult thrived further south in this Hellenistic region and perhaps explains some of those exuberant Neapolitan traits.

Modern Pompei → *For listings, see pages 95-96.*

Modern Pompei (as opposed to the architectural site Pompeii) has nondescript shopping streets fanning out from piazza B Longo, which has four patches of grass interspersed with a fountain, palm trees and benches. The focal point is the impressively flamboyant pilgrimage shrine dedicated to the Madonna of the Rosary, **Santuario della Madonna del Rosario** ① *piazza B Longo 1, T081-857 7111, www.santuario.it, May-Oct daily 0900-1300, 1530-1830, Nov-Apr Mon-Fri 1500-1700, Sat-Sun 0900-1300, free,* built in the late 19th century. Weekend and festival services are particularly worth attending, when you can inhale much Neapolitan piety and incense amid atmospheric surroundings.

Oplontis – Villa di Poppaea

① *Via Sepolcri, Torre Annunziata, T081-862 1755, www.pompeiisites.org. Circumvesuviana railway to Torre Annunziata. Turn left at the front of the station and walk for 5 mins.*

Villa di Poppaea is a large and lavish suburban Roman villa at Oplontis, near the port of Torre Annunziata, around 7 km from Pompei and 20 km southeast of Naples. It's reckoned that Nero's second wife Poppaea Sabina lived here. *Trompe l'œil* architectural details and lively landscape scenes filled with birds, butterflies, theatre players and fruits of the land fill the atrium, *triclinium*, *caldarium* and gardens. Bodies, gold jewellery, coins and statues were found crammed in the storeroom, making it likely that the villa was being restored at the time of the AD 79 eruption.

Boscoreale

① *Antiquarium Nazionale Uomo e Ambiente nel Territorio Vesuviano, via Settetermini 15, Località Villaregina, T081-857 5347, www.pompeiisites.org. Circumvesuviana railway to Boscotrecase, then shuttle bus to Villa Regina.*

Once a rural hamlet and Pompeian suburb, Boscoreale is located to the north of Pompei on the slopes of Vesuvius. It's worth seeking out for its archaeological museum which houses finds from the area's working Roman villas. Exhibits bring the workings of a Roman farm to life, and a visit to **Villa Regina**, with its vineyards, *torcularium* (grape press) and wine cellar, is a must for vino quaffers. Fabulous frescoes and a hoard of silver were discovered in the 1800s at two nearby villas, the **Villa di Pisanella** and **Villa di Publius Fannius Synistor**. Their treasures can be seen in the Archaeological Museum in Naples, the Louvre in Paris and the Metropolitan Museum of Art in New York.

Stabiae (Scavi di Stabia)

① *Via Passeggiata Archeologica, Castellammare di Stabia, T081-871 4541, www.pompeiisites. org. Circumvesuviana railway to Castellamare or via Nocera then red No 1 bus.*

Castellammare di Stabia, a spa town with shipbuilding traditions, is 33 km southeast of Naples and marks the start of the Sorrentine Peninsula. Its excavated Roman villas and *antiquarium* (museum) are currently being transformed by one of the largest archaeological projects in Europe since the Second World War. The plan is to create a 60-ha Stabiae archaeological park that will encompass the four villas already discovered at Roman Stabiae, which were excavated in the 18th century and from the 1950s onwards. Named after a wall painting of the mythological Ariadne found asleep by Dionysus, the **Villa di Ariana** ① *via Piana di Varano, T081-274200*, is just outside the modern town at Varano. Nearby is the **Villa di San Marco** ① *via Passeggiata Archeologica, T081-871 4541*, a wealthy residence with frescoes, stucco work and the remains of a swimming pool. The walk is well worth it for the views alone and you may even be lucky to glimpse ancient treasures coming to light.

Pompeii and around listings

For hotel and restaurant price codes and other relevant information, see pages 14-17.

🛏 Where to stay

Pompeii and around *p86*

€€€ Crowne Plaza Stabiae, SS145 Sorrentina, Località Pozzano, 80053 Castellammare di Stabia, T081-394 6700, www.ichotelsgroup.com. This former factory building has strangely alluring modernist shapes. Stylish accommodation, a choice of indoor and outdoor pools, and a private beach make this hotel far more glamorous than its industrial origins would suggest. The 157 rooms have clean contemporary lines and some have terraces with stunning views of the bay of Naples. There is one obvious downside: unless you have a car you'll have to rely on the free shuttle bus to Vico Equense and the train station.

€€ Hotel Forum, via Roma 99, 80045 Pompei, T081-850 1170, www.hotelforum.it. The **Forum** offers good value near the piazza Anfiteatro, the modern town and Santuario. The best of the 36 guest rooms are in the new wing, which have smart modern bathrooms and better soundproofing than the other rooms. Buffet breakfast is served in a leafy garden.

€€ Hotel Santa Caterina, via Vittorio Emanuele 4, Pompei, T081-856 7494, www.hotelsantacaterinapompei.com. Conveniently located on via Roma opposite the entrance to the ruins, this pleasant hotel has 20 cosy guest rooms in which Pompeian red hues and classical paintings abound. There are impressive views of either Vesuvius or the amphitheatre from some rooms while another 2 have been customized for disabled access. The English-speaking staff are helpful and there's free parking.

€ Hotel Diana, Vico Sant'Abbondio 10, 80045 Pompei, T081-863 1264, www.pompeihotel.com. This modern and well-run hotel is near the Pompei Scavi, Santuario

and town amenities. Expect good service and immaculate, brightly decorated rooms in various sizes to suit most needs, even if the bathrooms are a little on the small size. Facilities include a laundry and dry-cleaning service, while the garden filled with citrus and palm trees is a considerable bonus.

🍴 Restaurants

Pompeii and around *p86*

€€€ Il Principe, piazza Bartolo Longo 8, Pompei, T081-850 5566, www.ilprincipe.com. Tue-Sat 1200-1500, 1945-2230, Sun 1200-1500. Ancient Roman recipes with multi-ethnic origins (especially Arabic, African and Greek) dominate the menu at this large restaurant brimming with Pompeian design. Some courses have culinary antecedents from Roman times, including the *garum pompeianum*, a piquant anchovy-based sauce served with pasta. Other inventive creations include *arselle con scampi su timballo di riso selvatico*: clams and scampi with wild rice.

€€€ President, piazza Schettino 12, Pompei, T081-850 7245, www.ristorantepresident.com. Tue-Sun 1200-1500, 1930-2330. Il **President**'s elegant rooms often host themed evenings with historic culinary creations served from ancient times to the Bourbon era. Their *la cucina povera napoletana extravaganza* sees tiny 17th-century-style Neapolitan pizzas on the menu. They also organize candlelit walks around the ancient city – check the website for details of all their latest gastronomic events. Reservations recommended.

€€ Add'u Mimi, via Roma 61, Pompei, T081-863 5451. Sat-Thu 1200-1500, 1930-2300. This is a relaxing place to eat near the centre of modern Pompeii, serving good-value food, although service is often charmless and portions are not generous, so you will probably need a few courses. They serve salads and pizzas for veggies and tasty seafood pasta dishes.

Cafés and bars

Caffè Spagnolo, via Giuseppe Mazzini 45, Castellammare di Stabia, T081-871 1272. Thu-Tue 0800-2200. A *stile-Liberty* (Italian art nouveau) gem near Roman Stabiae at Castellammare di Stabia. The surroundings are handsome and everything is top quality, from the coffee and pastries to the focaccia and ice cream.

De Vivo, via Roma 36/38, Pompei, T081-863 1163. Daily 0730-2200. This *gelateria-pasticceria* on via Roma does savoury snacks including panini, a range of *gelati*, *sorbetti* and *semifreddi*, as well as sweet creations including *sfogliatelle*, *pastiera* and *Babà al limoncello*.

🛍 Shopping

Pompeii and around *p86*
Food and drink

Melius, via Lepanto 156, Pompei. Daily 0800-1300, 1600-2100. A fabulous deli with home-made meals as well as cheeses and salame to fill your panini bought from the *paneficio* (bakery) next door. Great too for food and wine to take home.

Mirto, via Lepanto 142, Pompei. Daily 0830-2000. A decent supermarket in the modern town – useful for picnic products and food to take home.

Photographic supplies

Foto Shop, via Sacra, Pompei, T081-850 7816. A handy shop for camera equipment.

🎯 What to do

Pompeii and around *p86*
Cultural

Itinera, corso Vittorio Emanuele 663, Naples, T081-664545, www.itineranapoli.com. Metro to corso V Emanuele. Friendly, English-speaking Francesca del Vecchio organizes trips around the Vesuvian sights.
Ufficio Scavi, Villa dei Misteri 2, T081-857 5347, www.pompeiisites.org. For details

about guided tours, themed adventures and latest access to restricted areas around the *scavi* (restorations), contact this office.

Wellbeing

Terme di Stabia, viale delle Terme 3/5, Castellammare di Stabia, T081-391 3111, www.termedistabia.com. Daily 0900-1900. Alas concrete and crazy paving covers most of the ancient baths here but the complex does still provide mineral waters with curative properties, a Centro Benessere offering spa beauty treatments and medical programmes for sports injuries.

🚇 Transport

Pompeii and around *p86*
Pompei Scavi-Villa dei Misteri Frequent Circumvesuviana train services to **Napoli** (35 mins), **Torre Annunziata-Oplonti** (5 mins), **Castellammare di Stabia** (10 mins), **Ercolano** (20 mins) and **Sorrento** (30 mins).

Torre Annunziata-Oplonti Frequent Circumvesuviana train services to **Napoli** (30 mins), **Castellammare di Stabia** (15 mins), **Pompei** (10 mins), **Ercolano** (20 mins) and **Sorrento** (35 mins).

Castellammare di Stabia Frequent Circumvesuviana train services to **Napoli** (45 mins), **Pompei** (10 mins), **Torre Annunziata-Oplonti** (15 mins), **Ercolano** (30 mins) and **Sorrento** (20 mins).

ℹ Directory

Pompeii and around *p86*
Medical services Hospital Pronto Soccorso, via Colle San Bartolomeo 50, T081-535 9111. Farmacia Pompeiana, via Roma 12, Pompei, T081-850 7264.
Money Banca Monte dei Paschi di Siena, piazza Longo B40, T081-863 6511 (ATM).
Post office Piazza Esedra 3, T081-536 5200 (Mon-Fri 0800-1330, Sat 0800-1230).

The Islands

The islands of the Bay of Naples all have their own unique fascination. Capri, *L'Isola Azzurra* (the Blue Island), parades the most glamour and dizzying beauty in its 10 sq km. Emperor Augustus was so smitten with its limestone coves and plunging cliffs that he swapped it for Ischia, which is nearly five times larger. His successor Tiberius ruled the empire from his Caprese villas, and according to some Roman accounts had a knee-tremblingly good and dastardly time. Lavish lifestyles, illustrious visitors, and the jet-set entourage followed.

Capri has a magical lustre but Ischia and Procida are no bogus rocks. The Campi Flegrei volcano system plopped these islands into the sea farther west – they share the geology and earthy characteristics of Naples while limestone love child Capri was chipped off the shoulder of the Sorrentine Peninsula. Ischia, L'Isola Verde (the Green Island), still vents its vulcanism at its thermal springs and spa resorts. There are some fine sandy beaches and varied landscapes (including a dead volcano or two) and microclimates that allow subtropical species to thrive.

You can get around cute Procida and its 4 sq km in no time; its charm is its intimacy, down-to-earth feel and picturesque sights, including pastel-coloured fishing villages, rolling lanes lined with market gardens and a half-dozen beaches.

Capri

Capri is just 5 km from Punta della Campanella on the Sorrentine Peninsula. Despite the invasion of day-trippers who throng its boutique-lined lanes and cram its cute orange buses, Capri still has that special allure, particularly in its gorgeous hidden bays beloved of emperors and film stars, and along its tranquil, flower-strewn paths. Out of season, and after the last boat to Naples has departed, you almost feel part of the privileged Capri set. Its chic epicentre is Capri Town, 142 m above sea level and 3 km by road from the island's main harbour, Marina Grande, which is always abuzz with the weaving and heaving of foaming boats, floppy-hatted tourists and *facchini* (porters). Anacapri, 3 km to the west by road, is less self-consciously exclusive and has a friendlier feel. The single-seat chairlift ride to Monte Solaro is a magical, must-do experience – from its summit there are wonderful walks across wild country.

Arriving on Capri

Getting there and around
Capri is just 6 km by 3 km and traffic is restricted so forget about using a car. Ferries from Naples and elsewhere arrive at Marina Grande. To reach Capri Town take the three-minute funicular ride (€1.80) or hop on a bus. Getting around on the tiny orange buses run by **SIPPC** ⓘ *T081-937 0420*, and **Staiano Autotrasporti** ⓘ *T081-837 1544*, is fun and exhilarating as you hurtle around hairpin bends and contemplate dizzying chasms. There are frequent services between Marina Grande, Capri Town, Marina Piccola, Anacapri, Damecuta, Faro, and the Grott'Azzurra; prices from €1.80 for a single bus ride to €8.60 for a day pass allowing unlimited bus travel and two funicular rides. ⏩ *See Transport, page 105.*

Tourist information
AASCT Capri ⓘ *piazzetta Cerio, Capri Town, T081-837 5308, www.capritourism.com.*

Capri Town → *For listings, see pages 102-105.*

Capri Town sits in a lush bowl between the limestone cliffs of Monte Solaro and Punta del Capo. Known as *La Piazzetta* (the little square), piazza Umberto I is the intimate and chic social hub of Capri Town and the island. Anyone and everyone over the past two centuries has sat at one of the cafés here, plonking their feet on the flagstones and glancing intermittently over a newspaper to do some people-watching – you never know who will walk by. It must have been a less pricey pleasure, though, for the likes of Dickens, Greene, Gorky and Lenin.

Gaze beyond the entertaining ebb and flow and you'll see the **Torre dell'Orologio** (clock tower), with its majolica-tiled clock face; the **Municipio** (town hall); the Baroque **Chiesa di Santo Stefano** (with fragments of Roman flooring from Emperor Tiberius's Villa Jovis); and **Palazzo Cerio** ① *T081-837 6218, Tue-Wed, Fri-Sat 1000-1300, Thu 1500-1900*, which has natural history collections amassed by naturalist and physician Ignazio Cerio.

A maze of medieval *vicoli* (alleyways) fans out from the Piazzetta. Via Madre Serafina, an atmospheric arcaded street, follows the town's old ramparts. Between the whitewashed buildings light-wells offer glimpses of flowery terraces. The locals would pour hot oil through the holes onto invading Saracen pirates. Via Lungano and Capri's main via Vittorio Emanuele III are lined with boutiques, bars, *pasticcerie* and glitzy hotels, including **Il Quisisana** (meaning 'here one heals'), originally a 19th-century sanatorium founded by a Scottish doctor.

Certosa di San Giacomo

① *Via Certosa, T081-837 6218. Tue-Sun 0900-1400, free.*

The Charterhouse, a 14th-century Carthusian monastery dedicated to the apostle Giacomo (James), is located southeast of the Piazzetta. The monks have long since packed their habits, but the serene atmosphere, sombre architecture and verdant gardens makes it worth the walk here. It's rather run down but there are things to see: two cloisters, a church, panoramic terraces and the intriguing refectory museum that contains Roman statues recovered from the Grotta Azzurra and haunting paintings by the German painter, Wilhelm Diefenbach.

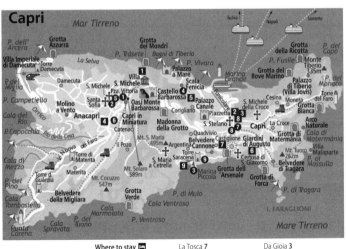

Where to stay 🛏	La Tosca 7	Da Gioia 3
Caesar Augustus 1	Stella Maris 8	Da Paolino 4
Caprihouse 2	Weber Ambassador 9	Il Solitario 5
Casa Malua 3		La Rondinella 6
Casa Mariantonia 4	**Restaurants** 🍴	Pasticceria Buonocore 7
JK Place 5	Bar Buchetto 1	Pulalli Wine Bar 8
La Minerva 6	Caffè Michelangelo 2	Torre Saracena 9

400 metres
400 yards

Continuing on via Giacomo Matteotti you come to the **Giardini di Augusto** (Gardens of Augustus), a vibrant profusion of flowers and vegetation with jowl-dropping terrace views to die for – just mind the chasm.

Belvedere Cannone

From the Piazzetta, follow the via Madre Serafina, linger at the Santa Teresa Church, then climb to the impressive **Castiglione** (a sprawling €40 million villa beloved of wealthy pop stars and celebrities). Steps lead to the belvedere that looks over the Faraglioni rocks, the Charterhouse, the Grotta delle Felci (where Bronze Age artefacts were found) and down towards the Marina Piccola.

Circular coastal walk from the Piazzetta

Starting at the Piazzetta, take via le Botteghe, then follow via Croce and via Matermania, before following the signs to steps that descend near the breathtaking natural archway, **Arco Naturale**. A path continues to the **Grotta di Matermania** – a cave with a Roman *nymphaeum* and lots of *opus reticulum* bricks. At the craggy outcrop **Punta Masullo** you'll glimpse red-hued **Villa Malaparte** with its trapezoidal staircase and angular shapes: this piece of Italian rationalist architecture was named after its eccentric owner, the writer Curzio Malaparte. It starred alongside Brigitte Bardot in Jean-Luc Godard's 1963 film *Le Mépris*. Climbing up to **Punta Tragara**, there are fabulous views of the Faraglioni and Monacone rocks rising from turquoise waters. Head northwest along leafy via Tragara to return to the Piazzetta. Allow at least three hours to do the entire route.

Villa Jovis and Il Salto di Tiberio

ⓘ *Viale Amedeo Matiuri. Daily 0900 till dusk.*

Villa Jovis, Emperor Tiberius's infamous 7000-sq-m palace from which he ruled the Roman Empire from AD 27 to 37, takes about an hour on foot to reach from Capri Town. Verdant lanes pass by colonnaded gardens (linger at Villa La Moneta at via Tiberio 32), prickly pears, abundant birdlife and lounging lizards. There's not much left of the lavish apartments (although Prime Minister Silvio Berlusconi had plans to allow luxury pads to be built here for him and his mates). Between orgies, gorging and torturing, Tiberius apparently enjoyed spending time in the loggia, with its sublime views, and in the *specularium*, where astrologers gave him the low-down perhaps. Within the site, at Monte Tiberio, there's a rustic church, **Santa Maria del Soccorso**, scene of the **Festa di Santa Maria del Soccorso** (7-8 September), a festival involving morning Mass, music and dance.

Tiberius's Leap, near Villa Jovis, is a 300-m cliff from where the emperor apparently flung his tortured victims. According to the Roman historian Gaius Suetonius Tranquillus, sailors would wait in the sea below to finish off the unfortunates. Suetonius flung a lot of juicy muck in his opus *The Lives of the Twelve Caesars*, and a reputation for perversion, madness and cruelty has certainly stuck to Tiberius.

Anacapri and around → *For listings, see pages 102-105.*

Sitting below Capri's highest point, Monte Solaro, Anacapri – a short bus ride from Capri – has a friendlier, more villagey feel than self-consciously chic Capri Town.

Piazza della Vittoria is always abuzz with buses, taxis, coaches and crowds. Up its steps is the chairlift to Monte Solaro, Villa San Michele and viale Axel Munthe, lined with perfumed boutiques and aristocratic *alberghi*. Anacapri's main lane, via Orlandi, heads past some interesting shops and friendly *chiaccheroni Anacapresi* (local chit-chatters) to an intimate piazza in front of the cheery, yellow-hued Chiesa di Santa Sofia, a favourite meeting place and wedding venue. On the way is the Chiesa di San Michele (with majolica marvels) and Casa Rossa, a building painted in Pompeian red with Moorish detailing, a gallery of Caprese landscape paintings and a courtyard displaying archaeological fragments. Along the craggy northwestern and western coastline are some magical natural and ancient attractions including the ethereal Grotta Azzurra cave and the fort, flora and fauna-studded trail, Il Sentiero dei Fortini (see page 102).

Chiesa San Michele

ⓘ *Piazza San Nicola, Anacapri. Apr-Sep daily 0900-1900, Oct-Mar 1000-1500 generally, €1.*
Built in 1761, the Baroque church has majolica flooring depicting Adam and Eve in a dreamlike scene, viewed from a special gallery. The beguiling small square here is a meeting place for the Anacapresi.

Villa San Michele

ⓘ *Viale Axel Munthe 34, Anacapri, T081-837 1401, www.villasanmichele.eu. Mar 0900-1630, Apr and Oct 0900-1700, May-Sep 0900-1800, Nov-Feb 0900-1530, €7.*
Swedish doctor and writer Axel Munthe (1857-1949) created this idyllic villa with an emphasis on bringing out the island's "light, light everywhere". After assisting the cholera epidemic relief effort in the 1880s, he put down his stethoscope and focused on constructing the villa's buildings and lush garden, with its loggia, pergolas, statues and columns, and a circular viewpoint with the most stunning views across the Gulf of Naples. Run as a museum by the Axel Munthe Foundation, temple-like interiors display Munthe's eclectic collection of art, antiquities, bric-a-brac and personal memorabilia. There are also the remains of a Roman imperial villa. Munthe's *The Story of San Michele*, published in 1929, charts his Caprese love affair and became a worldwide bestseller, drawing many a pilgrim to this enchanting place.

Monte Solaro chairlift

ⓘ *Seggiovia Monte Solaro, via Caposcuro 10, T081-837 1428. Mar-Oct 0930-1730, Nov-Feb 1030-1500, €10 return, €7.50 single, children up to 8 free.*
If you don't fancy the walk, the chairlift offers a quick and easy means of reaching the highest point of the island. Feet dangle over a hiking path weaving through terraced gardens dotted with quirky ornaments and abundant produce, and as you rise to the 600-m summit the craggy ridge, wild parched landscape and shimmering seascapes become ever more spectacular. After 12 minutes you arrive just below the one-bar terrace which is pleasingly slightly run-down. You can spend a couple of hours sitting in a deckchair slurping ice cream and exploring the rough terrain and knee-knocking drops, including the vertiginous cliffs down to Ventroso and limpid blue waters. Just watch your step though. There are lots of walks from here: to Monte Capello, the small church at Cetrella and along the very tricky Passetiello path back to Capri Town (note that the Passetiello has lots of loose rocks and steep scrambles, so should only be tackled with an experienced guide).

Grotta Azzurra

ⓘ *0900 till dusk. Bus or by foot (3 km) from Anacapri, or boat from Marina Grande, then entry to the cave by rowing boat.*

Once filled with statues from Tiberius's Gradola villa, the 'Blue Grotto' and its ethereal light atmospherics were 'rediscovered' in 1826 and turned into a Grand Tour day trip. The lighting effects inside the cave are caused by the refraction of the sun's rays in the waters, lighting the cave from below in an eerie shade of blue. The island's most popular tourist attraction can be approached via a footpath, lift or by boat, with many excursions around the island including a trip to the grotto. Joining the melee of bobbing rowing boats you pay €13 to board one of them and then it's time to duck down while going through the narrow entrance into the cavern beyond. It's usually all over after about five minutes, in which time the oarsmen sing and shout, point at strange rock formations and nudge you for a tip. For the best experience and lighting effects are between 1100 and 1300.

Il Sentiero dei Fortini

Along this stretch of coast there's a fabulous trail, Il Sentiero dei Fortini, which follows the crumbling forts built by Bourbon-backed British troops and enlarged by Napoleonic French after they retook the island in 1808. It passes the scenic ruins of a Roman complex, the **Villa Imperiale Romana di Damecuta**. Walking guide Luigi Esposito of **Capri Trails** ① *T347-368 1699, www.capritrails.com*, reckons, "It's best to walk southwards from the Grotta Azzurra to Faro as the sun and sea are in front of you, whereas going the other way you face the cliffs."

Capri listings

For hotel and restaurant price codes and other relevant information, see pages 14-17.

● Where to stay

Capri *p98, map p99*
€€€€ Caesar Augustus, via G Orlandi 4, Anacapri, T081-837 3395, www.caesar-augustus.com. Within walking distance of Anacapri, 'Cesare Augusto' – as the locals call it – is perched on cliffs, giving it the most spectacular views across the bay. A sprawling lounge with comfy sofas and piano bar looks onto the long terrace where a statue of Emperor Augustus watches the ferry and yacht traffic. Amid its citrus trees and flowers there's an infinity pool, spa and 2 restaurants. A secluded mini-terrace is laid out for candlelit meals served by your own butler. A shuttle service is available to the port and the Piazzetta.
€€€€ JK Place, via Prov Marina Grande 225, near Marina Grande, T081-838 4001, www.jkcapri.com. Capri's first quality inn – the **Hotel Continental** – was housed in this whitewashed 19th-century palazzo. A penthouse and roof terrace have been

added as well as all manner of luxuries including 2 pools (indoor and outdoor), spa facilities, stylish interiors filled with artworks and a sundeck.
€€€ Casa Mariantonia, via G Orlandi 180, Anacapri, T081-837 2923, www.casamariantonia.com. Expect beautifully tiled rooms, spacious suites and apartments with terraces overlooking a lemon grove where a Russian revolutionary allegedly laced his *limone* with vodka. Breakfasts are a little basic but overall this is a gem of a place and the Canale family are charming hosts.
€€€ La Minerva, via Occhio Marino 8, Capri Town, T081-837 7067, www.laminervacapri.com. Top-notch customer service, bright rooms and a tranquil garden setting make this a fine choice near the Capri Town *passeggiata* and Punta Tragara.
€€ Hotel Weber Ambassador, via Marina Piccola 118, Marina Piccola, T081-837 0141, info@hotelweber.com. Many rooms here look out over Marina Piccola's pebbly beaches, restaurants and shapely rocks. Rooms have tiled floors and some have small terraces with sea views. A shuttle service takes guests to and from the

Piazzetta. Table tennis, mountain biking, fishing and various watersports are on offer.

€€ **Stella Maris**, via Roma 27, Capri Town, T081-837 0452, albergostellamaris@libero.it. Up the tiled steps of this *pensione*, opposite the bus station, is a cosy B&B that has been run by the same family for over 25 years now. Expect kitsch decor in the charming lobby-cum-lounge-cum-breakfast room, which hasn't changed much since the late 1980s. The owners have a few apartments dotted around town. Avoid the rooms at the front unless you enjoy the sights and smells of Capri's cute buses.

€ **Hotel La Tosca**, via D Birago 5, Capri Town, T081-837 0989, h.tosca@capri.it. La Tosca is ensconced down a quiet lane and is a short swagger from the Piazzetta. Breakfasts are taken on the flower-filled terrace with views of the Faraglioni rocks. The clean, simple decor throughout extends to the 11 whitewashed guest rooms with their smallish bathrooms.

Self-catering

Renting an apartment or villa on Capri starts at about €100 per night off-season for 2-4 people. A useful list of places to stay can be found at www.capri.com, which includes small apartments such as **Caprihouse** (T328-152 8750, www.caprihouse.it) and **Casa Malua** (T081-837 9577, www.casamalua.it).

❼ Restaurants

Capri *p98, map p99*

€€€€ **Torre Saracena**, via Marina Piccola, T081-837 0646. Apr-Oct daily 1200-1500, Sat 1900-2300. The freshest of seafood – plucked from the day's catch tanks – served on the shore. Favourites include *pezzogna all'acqua pazza* (bream cooked in 'crazy' boiling water) and *zuppa di pesce con scorfano* (fish soup with scorpion fish).

€€€ **Da Gioia**, Marina Piccola, T081-837 7702. May-Oct daily 1200-1500, 1900-2300, rest of year times vary. The magical essence of Caprese dining can be found on this boardwalk platform

overlooking the Marina Piccola shoreline. The Mennillo family's simple Neapolitan classics like *spaghetti ai frutti di mare* (spaghetti with shellfish), pizza and salads, washed down with a Peroni or wine, hit the epicurean spot best when outside, looking over the sea and towards the Fariglioni rocks. Reservations recommended.

€€€ **Da Paolino**, via Palazzo a Mare 11, T081-837 6102. Thu-Tue 1230-1500, 1900-2400. Down a leafy lane on the way to Bagni di Tiberio, amid lemon groves and stray cats, is legendary Paolino's, famed for simply prepared seafood dishes such as *totano con patate* – a special, seasonal type of squid served with potatoes.

€€ **Il Solitario**, via G Orlandi 96, 80071 Anacapri, T081-837 1382, www.trattoria ilsolitario.it. Daily 1200-1500, 1900-2400. Under a pergola near the Santa Sofia church, charming Alessandra and Massimiliano carry on the family tradition started in 1960 when Il Solitario was a tavern for locals. Expect excellent pizzas (try their *pizza bianca*) and wonderful dishes like *calamari alla griglia* (grilled squid), cheese-dream filled *ravioli capresi* and their special *scialatelli pasta* (with some potato in the mix) *alle vongole*. Polish it off with home-made tiramisù.

€€ **La Rondinella**, via G Orlandi 295, 80071 Anacapri, T081-837 1223. Daily 1200-1500, 1900-2300. The *Rondinella* combines flavoursome food, relaxed dining and friendly service down the quiet end of Anacapri's main lane. There's a smallish but wonderful terrace (book it!) and a large dining room. The freshest seafood goes into dishes like *linguine al scampo* and *frittura di gambero e calamaro* (fried prawns and squid).

Cafés and bars

Bar Buchetto, via G Orlandi 38, Anacapri. Daily 0800-2200. Near the bus terminal, ever-reliable **Bar Buchetto**, with charming Michele Scarpato at the helm (70-odd years in the job), delivers *pizza al taglio*, ice cream and refreshments.

Caffè Michelangelo, via Trieste e Trento 1, Anacapri. Daily 0800 till late. The amiable bar staff at this swish bar serve *aperitivi* with *taralli di finocchietto* (savoury biscuits with fennel seeds) on the terrace while you watch the Anacapresi and tourists go by.

Pasticceria Buonocore, Vittorio Emanuele 35, Capri Town, T081-837 7826. Daily 0730-2100. The sweet smell of Buonocore's ice cream cones stays long in the olfactory memory. Its sweet and savoury treats, like lemon-and-almond *caprilù* biscuits and freshly prepared panini, are great for snacks and picnics.

Pulalli Wine Bar, 4 piazza Umberto I, Capri Town. Closed Tue. Up near the clocktower is an intimate terrace bar with views over the piazzetta serving drinks, nibbles and excellent dishes.

Sfizi di Pane, via le Botteghe 4, Capri Town, T081-837 0106. Tue-Sun 0700-1330, 1600-2000. Breaded treats including olive breads, cute and crusty rolls (*bacetti*) and *taralli* biscuits make this a good stop for snacks.

⏴ Entertainment

Capri *p98, map p99*
Nightlife

Anema e Core, via Sella Orta 39/e, Capri Town, T081-837 6461, www.anemaecore. com. Thu-Sat 2100 till late. The cheesiest Caprese night club, where Italian celebrities go cheek to cheek and dressed-up locals quaff cocktails, grin and gyrate to live Italo-latino music, including resident crooner Guido Lembo.

Lanterna Verde, via G Orlandi 1, Anacapri, T081-837 1427, www.lanternaverdecapri.it. Thu-Sat 2200 till late. Piano-bar Italian tunes, rock outfits and live latino sway young and ageing hips at **Hotel San Michele**'s chic nightspot.

✿ Festivals

Capri *p98, map p99*

14 May Procession of San Costanzo, Capri Town. According to legend, Capri's patron saint and protector was washed ashore here on his way back to Constantinople. A colourful procession to Marina Grande sees Capresi shower the garlanded statue with rose petals.

13 Jun Procession of Sant' Antonio, Anacapri. Anacapri's saintly protector is honoured with a colourful ceremony involving lots of flower petals and eating of sweets, followed by a concert in piazza Diaz.

Late Aug to early Sep Settembrata Anacaprese, Anacapri. The town's 4 *quartieri* (districts) pit their wits against each other in gastronomic and other quirky contests.

7-8 Sep Santa Maria del Soccorso, Villa Jovis. The ancient church at Villa Jovis is lit up on the evening of 7 Sep and the following morning a Mass is held in honour of the Virgin Mary. Music making, dancing and feasting follow.

✪ Shopping

Capri *p98, map p99*
Ceramics

Cose di Capri, via G Orlandi 50/a, Anacapri, T081-838 2111. Interesting ceramics in unusual colours and shapes made by Vittoria Staiano.

Clothing

100% Capri, via Fuorlovado 27-44, Capri Town, T081-837 7561. Quality luxuries such as fine cotton beach robes and scented candles fill this oh-so-white outlet.

Canfora, via Camerelle 3, Capri Town, T081-837 0487. Historic **Canfora** makes quality leather sandals in lots of colours.

Food and drink

Fairly cheap, basic picnic ingredients can be gathered at **Supermarket Al** (via Pagliaro 19,

Capri Town, and Anacapri) and **Deco** (via Matermania 1, Capri Town).

La Capannina Più, via le Botteghe 39, Capri Town, T081-837 8899. The posh restaurant's *enoteca* and gourmet shop has lots of wines and food for that very special picnic.

Limoncello di Capri, via Roma 79, Capri Town, T081-837 5561; via Capodimonte 27, Anacapri, T081-837 2927. Many places claim to have invented the syrupy *digestivo*, but the story that this family's first brew oiled the constitution of Russian revolutionary guests is hard not to like.

Perfumery

Carthusia Profumi, via Camerelle 10, Capri Town, T081-837 0368; via Capodimonte 26, Anacapri, T081-837 3668. Carthusia does famous scents – first created by monks and made from the fruit and flora of Capri – and gorgeous packaging.

⚫ What to do

Capri *p98, map p99*
Boat trips
Giovanni Aprea, T347-475 7277 (mobile), www.aprea.it. Giovanni Aprea takes groups around Capri's bays and grottoes in his mildly souped-up Sorrentine *gozzo* sailing boat from €40.

Gruppo Motoscafisti, via Provinciale Marina Grande 282, T081-837 7714/5648, www.motoscafisticapri.com. Capri must be experienced from the sea. Pack a picnic and hire a boat or join one of the many boat trips offered by the Società Cooperativa Motoscafisti – their distinctive wooden kiosk and fleet can be found at Marina Grande. Classic excursions include tours of the island, through the Fariglione di Mezzo and into the Grotta Verde, from €17 for a 2-hr trip.

Diving

Capri Sea Service, C Colombo 64, Marina Grande, T081-837 8781, T328-721 2920 (mobile), www.capriseaservice.com.

Scuba-diving courses, boat tours and rentals around Capri.

Sports

Capri Sporting Club, via G Orlandi 10, Anacapri, T081-837 2612, www.capri sportingclub.net. Tennis courts and *calcetto* (5-a-side) footie pitches in a spectacular setting.

Walking

Capri Trails, T081-837 5933, T3473-681699 (mobile), www.capritrails.com. Luigi Esposito takes walking tours, kayaking adventures and climbing on the cliffs near Faro (€30 per hr, €180 per day).

Wellbeing

Capri Palace, via Capodimonte 14, Anacapri, T081-978 0505, www.capripalace.com. Mar-Nov 0900-1300, 1600-2000. Specialist medical spa and beauty treatments in the most luxurious surroundings.

⊖ Transport

Capri *p98, map p99*
Boat Ferries, TMVs and hydrofoils go to **Naples**, **Ischia**, **Positano**, **Sorrento** and **Salerno**. Journey times 35-80 mins. Seasonal timetables apply.

Taxis Taxis (Capri T081-837 0543, Anacapri T081-837 1175) are very pricey, especially the open-topped vintage vehicles.

ⓘ Directory

Capri *p98, map p99*
Medical services ASL Na 5 Guardia Medica, piazza Umberto I 1, Capri Town, T081-837 5716. **Farmacia Internazionale**, via Roma 24, Capri Town, T081-837 0485. **Money** Banca di Roma, piazza Umberto I 19, Capri Town, T081-837 5942 (ATM). **Post office** Via Roma 50, Capri Town, T081-837 5829 (Mon-Fri 0800-1630, Sat 0800-1230).

Ischia

Ischia's dead volcanoes, steamy thermal fissures and curvaceous craters are evidence of its Campi Flegrei caldera origins. Follow in the sandal-steps of Greeks, Romans and today's ubiquitous German holidaymakers at one of Ischia's popular spa resorts. There are 67 fumaroles (volcanic vents) and a hundred-plus thermal springs across the island; the island's longest and most coveted stretch of volcanic sand, La Spiaggia dei Maronti, is dotted with them. Away from the swanky spas and bulging bathrobes are hilltop villages and exotic gardens sheltered by the shapely tufa-rock topped Mont Epomeo, an extinct volcano reachable on foot or donkey.

Arriving on Ischia

Getting there and around
Ferries from Naples (21 km), Pozzuoli (11 km) and elsewhere arrive at Porto d'Ischia. A system of 19 bus routes run by **SEPSA** ① *T081-991 1808*, circles the island in clockwise and anti-clockwise directions: the CD (Circolare Destra) goes clockwise and the CS (Circolare Sinistra) goes anticlockwise. Unico Ischia tickets (€1.90) allow 90 minutes of travel. If you are here for over a week, car hire is an option. Companies include: **Di Meglio** ① *T081-995222, www.ischia-rentacar.it*, and **Mazzella** ① *T081-991141, www.mazzellarent.it*. To see the island in comfort contact **Giuseppe Lauro** ① *T339-4052691, www.ischiataxiservice.com*.

Tourist information
AACST Ischia ① *via Sogliuzzo72, Ischia, T081-507 4211, www.infoischiaprocida.it*.

Ischia Porto and Ischia Ponte → *For listings, see pages 110-112.*

A volcanic crater was transformed into the island's main harbour, Ischia Porto, by Bourbon King Ferdinand II in 1854. The Riva Destra, along its right bank is lined with yachts and fishing boats, and popular bars and restaurants spill out onto the pitted flagstones of its quayside. Ischia's main shopping drag (via Pontano, corso Vittoria Colonna and then via Roma), known as *il corso* by the locals, connects the port with the medieval town Ischia Ponte via a 228-m-long causeway. A few sandy beaches lie to the east: Spiaggia dei Pescatori, Lido d'Ischia and the public beach, Spiaggia San Pietro e della Marina. Ischia Ponte's fortifications were first laid down in the fifth century BC and today's structure is due to the House of Aragon, hence the name Castello Aragonese.

Castello di Ischia
① *Piazzale Aragonese, Ischia Ponte, T081-992 834, www.castellodischia.it. Mar-Oct 0930-1700, €10.*

The first fortress here was built by Syracusan Greeks in 474 BC and the present towering citadel and bridge (more like a causeway these days) was begun by Alfonso of Aragon in the 1440s. Attacked by Romans, Arabs, Normans, Swabians, French and English, it was not only the strategic stronghold of the island but also a vital place of refuge for the locals. A fairytale romance is also attached to the castle: in the 1500s it became the home of the poet-princess Vittoria Colonna, who married Ferrante d'Avalos here then later became the platonic sweetheart of Michelangelo. Amid its maze of stone steps and higgledy-piggledy structures, there are atmospheric churches, spaces with art exhibitions and some creepy corners. The **Convento delle Clarisse** has the macabre sight of a ring of stone seating, where nuns were laid to rest and decompose, the fluids collected in vases beneath before their skeletons joined their sisters in the Ossarium. Other highlights of the citadel are the museum of torture instruments and the tall 15th-century tunnel.

Museo del Mare
ⓘ *Palazzo dell'Orologio, via Giovanni da Procida 3, Ischia Ponte, T081-981124, www.museodelmareischia.it. Apr-Jun 1030-1230, 1500-1900, Jul-Aug 1030-1230, 1830-2200, Nov-Mar 1030-1230, closed Feb, €5.*

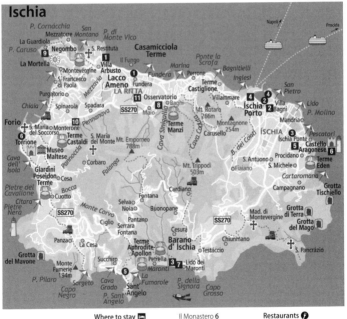

Ischia

Where to stay 🛏
Albergo della
 Regina Isabella 1
Aragona Palace 2
Camping Mirage 3
Continental Mare 4
Europa 5

Il Monastero 6
Parco Smeraldo Terme 7
Pera di Basso 8
Villa Caruso 9
Villa Olivia 10
Villa Serena 11

Restaurants 🍴
Al Triangolo 1
Bar Ciccio 2
Bar Pasticceria Calise 3
Mezzanotte 4
Neptunus 5
Umberto a Mare 6

800 metres
800 yards

Natural beauty spots off the beaten track

La Scarrupata A picturesque beach with chunky *ciottoli* (pebbles) that stretches from Punta San Pancrazio to Capo Grosso in the southeastern corner of the island. Spectacular layers of volcanic debris can be seen along this stretch of the Barano coastline, which is accessed via a path from Barano d'Ischia or by chartering a boat.

I Frassitelli a La Falanga These wild chestnut and acacia woods on the slopes of Monte Epomeo are criss-crossed with trails, where you may encounter the island's wild rabbits and abundant birdlife, including falcons. Like the locals who fled invasions and epidemics, you can live on nuts, mushrooms and berries and explore their ingenious stone dwellings hewn out of the volcanic tufa stone as well as colossal basins to store water and ice.

Spiagge di San Pancrazio e Sorgeto The stunning rocky southeastern coastline around the intimate and isolated San Pancrazio beach is reachable only by boat. Honey-coloured tufa rock cliffs are pocked with marine caves popular with snorkellers. A seafood restaurant and bar is open here in the summer.

Spiaggia dei Maronti In the southwestern corner of the island, just 2 km up the coastal road from Sant'Angelo, is one of Ischia's most beautiful beach hot spots – although it's volcanic thermal waters and steamy vents seldom scorch a non-Italian culo. Its balmy pebbles and pools are accessed via a long set of steps near Panza or else by taking a boat from Sant'Angelo for a few euros. After a dip in the clear waters, take care not to burn your backside on the hot rocks. When tides are low, its tepid waters make it popular with winter skinny-dippers.

Approaching the Aragonese citadel you come to the attractive Palazzo dell'Orologio which houses the Museum of the Sea. The engaging collection is awash with maritime curios, nautical instruments, fishermen's tackle, marine creatures, Marconi's radio equipment and intriguing archaeological finds.

Torre di Michelangelo and Baia di Cartaromana

ⓘ *Torre di Guevara, via Nuova Cartaromana, T081-333 1146. Tue-Sun, times vary, free.*

The fine sands of the Cartaromana Bay have thermal spring waters and are backed by a rectangular tower, the Torre di Guevara, also known as Michelangelo's Tower. The story goes that Michelangelo stayed here and had a relationship with the poetess Vittoria Collana, who resided in the Aragonese castle over the water, spawning the romantic myth that a secret tunnel connecting the two castles enabled hush-hush rendezvous. The tower is now a cultural centre with occasional art shows.

Around the island → *For listings, see pages 110-112.*

Casamicciola Terme

This popular spa resort 6 km northwest of Ischia Porto is renowned for its 85°C iodine-rich springs. Inventive Iron Age inhabitants tapped into the area's vulcanism for cooking and pottery. In 1883 an earthquake decimated the village. The European aristocracy flocked to its spas on piazza Bagni in the 18th and 19th centuries and many offer state-of-the-art facilities today. Casamicciola Terme's beaches may have some fine grains of sand but they can get mighty busy in the summer and are not the island's most picturesque.

Lacco Ameno

More laid-back than Casamicciola Terme, Lacco Ameno has the most naturally radioactive waters in Italy, with alleged curative powers. The first colony of Neapolitan Magna Graecia was established here at Monte Vico before one too many earth tremors persuaded them to set sail to nearby Cumae and Megaride. The sleepy fishing village was transformed in the 1950s into an exclusive spa resort. Among its famous spa establishments today are the **Hotel Regina Elisabetta** on piazza Santa Restituta and the exclusive **Negombo** resort just out of town. Lacco Ameno's logo is the mushroom-shaped volcanic rock offshore, known as *il fungo*.

The local archaeological museum, **Museo Civico Archeologico di Pithecusae** ① *corso Angelo Rizzoli, T081-900356, Tue-Sun 0930-1300, 1600-2000, €5, free with Artecard*, is housed in the 18th-century Villa Arbusto. It contains Roman tombs, geological exhibits and archaeological finds including the Coppa di Nestore (Nestor's Cup), a terracotta *kotyle* made in 700 BC on Rhodes and found in the tomb of a child in 1995. Further reminders of Lacco Ameno's past can be found in the **Sanctuary and Church of Santa Restituta** ① *piazza Santa Restituta 1, T081-980706*. Next to the pink-hued church is a museum with archaeological finds (don't miss the Egyptian amulets in the form of beetles) and subterranean Graeco-Roman ruins.

Giardini La Mortella

① *Località Zaro, T081-986220, www.lamortella.it. Apr-Oct Tue, Thu, Sat, Sun 0900-1900, €12 plus concessions. Take the SS Forio–Lacco Ameno, towards Chiaia.*

The brainchild of garden architect Russell Page, Argentinian Susana Walton and composer English composer William Walton, La Mortella offers a dreamlike garden experience, with fountains, lily ponds, zen water features and subtropical species that thrive in this microclimate beneath the lava flows of Monte Zaro. Pavilions, temples and a tea room add contemplative English and Eastern atmospheres. Check online for details of their programme of spring and autumn chamber recitals and **Summer Festival of Youth Orchestras**.

Forio

The port and town of Forio, on Ischia's western coast, has traditionally been the island's home of winemaking and fishing. From the 1950s to 1970s it became an enclave for artistic types like poet Pablo Neruda and writer-directors Luchino Visconti and Pier Paolo Pasolini. Germans especially enjoy its scenic ramparts and towers. The rotund watchtower that dominates the Forio skyline is home to the **Museo Civico** ① *via del Torrione, T081-333 2934*, with exhibits relating to Neapolitan song, artworks (lots by landscapist local hero Giovanni Maltese) and temporary exhibitions.

The elegantly outlined **Santuario della Madonna del Soccorso** ① *via del Soccorso*, is a whitewashed church with majolica-tiled flourishes. Its terrace is the perfect place to watch the setting sun. To the north is the picturesque Spiaggia di San Francesco, with its coarse sand, and beyond it the rocky promontory Punta Caruso. Long and scruffy (but popular) Spiaggia Citara lies to the south of the town, backed by the beach-front gardens of the **Parco Termale Giardini di Poseidon** ① *T081-907122*, one of the most attractive spas.

Panza, Sant'Angelo and Lido di Maronti

Panza, with its restaurants, roadside bustle and joyously yellow San Leonardo church runs into **Sant'Angelo**, the island's most appealing village, which looks over a harbour with a mound-like islet connected by a sandy isthmus. It's a sublime place to saunter, shop, eat alfresco and visit the beach **Lido di Maronti**, reached by water taxi in five minutes.

This 2-km-long stretch of beach formed from volcanic sand and studded with steaming fumaroles, has some relaxing bar-restaurants. Close to this *spiaggia calda* (hot beach) is the Roman spa resort of **Cava Scura**. For a tad more exertion trek to Ischia's highest point, **Monte Epomeo**, for a scramble over smooth tufa rocks and gasp at some stunning views.

Ischia listings

For hotel and restaurant price codes and other relevant information, see pages 14-17.

😑 Where to stay

Ischia *p106, map p107*
€€€€ Albergo della Regina Isabella, piazza Santa Restituta 1, Lacco Ameno, T081-994322, www.reginaisabella.it. Set up by the legendary film producer Angelo Rizzoli, this luxury hotel retains some 1950s lustre. Spacious suites have terraces overlooking shore-side pools. Spa facilities and treatments are excellent, but not quite up there with **Terme Manzi**, see page 112.
€€€ Aragona Palace Hotel, via Porto 12, Ischia Porto, T081-333 1229, www.hotel aragona.it. Comfort and location – it's right on the Riva Destra with its harbourside restaurants – make this a popular choice. Many of the spacious, blue-tiled rooms have terraces with harbour views. Facilities include a smart spa offering treatments.
€€€ Hotel Parco Smeraldo Terme, Spiaggia dei Maronti, Barano d'Ischia, T081-990127, www.hotelparcosmeraldo.com. The bright, cheery and airy hotel is well situated on Maronti beach and many of the 64 rooms have sea views and balconies. Relax in the hotel's subtropical gardens or its wellness centre (with 2 pools and spa treatments) or hit some balls on the tennis court. Most beach facilities are included and there's a choice of restaurants along the volcanic sands.
€€ Albergo Il Monastero, Castello Aragonese, Ischia Ponte, T081-992435, www.albergoilmonastero.it. Atmosphere and stylish understated interiors make this hotel, housed in the former Convent of Santa Maria della Consolazione within the Castello Aragonese, a special place to stay. Room 21

has a balcony with stunning views of the Chiesa dell'Immacolata and beyond. Their café also serves delicious pastries and looks over the Baia di Sant' Anna.
€€ Hotel Continental Mare, via B Cossa 25, Ischia, T081-982577, www.continentalmare.it. Whitewashed walls and tiles throughout give this sprawling clifftop hotel a clean fresh feel. Head waiter Luigi is the embodiment of efficiency. There are 2 pools –a thermal pool within the leafy grounds and a larger pool on an upper terrace. Down some stone steps is a pebbly beach, which alas is not ideal for swimming. Most rooms have small outdoor terraces. Spa treatments are offered at their sister hotel, **Continental Terme**.
€ Hotel Europa, via A Sogliuzzo 25, Ischia Ponte, T081-991427, www.hoteleuropa ischia.it. The **Europa** has been run by the same family since the 1950s and is near to Ischia Ponte's historic quarter and Ischia Porto's restaurants, with lots of shops in between. There are 34 reasonably priced rooms with tiled floors and unfussy decor. The hotel provides a thermal pool and spa treatments and organizes excursions and boat trips.
€ Villa Serena, via Calata S Antonio 8, Casamiciola Terme, T081-994738, www.hotel villasirena.eu. A solid budget choice with spa pools, colourful tiles aplenty and a homely restaurant. Warm hospitality and green, quiet surroundings.

Camping
Camping Mirage, Spiaggia dei Maronti, Barano d'Ischia, T081-990551, www.camping mirage.it. €31 for a small tent and 2 people. This typically dusty Italian campsite is right next to Maronti beach and has the usual campsite basics including washing facilities and a no-frills bar-restaurant.

Self-catering

Pera di Basso, via Pera di Basso (loc Rarone), T081-900122, www.peradibasso.it. Deep in the woods above Casamicciola Terme, this stone farm building has comfortable accommodation and offers tranquillity and outdoor pursuits including trekking and mountain biking. The suite for 2 costs from €130 per night half-board. The most basic studio apartment at **Villa Olivia** (via Baiola 129, Forio, T081-998426, www.villaolivia.it), which has gardens and 2 pools, starts at €350 per week for 2 people, with various options for different-sized parties. At the other end of the scale is the luxurious **Villa Caruso** (Ville in Italia, T055-412058, www.villeinitalia.com/houses/puntacaruso.jsp), in Forio, which sleeps up to 18, will set you back over €12,000 for a week.

⑦ Restaurants

Ischia *p106, map p107*
€€€ Umberto a Mare, via Soccorso 2, Forio, T081-997171, www.umbertoamare.it. Tue-Sun 1200-1530, 1930-2300. Sophisticated dining and spellbinding views of the Soccorso shoreline make this a special restaurant. Innovative dishes like local *ricciola* fish with sweet artichokes, fresh basil and lemon can be accompanied by an impressive range of wines. Phone to book a table near the window to enjoy the sunset.
€€ Mezzanotte, via Porto 72, 80077 Ischia Porto, T081-981653. Daily 1200-1500, 1900 till late. A youthful throng spills out onto the Riva at weekends here and there's a cocktail bar upstairs. Expect classic seafood dishes like *spaghetti alle vongole* and a choice of pizzas.
€€ Neptunus, via delle Rose 11, Sant'Angelo, T081-999702. Daily 1200-1500, 1930-2400. Eating the freshest seafood on the terrace here, overlooking Sant'Angelo, is an archetypal Ischian experience. Start with the seafood salad of squid and octopus, squeeze your lemon wedge and let Giuseppe Jacono and team guide you through the

menu – it may just climax with a sugar, alcohol and caffeine-combined rush of *torta caprese*, grappa and a shot of espresso.

Cafés and bars

Al Triangolo, via Roma, Lacco Ameno, T081-099 4364. Daily 0700-2200. Near *il fungo*, this is the place for refreshing *granite* in classic and crazy flavours like lemon, melon, coffee, strawberry and yoghurt.
Bar Ciccio, via Porto 1, Ischia Porto. Daily 0700-2200. Open for over 100 years, **Bar Ciccio** does interesting ice-cream flavours including healthy options such as organic, fat-free, *doppio-zero* and gluten-free.
Bar Pasticceria Calise, via Sogliuzzo 69, Ischia Porto, T081-991270. Sweet filled *cornetti* including the devilish *alla crema e amarene* (with cream and sour cherries) are just some of the pastries enjoyed at this popular spot.

⑪ Entertainment

Ischia *p106, map p107*
Nightlife
L'Ecstasy, Piazzetta dei Pini 3, Ischia Porto, T081-992653. Daily 2000 till late. A bar-*discoteca* that hosts club nights and live music including jazz acts.
New Valentino, corso Vittoria Colonna 97, Ischia Porto, T081-982569, www.valentinoischia.eu. Daily 2100 till late. A bizarre mix of majolica tiling and lurid lighting is the backdrop to wild nights of piano bar and dance music.

✪ Festivals

Ischia *p106, map p107*
Jun Ischia Film Festival, www.ischiafilmfestival.it. Each Jun, Ischia hosts a 2-week film festival dedicated to film locations.
26 Jul Festa di Sant' Anna. The island's patron saint is honoured with a lively procession of boats, fireworks and feasting around the Castello Aragonese.

O Shopping

Ischia *p106, map p107*
Ceramics
Di Meglio, via Roma 42, Ischia Porto,
T081-991176. A large space brimming
with colourful ceramic plates and tiles.

Food and drink
Ischia Sapori, via R Gianturco 2, Ischia
Porto, T081-984482. Gastronomic goodies,
including liqueurs, olive oils, wines,
handmade pasta and preserves.
Salumeria Manzi, via Roma 16, Lacco
Ameno. With lots of reasonably priced
bread, cheese, meats and fruit and
vegetables, this is a good place to buy
picnic or self-catering provisions.

Souvenirs
Napoli Mania, Il Corso, Ischia Porto,
www.napolimania.com. Novelties in
Neapolitan dialect that many Italians
don't understand: from T-shirts and mugs
to baby bibs and Maradona-related items.

O What to do

Ischia *p106, map p107*
Adventure sports
Indiana Park Pineta, Loc Fiaiano, Barano,
T0773-474473. Apr-Oct. 6 colour-coded
arboreal assault courses (they call it) allow
anyone over 110 cm in height to experience
adrenalin-fuelled 'tarzanning', which involves
lots of climbing, swinging and abseiling
around this forest park.

Fishing
Fishing trips with local fishermen from Ischia
Porto and other harbours make for a magical
morning on the waves. **Hotel Tre Sorelle**
(T081-907792, www.hoteltresorelleischia.it)
organizes regular forays at Succhivo.

Sailing
Scuola Vela Ischia, Hotel Villa Carolina,
Forio, T081-997119, www.scuolavelaischia.it.
Sailing school in Forio with courses starting
at €100 for 2 outings.

Walking
Ischia Trekking, T368-335 0074 (mobile),
www.ischiatrekking.it. Guided treks
exploring the caves of Pizzi Bianchi,
Piano Liguori and Mont' Epomeo (4 hrs)
from €15 per person.

Wellbeing
Parco Termale Castiglione, via
Castiglione 62, Casamicciola Terme, T081-
982551, www.termecastiglione.it. Historic
spa now with luxurious spaces and outdoor
pools. A day ticket costs €27 and entitles
use of thermal pools, sauna, sunbeds and
changing facilities.
Spa Resort Negombo, Baia San Montano,
T081-986152, www.negombo.it. Arguably
Ischia's most beautiful spa resort, frequented
by both minted megalomaniacs and everyday
Giuseppes. Massage treatments involving the
use of hot healing stones start at €90.
Terme Manzi, piazza Bagni, Casamicciola
Terme, T081-994722, www.termemanzi
hotel.com. Amid the chic interiors, mood
lighting and techie spa equipment is the
tub a wounded Giuseppe Garibaldi sat
in when convalescing during his 1862
Risorgimento campaign. A pricey yet
serene and stylish spa.

O Directory

Ischia *p106, map p107*
Medical services Guardia Medica,
T081-983499/ 998989. Farmacia
Internazionale, via de Luca Alfredo 117,
T081-333 1275. **Money** Banca Monte
dei Paschi di Siena, via Sogliuzzo 44,
T081-982310. **Post office** Via Morgioni,
Porto d'Ischia, T081-507 4611 (Mon-Fri
0800-1630, Sat 0800-1230).

Procida

Located between Capo Miseno and Ischia, Procida is less than 4 km long and has a paint-peeling, down-to-earth charm. Its old fishing villages of dishevelled pastel-painted buildings have become a favourite film backdrop, most famously in *Il Postino* and *The Talented Mr Ripley*. Don't expect tourist hordes and glitz here – although its 11,000 inhabitants and summer influx do create traffic mayhem in its centre. There are leafy lanes with attractive villas and market gardens to explore, and the island's fishing tradition lives on, making dining here a treat. Procida's circular bays, Corricella and Chiaiolella, are dead volcanic craters created by the Phlegrean caldera system, between which are some fine but scruffy beaches.

Arriving on Procida

Getting there and around

Boat services from Naples and Pozzuoli arrive at Marina Grande. The island is so small that you can get around on foot, but there are times when you'll need some wheels to take the strain. Four bus routes run by **SEPSA** ① *T081-542 9965, www.sepsa.it*, cover just about all the island. Walking is not pleasant after dark, especially as there are no pavements, and often piles of rubbish on the roadside. Taxis and microtaxis are pretty cheap and cycling around the quieter lanes can be fun. At Marina Grande there's a **taxi rank** ① *T081-896 8785*, and nearby you can hire scooters and basic bicycles from **Ricambio Giuseppe** ① *via Roma 107, T081-896 0060*). **Sprint** ① *via Roma 28, T081-896 9435*, also hires out scooters and electric bikes. In the spring of 2013 Mayor Capezzuto introduced an experimental free electric bike scheme for tourists at the port and limited vehicular traffic in the summer months to ease the noise and congestion. ►► *See Transport, page 118.*

Tourist information

Ufficio di Turismo ① *via Roma, Marina Grande, T081-810968, www.infoischiaprocida.it.*

Marina Grande and Terra Murata → *For listings, see pages 116-118.*

On arrival at **Marina Grande** (Porto Sancio Cattolico or, as the locals call it, Sent' Cò) you are greeted by an expanse of sticky, uneven flagstones hosting the usual Neapolitan traffic chaos backed by a ramshackle row of high, pastel-coloured former fishermen's dwellings. The eye-catching arches of these via Roma buildings, under which fishing boats used to be stored, are now occupied by bars and restaurants. Ischia's high street, via Principe Umberto, leads to piazza dei Martiri where the Baroque **Chiesa della Madonna delle Grazie** stands alongside a memorial to 12 *procidani* – Republican martyrs killed during a Royalist backlash to a 1799 uprising.

Terra Murata ('walled land'), the highest point on the island at 91 m, offers wonderful views of the fishing port, Marina di Corricella, and beyond. The medieval quarter Terra Casata and the *cittadella* Castello d'Avolos have atmosphere aplenty: the latter was a castle turned Aragonese-built prison (1560s). The prison held political activists in the Fascist period and closed in 1988. On the way up the hill to the castle is housed the **Ragazzi dei Misteri** ⓘ *www.ragazzideimisteri. com, Mon-Sat 1600-2000; Sun 1000-1200*, cultural centre which exhibits vibrant and surreal iconographic sculptures from previous **Venerdì Santo** (Good Friday) processions. Talk to one of the volunteers here to find out about the latest exhibits. You may find out about the latest plans to transform the huge castle complex into a cultural quarter with accommodation. Nearby is the impressive noble residence Palazzo de Iorio – also due a refurbishment.

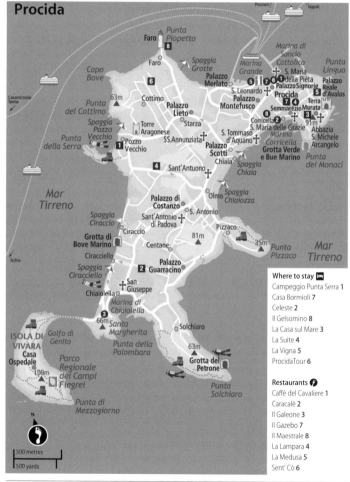

Where to stay 🛏
Campeggio Punta Serra **1**
Casa Bormioli **7**
Celeste **2**
Il Gelsomino **8**
La Casa sul Mare **3**
La Suite **4**
La Vigna **5**
ProcidaTour **6**

Restaurants 🍴
Caffè del Cavaliere **1**
Caracalè **2**
Il Galeone **3**
Il Gazebo **7**
Il Maestrale **8**
La Lampara **4**
La Medusa **5**
Sent' Cò **6**

Procida's patron saint

The Abbazia contains Nicola Russo's painting *Saint Michael Protects the Island* which portrays Procida's patron saint stopping a 1535 Saracen attack. According to the legend, St Michael appeared as a vision in the sky, whipped up some waves and overwhelmed Barbarossa Hayreddin Pasha's pirates. Perhaps it was that disorientating meteorological phenomenon St Elmo's Fire that did the saintly work?

Abbazia di San Michele Arcangelo

① *Via Terra Murata, T081-896 7612, www.abbaziasanmichele.it. Daily 1000-1245, 1500-1730, closed Sun and Mon afternoon, church free, museum €3.*

This abbey deep in the Terra Murata was originally built in the 11th century and was repeatedly ransacked by Saracen pirates in the 16th and 18th centuries. Contrasting with the uplifting artistic highs of the exquisite inlaid marble altar, coffered ceiling and flourishes of gold leaf are some macabre sights in the catacombs.

Marina della Corricella, Marina di Chiaiolella and Isola di Vivara

The pastel-coloured buildings and alleyways of Marina della Corricella were the backdrop of the film *Il Postino*, starring the late Massimo Troisi, a Neapolitan comedy genius. Marina della Chiaiolella is a crescent-shaped harbour, and also has a fair catch of fishing-harbour lure, with some swanky yachts and bar-restaurants to boot. Another curvaceous crater ridge forms the **Isola di Vivara** ① *accessed via a bridge, www.isoladivivara.it*, an island nature reserve with a 109-m-high lump of Mediterranean scrub teeming with birdlife and other animals. The reserve is only open to the public a few days per year.

Procida beaches

Although often littered with plastic flotsam and jetsam, Procida's beaches have their charms and lie in stunning positions:

La Spiaggia del Ciraccio Procida's longest and most popular beach is a continuation of Spiaggia della Chiaiolella and just around the corner from Marina di Chiaiolella, on the western shore. Afternoon breezes are welcomed by its sun-worshippers and windsurfers.

Spiaggia della Silurenza Just west of Marina Grande, with ample beach facilities and restaurants. Locals fire themselves off Il Cannone (named after an old cannon placed on the rocks).

Spiaggia della Lingua East of the port, off piazza della Marina Grande, is this intimate beach with limpid waters, popular with swimmers, snorkellers and fishermen.

Spiaggia di Chiaia Access to this busy beach's dark coarse sands on Procida's eastern shore involves a descent down 200 steps off piazza San Giacomo, or a boat ride.

Spiaggia Pozzo Vecchio In the northwestern corner of the island (reached from via Battisti) is the Pozzo Vecchio beach, which appeared in *Il Postino* – it is enclosed within a semicircular bay, making it popular with swimmers.

Pick of the picnic spots

Pick up picnic treats from a local *alimentari* (food shop) or splash out on something special at one these gourmet gems: **Pasticceria Buonocore**, Capri, see page 104; **Ischia Sapori**, Ischia (see page 112); **Il Ghiottone di Imputato M**, Procida, see page 118.

Monte Solaro, Capri After ascending serenely on the chairlift or by foot to Capri's limestone peak, there are shimmering views to savour over the rolling island, ocean and even as far as smoking Stromboli, towards Sicily.

La Migliera, Capri The buzz of Anacapri fades as you walk down flowery lanes, through woods and grapevines to the clifftop Belvedere del Tuono, with heart-pounding panoramas down jagged cliffs to Punta Carena, Il Faro and along the spectacular coast with its forts and yacht-studded coves.

Monte Epomeo, Ischia A walk to Ischia's volcanic zenith is rewarded with the chance to eat and drink in the breathtaking views while lounging on the smooth sculptured rocks.

La Mortella, Ischia Exotic plant species, trickling water features and idyllic garden corners make this a mellifluous venue for a *merenda* (snack) – just don't leave a mess – and perhaps enjoy a drink in La Mortella's tea room.

Marina della Corricella, Procida Take a pew near the rusty rings and flaking boats on the fishing village quayside. Between bites and glimpses of salty Procida lives you can snap away at pastel and marine blue-hued views.

Procida listings

For hotel and restaurant price codes and other relevant information, see pages 14-17.

⊖ Where to stay

Procida *p113, map p114*

€€€ Casa Bormioli, via Principe Umberto 86, T081-986 0090, www.casabormioli.it. A luxury B&B with cool interiors mixing contemporary artworks and vibrant fabrics with North African pieces. There are 4 double bed suites and a quad ideal for families. A gorgeous terrace overlooks an orange grove. Prices drop considerably outside Jul-Aug.

€€€ La Vigna, via Principessa Margherita 46, T081-896 0469, www.albergolavigna.it. The crenellated parapet of **La Vigna**'s red-hued tower pokes above the vines in its clifftop vineyard setting. Atmosphere, tranquillity and luxury reign at this *castellino* in the country, a 10-min walk from the harbour; you can quaff their vino, indulge in therapeutic baths and massages and revel in the effortless style of the place. For those fancying a splurge, the Malvasia suite has a luxury bath and private roof terrace.

€€ Hotel La Casa sul Mare, via Salita Castello 13, T081-896 8799, www.lacasa sulmare.it. Deep in the Terra Murata historic quarter, this 18th-century residence has 10 elegant rooms decked out in cool hues and tiled floors. Many have small balconies with views. Wonderful breakfasts are taken in a small garden. As it sits on a hill, some fitness is required to get around, although a handy beach shuttle service is provided.

€€ La Suite, via Flavio Gioia 81, T081-810 1564. New boutique hotel with whitewashed, minimalist rooms and spacious suites with sea and garden views. There's a spa, pool, bar and access to the beach made famous in *Il Postino*.

€ Hotel Celeste, via Rivoli 6, T081-896 7488, www.hotelceleste.it. Basic accommodation near Marina di Chiaiolella. Many of the 35 rooms have a balcony or terrace.

€ Il Gelsomino, Faro, T333 4350755, procida2006@libero.it. A small B&B in a verdant garden setting run by the wonderful Borgogna family. You can enjoy proper Procida hospitality here with rosy-cheeked smiley hosts: Luciana makes a mean lemon and garlic salad while her *marito*, Francesco, gives tours of the Limoneto garden where he breeds rabbits and grows wonderful produce.

Camping

Campeggio Punta Serra, via Serra 4, T081-896 9519, campeggioserra@simail.it. Open Jun-Sep. Pozzo Vecchio beach, granular star of *Il Postino*, is a short walk from this campsite which has pitches for tents and caravans and bungalows for rent (sleeps 2-6, €65-170 per night).

Self-catering

ProcidaTour, via Santo Ianno 20, T081-896 9393, www.procidatour.it. This family-run enterprise rents out a number of apartments and studios in the Collinetta di Cottimo area. Punto Faro and Pozzo Vecchio beaches are nearby.

🍴 Restaurants

Procida *p113, map p114*

€€€ La Medusa, via Roma 116, Marina Grande, T081-896 7481. Daily 1200-1500, 1900-2300. An idiosyncratic owner and excellent seafood dishes including *spaghetti ai ricci di mare* (sea urchin sauce) make this a memorable place to dine. If the *padrone* (main man) takes a liking to you expect copious amounts of charm and *cibo* (food).

€€ Caracalè, via Marina Corricella 62, Corricella, T081-896 9192. Daily 1200-1500, 1900-2300. **Caracalè** offers seafood creations like swordfish with aubergine and is a fine spot for absorbing the picturesque Corricella harbour scene. Expect the freshest octopus salad, grilled catch of the day and fruity desserts. The laid-back atmosphere and unfussy preparation of the freshest catch

make it a beguiling eatery right on the *banchina* (quayside).

€€ Il Gazebo, via Roma 140, T081-810 1071. Hidden down the end of the port area and very popular with locals. Don't be put off by the simple interiors and brisk trade in panini in the early evening. Beaming gentleman cook Pio has worked all over Italy and Europe and brings those influences to some superb dishes. Young chef Bruno is equally talented. Starters include the freshest marinated anchovies and ricotta-stuffed zucchini flowers. *Primi* include prawn and prosecco risotto, and spaghetti with cuttlefish and asparagus. Pio really knows his wine and includes quality northern Italian labels alongside southern classics.

€€ Il Maestrale, via Marina di Corricella 29, T081-810 1889. Corricella quayside place run by the serene and friendly couple Rosaria and Bruno, who look after the guests and resident cats with style. Fabulous choice of seafood including: linguine with *orata* (gilt-head bream) and tomato sauce, and *spigola all'acquapazza* (sea bass cooked "crazy water" style) with a kick of chilli an herbs. Chef Mario's creamy lemon risotto with a parmesan crostata (crust) is wonderful.

€€ La Lampara, via Marina Corricella 88, T081-896 0609. Wonderful terrace restaurant overlooking Marina di Corricella. Tasty marinated seafood antipasti and spicy clams followed by **Lampara**-caught octopus and whatever's in the net.

€€ Sent' Cò, via Roma 167, Marina Grande, T081-810 1120. Tue-Sun 1200-1500, 1900-2300. **Sent' Cò** is a no-frills ristorante-pizzeria serving the catch of the day and a popular fish soup. Also worth trying are the *orecchiette* (small ear-shaped pasta) with a sauce made from the island's vegetables.

Cafés and bars

Caffè dal Cavaliere, via Roma 42, Marina Grande, T081-810 1074. Daily 0700-2100. Famed for their creamy pastries – *lingue di bue* (cow's tongues) – containing Procida's mightily pithy lemons.

Il Galeone, via Marina Chiaiolella, Marina di Chiaiolella, T081-896 9622. Daily 0800-2400. A largish café-bar-restaurant by the harbour serving drinks, pizzas, snacks like *bruschette*, as well as meat dishes and grilled fish.

🎭 Entertainment

Procida *p113, map p114*
Nightlife
GM Bar, via Roma 117, Marina Grande, T081-896 7560, www.gmbar.it. Thu-Sat 2200 till late. According to the locals this bar-discoteca is '*il boom*' at the moment – and it's certainly popular with the young Procidiani who cram in here at weekends for live music, DJs and free buffet food.

✺ Festivals

Procida *p113, map p114*
Easter Good Friday Procession. Dating back to 1627, this Easter procession was inspired by the Spanish tradition of the mysteries. Representations of Christ's suffering made by local children are displayed and then a dozen white-robed locals haul an 18th-century wooden statue of the dead Christ to Terra Murata. A funereal procession takes place the following morning.
2 Jul Madonna delle Grazie, a colourful religious procession with much feasting.
Late Jul Sagra del Mar (Festival of the Sea).
Mid-Aug Sagra del Pesce Azzurro, a fish festival in Corricella involving lots of eating and drinking.
Nov Sagra del Vino, Procida's wine festival.

🛍 Shopping

Procida *p113, map p114*
Food and drink
Il Ghiottone di Imputato M, via Vittorio Emanuele 15, T081-896 0349. Gastronomic establishment – great for gifts and all you need for a lavish Procidiano picnic. On the right hand side heading up the hill from the port on the same street is an *alimentari* food shop run by the friendly and honest Gennaro and his 90-year-old father – good for picnics and seasonal produce.

Souvenirs
Izzo Rosana, via Vittorio Emanuele 36, T081-896 9118. Funky stationery and knick-knacks.

⛳ What to do

Procida *p113, map p114*
De Sanctis, via G da Procida, Procida, T081-896 7571. Tennis and *calcetto* (5-a-side) facilities, best booked for the cool evenings.

⊖ Transport

Procida *p113, map p114*
Boat Ferries, TMVs and hydrofoils to **Ischia**, **Pozzuoli** and **Naples**. Journey times 20-60 mins. Seasonal timetables apply.

ⓘ Directory

Procida *p113, map p114*
Medical services Guardia Medica, T081-983499. Farmacia Madonna Delle Grazie, piazza dei Martiri 1, Corricella, T081-896 8883. **Money** Banco di Napoli, via V Emanuele 158, T081-810 1489. **Post office** Via Libertà 34, T081-896 0711.

Contents

Footnotes

Language

In hotels and bigger restaurants, you'll usually find English is spoken. The further you go from the tourist centre, however, the more trouble you may have, unless you have at least a smattering of Italian. Luckily, Neapolitans are generally gregarious and very encouraging of anyone speaking Italian, although many of them communicate between themselves in Neapolitan dialect, a branch of the Napoletano-Calabrese language spoken throughout Southern Italy.

Napoletano (pronounced 'nabuledan') has a very different rhythm and phonology to the Tuscan dialect that forms the basis of standard Italian – indeed most Northern Italians find it very tricky deciphering a Neapolitan's clipped vowels, voiced and double consonantal sounds, and exotic Greek, Arabic and Spanish linguistic influences. So a trip to Naples not only gives visitors the opportunity to dip into the city's rich tradition of music, literature and theatre: there's also the chance to hear Neapolitan language and its witty proverbs.

When communicating in shops and restaurants stick to Italian. Stress in spoken Italian usually falls on the penultimate syllable. Italian has standard sounds and is the most phonetically true language: unlike English you can work out how it sounds from how it is written and vice versa.

Vowels

a like 'a' in cat
e like 'e' in vet, or slightly more open, like the 'ai'in air (except after c or g, see consonants below)
i like 'i' in sip (except after c or g, see below)
o like 'o' in fox
u like 'ou' in soup

Consonants

Generally consonants sound the same as in English, though 'e' and 'i' after 'c' or 'g' make them soft (a 'ch' or a 'j' sound) and are silent themselves, whereas 'h' makes them hard (a 'k' or 'g' sound), the opposite to English. So *ciao* is pronounced 'chaow', but *chiesa* (church) is pronounced 'kee-ay-sa'.

The combination 'gli' is pronounced like the 'lli' in million, and 'gn' like 'ny' in Tanya.

Basics

thank you	*grazie*
hi/goodbye	*ciao*
good day (until after lunch/mid-afternoon)	*buongiorno*
good evening (after lunch)	*buonasera*
goodnight	*buonanotte*
goodbye	*arrivederci*
please	*per favore*
I'm sorry	*mi dispiace*
excuse me	*permesso*
yes	*sì*
no	*no*

Numbers

one	*uno*	17	*diciassette*
two	*due*	18	*diciotto*
three	*tre*	19	*diciannove*
four	*quattro*	20	*venti*
five	*cinque*	21	*ventuno*
six	*sei*	22	*ventidue*
seven	*sette*	30	*trenta*
eight	*otto*	40	*quaranta*
nine	*nove*	50	*cinquanta*
10	*dieci*	60	*sessanta*
11	*undici*	70	*settanta*
12	*dodici*	80	*ottanta*
13	*tredici*	90	*novanta*
14	*quattordici*	100	*cento*
15	*quindici*	200	*due cento*
16	*sedici*	1000	*mille*

Questions

how?	*come?*	where?	*dove?*
how much?	*quanto?*	why?	*perché?*
when?	*quando?*	what?	*che cosa?*

Problems

I don't understand	*non capisco*
I don't know	*non lo so*
I don't speak Italian	*non parlo italiano*
How do you say ... (in Italian)?	*come si dice ... (in italiano)?*
Is there anyone who speaks English?	*c'è qualcuno che parla inglese?*

Shopping

this one/that one	*questo/quello*
less	*meno*
more	*di più*
how much is it/are they?	*quanto costa/costano?*
can I have ...?	*posso avere ...?*

Travelling

one ticket for...	*un biglietto per...*
single	*solo andata*
return	*andata e ritorno*
does this go to Pompeii?	*questo va a Pompeii?*
airport	*aeroporto*
bus stop	*fermata*
train	*treno*
car	*macchina*
taxi	*tassi*

Hotels

a double/single room	*una camera doppia/singola*
a double bed	*un letto matrimoniale*
bathroom	*bagno*
Is there a view?	*c'è un bel panorama?*
can I see the room?	*posso vedere la camera?*
when is breakfast?	*a che ora è la colazione?*
can I have the key?	*posso avere la chiave?*

Time

morning	*mattina*
afternoon	*pomeriggio*
evening	*sera*
night	*notte*
soon	*presto/fra poco*
later	*più tardi*
what time is it?	*che ore sono?*
today/tomorrow/yesterday	*oggi/domani/ieri*

Days

Monday	*lunedi*
Tuesday	*martedi*
Wednesday	*mercoledi*
Thursday	*giovedi*
Friday	*venerdi*
Saturday	*sabato*
Sunday	*domenica*

Conversation

alright	*va bene*
right then	*allora*
who knows!	*bo! / chi sa*
good luck!	*in bocca al lupo!*
	(literally, 'in the mouth of the wolf')
one moment	*un attimo*
hello (when answering a phone)	*pronto* (literally, 'ready')
let's go!	*andiamo!*
enough/stop	*basta!*
give up!	*dai!*
I like ...	*mi piace ...*
how's it going? (well, thanks)	*come va? (bene, grazie)*
how are you?	*come sta/stai?* (polite/informal)

Menu reader → See also Food and drink in Naples, page 15.

General

affumicato smoked
al sangue rare
alla griglia grilled
antipasto starter/appetizer
aperto/chiuso open/closed
arrosto roasted
ben cotto well done
bollito boiled
caldo hot
cameriere/cameriera waiter/waitress
conto the bill
contorni side dishes
coperto cover charge
coppa/cono cone/cup
cotto cooked

cottura media medium
crudo raw
degustazione tasting menu of several dishes
dolce dessert
fatto in casa home-made
forno a legna wood-fired oven
freddo cold
fresco fresh, uncooked
fritto fried
menu turistico tourist menu
piccante spicy
prenotazione reservation
primo first course
ripieno a stuffing or something that is stuffed
secondo second course

Drinks (bevande)

acqua naturale/gassata/frizzante
    still/sparkling water
aperitivo drinks taken before dinner, often
    served with free snacks
bicchiere glass
birra beer
birra alla spina draught beer

bottiglia bottle
caffè coffee (ie espresso)
caffè macchiato/ristretto espresso with a
    dash of foamed milk/strong
spremuta freshly squeezed fruit juice
succo juice
vino bianco/rosato/rosso white/rosé/red wine

Fruit (*frutti*) and vegetables (*legumi*)

agrumi citrus fruits
amarena sour cherry
arancia orange
carciofo globe artichoke
castagne chestnuts
cipolle onions
cocomero water melon
contorno side dish, usually grilled
    vegetables or oven baked potatoes
fichi figs
finocchio fennel
fragole strawberries
friarelli strong flavoured leaves of the
    broccoli family eaten with sausages
frutta fresca fresh fruit
funghi mushroom
lamponi raspberries
melagrana pomegranate

melanzana eggplant/aubergine
melone light coloured melon
mele apples
noci/nocciole walnuts/hazelnuts
patate potatoes, which can be *arroste* (roast),
    fritte (fried), *novelle* (new), *pure'di* (mashed)
patatine fritte chips
peperoncino chilli pepper
peperone peppers
pesche peaches
piselli peas
pomodoro tomato
rucola rocket
scarola leafy green vegetable
sciurilli or *fiorilli* tempura courgette flowers
spinaci spinach
verdure vegetables
zucca pumpkin

Meat (*carne*)

affettati misti mixed cured meat
agnello lamb
bistecca beef steak
braciola chop, steak or slice of meat
carpaccio finely sliced raw meat
  (usually beef)
cinghiale boar
coda alla vaccinara oxtail
coniglio rabbit
coniglio all'ischiatana Ischia-style rabbit
involtini thinly sliced meat, rolled and
  stuffed
manzo beef

pollo chicken
polpette meatballs
polpettone meat loaf
porchetta roasted whole suckling pig
prosciutto ham – cotto cooked, crudo cured
salsicce pork sausage
salumi cured meats, usually served mixed
  (*salumi misto*) on a wooden platter
speck a type of cured, smoked ham
spiedini meat pieces grilled on a skewer
stufato meat stew
trippa tripe
vitello veal

Fish (*pesce*) and seafood (*frutti di mare*)

acciughe anchovies
aragosta lobster
baccalà salt cod
bottarga mullet-roe
branzino sea bass
calamari squid
cozze mussels
frittura di mare/frittura di paranza small fish,
  squid and shellfish lightly covered with
  flour and fried
frutti di mare seafood
gamberi shrimps/prawns
grigliata mista di pesce mixed grilled fish

orata gilt-head/sea bream
ostriche oysters
pesce spada swordfish
polpo octopus
sarde, sardine sardines
seppia cuttlefish
sogliola sole
spigola bass
stoccafisso stockfish
tonno tuna
triglia red mullet
trota trout
vongole clams

Dessert (*dolce*)

cornetto sweet croissant
crema custard
dolce dessert
gelato ice cream
granita flavoured crushed ice
macedonia (di frutta) fruit cocktail dessert
  with white wine
panettone fruit bread eaten at Christmas

semifreddo a partially frozen dessert
sorbetto sorbet
tiramisù rich 'pick-me-up' dessert
torta cake
zabaglione whipped egg yolks flavoured
  with Marsala wine
zuppa inglese English-style trifle

Other

aceto balsamico balsamic vinegar
arborio type of rice used to make risotto
burro butter
calzone pizza dough rolled with the chef's
  choice of filling and then baked
casatiello lard bread
fagioli white beans

formaggi misti mixed cheese plate
formaggio cheese
frittata omelette
insalata salad
insalata Caprese salad of tomatoes,
  mozzarella and basil
latte milk

Eleven classic Neapolitan dishes

ragù di carne alla Genovese Not from Genova but invented by the Genovese family. Small pieces of beef cooked with onions and served with smooth and long tubular *pasta liscia* like *mezzanelli*.

spaghetti alle vongole The classic summer dish is often served with the freshest Vesuvian tomatoes combined with clams. Often called *vermicelli alle vongole*.

baccalà alla Napoletana Preserved cod fried and cooked with tomatoes and onions.

polipetti affogati/polipetti con pomodori Octopus cooked in *bianco* (stewed in its own juices) with wine and black olives, or cooked with tomatoes.

frittura di pesce Medley of lightly fried seafood served with a wedge of lemon.

mozzarella in carozza Mozzarella goes gooey in its fried bread 'carriage'.

parmigiana di melanzane Layers of fried aubergine slices, mozzarella, parmesan, basil and *passata di pomodoro*. Umberto's (see page 59) does a meaty *ragù* version.

zucchini alla scapece A *contorno* (side dish) of thin courgette slices marinated in garlic, vinegar and mint.

zuppa di soffritto di maiale A hearty soup of pig offal, tomatoes and chilli.

sartù di riso/timpano di maccheroni A tasty ragù sauce is poured over a mound of rice that contains pieces of *polpettine* (meat balls), aubergine, peas, sausage meat and sometimes provola cheese, then it's baked. There's an *in bianco* (literally white) version without the *ragù* sauce. It often takes the form of a *ciambellone* (large ring). On the same lines is the *timballo o timpano di maccheroni*, a 19th-century dish that consists of a mound of macaroni (a timbale mould resembling a kettle drum is used, hence the name) mixed with layers of filling typically including meaty *ragù*, *salsicciotto piccante* (spicy sausage), hard-boiled egg, tomato salsa and sometimes even brains. It's covered in *pasta frolla* (pastry).

bucatini alla Siciliana Long pasta tubes popular in Naples are typically served with a rich sauce consisting of aubergine, meatballs, plus *ragù napoletano*, fried mushrooms, parmigiano and mozzarella. It's covered with more meaty ragù and baked in an oven.

"Naples was ruled by Ferdinando I di Borbone and the Regno delle due Sicilie," adds Massimo, "so everything was called 'Siciliano' for a while."
Massimo di Porzio, Ristorante-Pizzeria Umberto, Chiaia, Napoli (see page 59).

---

lenticchie lentils
mandorla almond
miele honey
olio oil
polenta cornmeal
pane bread
pane-integrale brown bread
pinoli pine nuts

provola cheese, sometimes with a smoky flavour
ragù a meaty sauce or ragout
riso rice
salsa sauce
sugo sauce or gravy
zuppa soup
zuppa di pasta e fagioli Neapolitan soup

Useful phrases

can I have the bill please?
  posso avere il conto per favore?
is there a menu? *c'è un menù?*
what's this? *cos'è questo?*

what do you recommend?
  che cosa mi consegna?
where's the toilet? *dov'è il bagno?*

Index

Titles available in the Footprint *Focus* range

Latin America	UK RRP	US RRP
Bahia & Salvador	£7.99	$11.95
Brazilian Amazon	£7.99	$11.95
Brazilian Pantanal	£6.99	$9.95
Buenos Aires & Pampas	£7.99	$11.95
Cartagena & Caribbean Coast	£7.99	$11.95
Costa Rica	£8.99	$12.95
Cuzco, La Paz & Lake Titicaca	£8.99	$12.95
El Salvador	£5.99	$8.95
Guadalajara & Pacific Coast	£6.99	$9.95
Guatemala	£8.99	$12.95
Guyana, Guyane & Suriname	£5.99	$8.95
Havana	£6.99	$9.95
Honduras	£7.99	$11.95
Nicaragua	£7.99	$11.95
Northeast Argentina & Uruguay	£8.99	$12.95
Paraguay	£5.99	$8.95
Quito & Galápagos Islands	£7.99	$11.95
Recife & Northeast Brazil	£7.99	$11.95
Rio de Janeiro	£8.99	$12.95
São Paulo	£5.99	$8.95
Uruguay	£6.99	$9.95
Venezuela	£8.99	$12.95
Yucatán Peninsula	£6.99	$9.95

Asia	UK RRP	US RRP
Angkor Wat	£5.99	$8.95
Bali & Lombok	£8.99	$12.95
Chennai & Tamil Nadu	£8.99	$12.95
Chiang Mai & Northern Thailand	£7.99	$11.95
Goa	£6.99	$9.95
Gulf of Thailand	£8.99	$12.95
Hanoi & Northern Vietnam	£8.99	$12.95
Ho Chi Minh City & Mekong Delta	£7.99	$11.95
Java	£7.99	$11.95
Kerala	£7.99	$11.95
Kolkata & West Bengal	£5.99	$8.95
Mumbai & Gujarat	£8.99	$12.95

Africa & Middle East	UK RRP	US RRP
Beirut	£6.99	$9.95
Cairo & Nile Delta	£8.99	$12.95
Damascus	£5.99	$8.95
Durban & KwaZulu Natal	£8.99	$12.95
Fès & Northern Morocco	£8.99	$12.95
Jerusalem	£8.99	$12.95
Johannesburg & Kruger National Park	£7.99	$11.95
Kenya's Beaches	£8.99	$12.95
Kilimanjaro & Northern Tanzania	£8.99	$12.95
Luxor to Aswan	£8.99	$12.95
Nairobi & Rift Valley	£7.99	$11.95
Red Sea & Sinai	£7.99	$11.95
Zanzibar & Pemba	£7.99	$11.95

Europe	UK RRP	US RRP
Bilbao & Basque Region	£6.99	$9.95
Brittany West Coast	£7.99	$11.95
Cádiz & Costa de la Luz	£6.99	$9.95
Granada & Sierra Nevada	£6.99	$9.95
Languedoc: Carcassonne to Montpellier	£7.99	$11.95
Málaga	£5.99	$8.95
Marseille & Western Provence	£7.99	$11.95
Orkney & Shetland Islands	£5.99	$8.95
Santander & Picos de Europa	£7.99	$11.95
Sardinia: Alghero & the North	£7.99	$11.95
Sardinia: Cagliari & the South	£7.99	$11.95
Seville	£5.99	$8.95
Sicily: Palermo & the Northwest	£7.99	$11.95
Sicily: Catania & the Southeast	£7.99	$11.95
Siena & Southern Tuscany	£7.99	$11.95
Sorrento, Capri & Amalfi Coast	£6.99	$9.95
Skye & Outer Hebrides	£6.99	$9.95
Verona & Lake Garda	£7.99	$11.95

North America	UK RRP	US RRP
Vancouver & Rockies	£8.99	$12.95

Australasia	UK RRP	US RRP
Brisbane & Queensland	£8.99	$12.95
Perth	£7.99	$11.95

For the latest books, e-books and a wealth of travel information, visit us at: www.footprinttravelguides.com.

Join us on facebook for the latest travel news, product releases, offers and amazing competitions: www.facebook.com/footprintbooks.